CHELSEA HOUSE PUBLISHERS

Modern Critical Views

Further titles in preparation.

Modern Critical Views

WALLACE STEVENS

Modern Critical Views

WALLACE STEVENS

Edited with an introduction by

Harold Bloom

Sterling Professor of the Humanities
Yale University

1985
CHELSEA HOUSE PUBLISHERS
New York

THE COVER:

The cover illustrates "The Auroras of Autumn," Stevens' crisis-poem, where the poet walks the shore at twilight, while staring in numb wonder at the great sweep of the Northern lights.—H.B.

PROJECT EDITORS: Emily Bestler, James Uebbing
ASSOCIATE EDITOR: Maria Behan
EDITORIAL COORDINATOR: Karyn Gullen Browne
EDITORIAL STAFF: Sally Stepanek, Linda Grossman, Joy Johannessen
DESIGN: Susan Lusk

Cover illustration by Neil Waldman

Library of Congress Cataloging in Publication Data

Wallace Stevens
     (Modern critical views)
     Bibliography: p.
     Includes index.
     Contents: The sausage maker / Helen Vendler—
Stevens' rock and criticism as cure / J. Hillis Miller
—The rejection of metaphor / Helen Regueiro—[etc.]
     1. Stevens, Wallace, 1879–1955—Criticism and
interpretation—Addresses, essays, lectures. I. Bloom,
Harold.
PS3537.T4753Z87 1984   811'.52   84–27431
ISBN 0–87754–607–X

Chelsea House Publishers
Harold Steinberg, Chairman and Publisher
Susan Lusk, Vice President
A Division of Chelsea House Educational Communications, Inc.
133 Christopher Street, New York, NY 10014

Contents

Editor's Note

This volume gathers together a representative selection of the best and most deeply informed criticism devoted to Wallace Stevens during the past fifteen years (1969–1984). It begins with the editor's portrait of Steven's as the central modern poet of the American Sublime, and continues with Helen Vendler's remarkable analysis of the poet's early attempts to write disjunctive sequences as versions of a long poem. J. Hillis Miller's strong reading of "The Rock" is an instance of Deconstructionist criticism, in the mode of Derrida and the late Paul de Man. Helen Regueiro charts the poet's evasions of metaphor in his quest for the limits of imagination, while the editor's detailed reading of "An Ordinary Evening in New Haven" sets itself against both Vendler's decreative analysis and the critical mode of Deconstruction.

Marie Borroff acutely describes the particular contours of Stevens' language, while Patricia Parker and the late Isabel G. MacCaffrey contribute profound studies of the poet's continuity with the conventions of Romance tradition. The essays by John Hollander and Eleanor Cook center definitively on Stevens' allusiveness, while Charles Berger concludes with an advanced estimate of Stevens' achievement as an elegist.

Introduction

Poets influence us because we fall in love with their poems. All love unfortunately changes, if indeed it does not end, and since nothing is got for nothing, we also get hurt when we abandon, or are abandoned by, poems. Criticism is as much a series of metaphors for the acts of loving what we have read as for the acts of reading themselves. Walter Pater liked to use the word "appreciations" for his critical essays, and I present this particular series of metaphors as an appreciation of Wallace Stevens. Precisely, I mean to appreciate his success in writing the poems of our climate more definitively than any American since Whitman and Dickinson. What justifies an estimate that sets him higher than Frost, Pound, Eliot and Williams? If he is, as so many readers now believe, a great poet, at least the equal of such contemporaries as Hardy, Yeats, Rilke and Valéry, what are the qualities that make for greatness in him? How and why does he move us, enlighten us, enlarge our existences, and help us to live our lives?

Though the admirers of Stevens are a mighty band these days, they have not convinced all skeptics or detractors. We have had some difficulty in exporting him to the British, who with a few noble exceptions continue to regard him as a rather luxurious and Frenchified exquisite, a kind of upper-middle-class mock-Platonist who represents at best an American Aestheticism, replete with tropical fruits and aroma-laden invitations to the voyage. Their Stevens is the celebrator of Florida and of pre-Castro Havana, a vulgarian-in-spite-of-himself. Some American apostles of the Pound-Eliot-Williams-Olson axis are holdouts also; thus we find Hugh Kenner growling, in his recent *The Pound Era*, that all Stevens comes to is the ultimate realization of the poetics of Edward Lear. We can find also, apart from different adherents of the Gorgeous Nonsense school, those critics who complain that Stevens increasingly became desiccated and mock-philosophical; here one can remember Jarrell's crack about G. E. Moore at the spinet. Finally, sometimes we can hear the complaint of those who insist they are weary of poems about poetry, and so are rendered weariest by the recorder of *Notes Toward a Supreme Fiction*. Probably new fault-findings, more soundly based upon Stevens' actual limitations, will arrive as the decades pass. Someone will rise to ask the hard question: How many qualifications can you get into a single poem and still have a poem? Do we not get more than enough of these interjections that Stevens himself describes as "a few words, an and yet, and yet, and yet—"?

But an appreciation does not address itself to answering negative critics, or to proposing fresh negations. The reader who loves Stevens learns a passion for Yes, and learns also that such a passion, like the imagination, needs to be indulged. "It must give pleasure," Stevens says, following a supreme tradition, and his poems do give pleasure. This pleasure, though naturalistic, essentially helps to satisfy the never-satisfied mind, and to the pursuit of the meaning of that satisfaction I now turn. Courageously waving before me the gaudy banners of the Affective Fallacy, I ask myself what it is that reading Stevens does for me, and what is it that I then attempt to do for other readers of Stevens? Is it an effectual though reduced Romantic Humanism that is rekindled for us? Is it a last splendid if willfully grotesque triumph of the American Sublime? Is it, O glorious if this be so, an achieved survival of the Genteel Tradition, another final hedge against the barbarians who are, as we all know, not only within the gates but also indistinguishable, alas, except upon certain moonlit nights, from our very selves? Is the prudential Seer of Hartford only the most eloquent elaborator of our way of life, the Grand Defender of our sanctified evasions, our privileged status as the secular clergy of a society we cannot serve, let alone save? Have we committed the further and grievous sin of making a Stevens in our own image, a poet of professors as Auden and Eliot and Arnold used to be? Having employed Stevens as a weapon in the mimic wars of criticism against the anti-Romantic legions of the Eliotics and Arnoldians, are we now confronted by his poems as so many statues in the formal parks of our university culture? Are his poems still Spirit to us, or are they only what Emerson, most prudent of New England seers, shrewdly called Commodity? Have we made him too into Literature? Do we need now to defend him against ourselves?

Several critics have regarded Stevens as essentially a comic poet. I think this characterization is not adequate to even his more sardonic aspect, but at least it reminds us of how humorous he could be. One of my favorite poems in *Harmonium*, which I rarely persuade anyone else to like, is called "Two Figures in Dense Violet Light." I take it as being a superbly American kind of defeated eroticism, the complaint of a would-be lover who is ruefully content to be discontent, because he rather doubts that high romance can be domesticated anyway in a world still so ruggedly

New. One might think of this poem's speaker as being a decadent Huckleberry Finn dressed up to play the part of Romeo:

> I had as lief be embraced by the porter at the hotel
> As to get no more from the moonlight
> Than your moist hand.
>
> Be the voice of night and Florida in my ear.
> Use dusky words and dusky images.
> Darken your speech.
>
> Speak, even, as if I did not hear you speaking,
> But spoke for you perfectly in my thoughts,
> Conceiving words,
>
> As the night conceives the sea-sounds in silence,
> And out of their droning sibilants makes
> A serenade.
>
> Say, puerile, that the buzzards crouch on the ridge-pole
> And sleep with one eye watching the stars fall
> Below Key West.
>
> Say that the palms are clear in a total blue,
> Are clear and are obscure; that it is night;
> That the moon shines.

Though more than usually mocking and self-mocking, this is surely another of Stevens' hymns to the Interior Paramour, another invocation of his Muse, his version of Whitman's Fancy. But Whitman's Fancy, though she rarely emanated very far out from him, did have a touch or two of an exterior existence. Stevens' Paramour, poor girl, is the most firmly Interior being in Romantic tradition. Compared to her, the epipsyches of Nerval, Poe, Shelley and the young Yeats are buxom, open-air, Renoir-like ladies. Stevens knows this, and the violet light of his poem is so dense that the two figures might as well be one. "What a love affair!" we cannot help exclaiming, as the Grand Solipsist murmurs to his Paramour: "Speak, even, as if I did not hear you speaking, / But spoke for you perfectly in my thoughts." This is a delicious Dialogue of One, all right, and we find its true father in some of Emerson's slyly bland observations on the Self-Reliance of Spheral Man. Recalling one Boscovich, an Italian Newtonian who had formulated a more-than-usually crazy version of the molecular theory of matter, Emerson mused: "Was it Boscovich who found that our bodies never come in contact? Well, souls never touch their objects. An innavigable sea washes with silent waves between us and the things we aim at and converse with."

In Stevens, this "innavigable sea" is called "the dumbfoundering abyss / Between us and the object," and no poet has been more honestly ruthless about the actual dualism of our everyday perceptions and imperceptions. Except for a peculiar roster of fabulistic caricatures, there aren't any *people* in Stevens' poems, and this exclusion is comprehensive enough to include Stevens himself as whole man or as person. But the "whole man" or "person" in a poem is generally only another formalizing device or dramatizing convention anyway, a means of self-presentation that Stevens did not care to employ. In the difficult poem, "The Creations of Sound," written against Eliot, who appears in it as X, Stevens declares himself as:

> . . . a separate author, a different poet,
> An accretion from ourselves, intelligent
> Beyond intelligence, an artificial man
>
> At a distance, a secondary expositor,
> A being of sound, whom one does not approach
> Through any exaggeration.

For all his antimythological bias, the old Stevens turned to Ulysses, "symbol of the seeker," to present his own final quest for a transcendental self. Unlike the Ulysses of Tennyson, at once somewhat Homeric, Dantesque, Shakespearean and Miltonic, the Ulysses of Stevens is not seeking to meet anything even partly external to himself. What other Ulysses would start out by saying: "As I know, I am and have / The right to be"? For Stevens, "the right to know / And the right to be are one," but his Ulysses must go on questing because:

> Yet always there is another life,
> A life beyond this present knowing,
> A life lighter than this present splendor,
> Brighter, perfected and distant away,
> Not to be reached but to be known,
> Not an attainment of the will
> But something illogically received,
> A divination, a letting down
> From loftiness, misgivings dazzlingly
> Resolved in dazzling discovery.

There is, despite so many of his critics, no doubt concerning the precursor of this ultimate Stevens. For that "something illogically received," we can recall the divinations of the inescapable father of the American Sublime, who uttered the grand formula: "All I know is reception; I am and I have: but I do not get, and when I have fancied I had gotten anything, I found I did not." In the same essay, the superb "Experience," Emerson mused: "I am very content with knowing, if only I could know." Both Emerson and Stevens hold hard to what both call "poverty," imaginative need, and they believe that holding hard long enough will compel the self to attain its due sphericity. Between the skeptically transcendental grandfather and the transcendentally skeptical grandson came the heroic father, spheral man himself, unqualified in his divinations, who tells us what we miss in Emerson and Stevens alike, and what we cannot resist in him:

> Encompass worlds, but never try to encompass me,
> I crowd your sleekest and best by simply looking toward you.
>
> Writing and talk do not prove me,
> I carry the plenum of proof and every thing else in my face,
> With the hush of my lips I wholly confound the skeptic.

For the absolutely transcendental self, the man-god, we read Whitman only, but I am astonished always how much of it abides in Stevens, despite nearly all his critics, and despite the Idiot Questioner in Stevens himself. His evasive glory is hardly distinguishable from his imperfect solipsism, or from ours. And there I verge upon what I take as the clue to his greatness; in the curiously esoteric but centrally American tradition of Emerson, Whitman, Thoreau and Dickinson, Stevens is uniquely the twentieth century poet of that solitary and inward glory we can none of us share with others. His value is that he describes and even celebrates (occasionally) our selfhood-communings as no one else can or does. He knows that "the sublime comes down / To the spirit and space," and though he keeps acknowledging the spirit's emptiness and space's vacancy, he keeps demonstrating a violent abundance of spirit and a florabundance of the consolations of space. He is the poet we always needed, who would speak for the solitude at our center, who would do for us what his own "Large Red Man Reading" did for those ghosts that returned to earth to hear his phrases, "and spoke the feeling for them, which was what they had lacked." Or, to state this function positively, Stevens, more even than Wordsworth, is the essential poet who can recognize that:

> There is a human loneliness,
> A part of space and solitude,
> In which knowledge cannot be denied,
> In which nothing of knowledge fails,
> The luminous companion, the hand,
> The fortifying arm, the profound
> Response, the completely answering voice,

> That which is more than anything else
> The right within us and about us,
> Joined, the triumphant vigor, felt,
> The inner direction on which we depend,
> That which keeps us the little that we are,
> The aid of greatness to be and the force.

There is nothing communal here. Stevens celebrates an apprehension that has no social aspect whatsoever and that indeed appears resistant to any psychological reductions we might apply. As no one is going to be tempted to call Stevens a mystical poet, or in any way religious, we rightly confront a considerable problem in description whenever Stevens is most himself. His True Subject appears to be his own sense of glory, and his true value for his readers appears to be that he reminds us of our own moments of solipsistic bliss, or at least of our aspirations for such moments.

The Stevens I begin to sketch has little in common with the poet of "decreation" most of his better critics have described for us. There is indeed a Stevens as seen by Hillis Miller, a poet of the almost-Paterian flux of sensations, of a cyclic near-nihilism returning always upon itself. There is also truly a Stevens as seen by Helen Vendler: Stevens the venerable ironist, apostle of "the total leaflessness." I do not assert that these are merely peripheral aspects of the poet, but they seem to me aspects only, darker saliences that surround the central man, shadows flickering beyond that crucial light cast by the single candle of Stevens' self-joying imagination, his version of "A Quiet Normal Life":

> His place, as he sat and as he thought, was not
> In anything that he constructed, so frail,
> So barely lit, so shadowed over and naught,
>
> As, for example, a world in which, like snow,
> He became an inhabitant, obedient
> To gallant notions on the part of cold.
>
> It was here. This was the setting and the time
> Of year. Here in his house and in his room,
> In his chair, the most tranquil thought grew peaked
>
> And the oldest and the warmest heart was cut
> By gallant notions on the part of night—
> Both late and alone, above the crickets' chords,
>
> Babbling, each one, the uniqueness of its sound.
> There was no fury in transcendent forms.
> But his actual candle blazed with artifice.

Stevens' customary anxiety about transcendent forms is evident, yet it is also evident that his actual candle is precisely a transcendent form. Wordsworth was sanely English in refusing to go too far into his True Subject, which was his own sense of actual sublimity. Emerson, deliberately and wildly American, made possible for all his descendants the outrageous True Subject of the American Sublime. Mocking as always where he is most vulnerable and most involved, here is Stevens' "The American Sublime":

> How does one stand
> To behold the sublime,
> To confront the mockers,
> The mickey mockers
> And plated pairs?
>
> When General Jackson
> Posed for his statue
> He knew how one feels.
> Shall a man go barefoot
> Blinking and blank?
>
> But how does one feel?
> One grows used to the weather,
> The landscape and that;
> And the sublime comes down
> To the spirit itself,
>
> The spirit and space,
> The empty spirit
> In vacant space.
> What wine does one drink?
> What bread does one eat?

Juxtapose this to one of the pure versions of the American Sublime:

In the highest moments, we are a vision. There is nothing that can be called gratitude nor properly joy. The soul is raised over passion. It seeth nothing so much as Identity. It is a Perceiving that Truth and Right ARE. Hence it becomes a perfect Peace out of the knowing that all things will go well. Vast spaces of nature, the Atlantic Ocean, the South Sea; vast intervals of time, years, centuries, are annihilated to it; this which I think and feel underlay that former state of life and circumstances, as it does underlie my present, and will always all circumstance, and what is called life and what is called death.

This excerpt from Emerson's 1838 Journal was modified into one of the most famous passages in the essay, "Self-Reliance." Nervous as Stevens is at confronting possible mockers, his American Sublime is no appreciable distance from Emerson's. One doesn't see Stevens posing for his statue, but he still admits that the Sublime comes down to what one feels and what one sees, and his emptiness of spirit and vacancy of space were part of the weather, inner and outer, and not permanent metaphysical reductions. That which he was, that only could he see, and he never wearied of affirming his version of Self-Reliance:

> . . . What
> One believes is what matters. Ecstatic identities
> Between one's self and the weather and the things
> Of the weather are the belief in one's element,
> The casual reunions, the long-pondered
> Surrenders, the repeated sayings that
> There is nothing more and that it is enough
> To believe in the weather and in the things and men
> Of the weather and in one's self, as part of that
> And nothing more.

How can a solipsism present itself in the accents of glory, we may be uneasy enough to ask, and again, can a solipsism be a possible humanism? I begin an answer with the dark Wittgensteinian aphorism: What the solipsist *means* is right. For, though solipsism is refutable by its status as tautology, this is what Wittgenstein means when he speaks of a *deep* tautology, which leads to a true realism. Stevens too knows, as Emerson knew, that what he *says* is wrong, but that his meaning is right. The European Sublime had a communal aspect, however solitary its stimulus, but we are of an even more displaced Protestant national sensibility, and, accordingly, we come to reality only through knowing first the scandalous reality of our own selves. Or, as Stevens said:

> The lean cats of the arches of the churches,
> That's the old world. In the new, all men are priests.

Stevens is a priest, not of the invisible, but of that visible he labors to make a little hard to see. He serves that visible, not for its own sake, but because he wants to make his own sublimity more visible to himself. Endlessly qualifying his sense of his own greatness, he still endlessly returns to rest upon such a sense. Yet he knows that he needs us, his possible readers, to do for him "what he cannot do for himself, that is to say, receive his poetry." As he proudly tells us, he addresses us as an elite, being in this one respect, at least, more honest than a far more esoteric and difficult poet, Whitman. In *The Noble Rider and the Sound of Words*, Stevens says:

> . . . all poets address themselves to someone and it is of the essence of that instinct, and it seems to amount to an instinct, that it should be to

an elite, not to a drab but to a woman with the hair of pythoness, not to a chamber of commerce but to a gallery of one's own, if there are enough of one's own to fill a gallery. And that elite, if it responds, not out of complaisance, but because the poet has quickened it, because he has educed from it that for which it was searching in itself and in the life around it and which it had not yet quite found, will thereafter do for the poet what he cannot do for himself, that is to say, receive his poetry.

There are two questions to be asked of this passage: What is it in this poet that gives him the instinct to address himself not to a drab but to a woman with the hair of a pythoness, and what is it that we keep searching for in ourselves that Stevens would quicken in us, that he would educe from us? The answer to both questions must be the same answer: a quality that Stevens calls "nobility." As he knew, it is hardly a word that now moves us, and I suspect he chose the word defiantly and therefore wrongly. Stevens says, in the same essay, that "It is one of the peculiarities of the imagination that it is always at the end of an era." Certainly Stevens now seems peculiarly to have been at the end of an era, where he himself could still be visualized as a *noble* rider moving to the sound of words. I myself have come to think that the principal peculiarity of the imagination is that it does not exist, or to state my thought another way, that people talking about the arts do better when they begin to talk as though the imagination did not exist. Let us reduce to the rocky level, and say, as Hobbes did, that "decaying sense" most certainly does exist. Stevens had then a decaying sense of nobility, which he called an imagination of nobility. "Noble," in its root, means to be knowing or seeing, and Stevens had therefore a decaying sense of a certain seeing that was also a knowing. I turn again to Stevens' central precursor for the inevitable vision of this nobility in its American variety:

> . . . This insight, which expresses itself by what is called Imagination, is a very high sort of seeing, which does not come by study, but by the intellect being where and what it sees; by sharing the path or circuit of things through forms, and so making them translucid to others.

"Leave the many and hold the few," Emerson also advises in his late poem, "Terminus," thus sanctioning the democratic poet, like Whitman, in the pragmatic address to an actual elite. Stevens needed little sanctioning as to audience, but he was rather anxious about his own constant emphasis upon the self as solitary "scholar," and his recourse was to plead "poverty." He cannot have been unaware that both "scholar" and "poverty" in his rather precise senses were Emersonian usages. A great coverer of traces, Stevens may be judged nevertheless to have turned more to a tradition than to a man. American Romanticism found its last giant in Stevens, who defines the tradition quite as strongly as it informs him.

"The prologues are over. . . . It is time to choose," and the Stevens I think we must choose writes the poems not of an empty spirit in vacant space, but of a spirit so full of itself that there is room for nothing else. This description hardly appears to flatter Stevens, yet I render it in his praise. Another of his still neglected poems, for which my own love is intense, is entitled simply, "Poem With Rhythms":

> The hand between the candle and the wall
> Grows large on the wall.
>
> The mind between this light or that and space,
> (This man in a room with an image of the world,
> That woman waiting for the man she loves,)
> Grows large against space:
>
> *There the man sees the image clearly at last.*
> *There the woman receives her lover into her heart*
> *And weeps on his breast, though he never comes.*
>
> It must be that the hand
> Has a will to grow larger on the wall,
> To grow larger and heavier and stronger than
> The wall; and that the mind
> Turns to its own figurations and declares,
> *"This image, this love, I compose myself*
> *Of these. In these, I come forth outwardly.*
> *In these, I wear a vital cleanliness,*
> *Not as in air, bright-blue-resembling air,*
> *But as in the powerful mirror of my wish and will."*

The principal difference between Stevens and Whitman appears to be that Stevens admits his mind is alone with its own figurations, while Whitman keeps inaccurately but movingly insisting he wants "contact" with other selves. His "contact" is an Emersonian term, and we know, as Whitman's readers, that he actually cannot bear "contact," any more than Emerson, Dickinson, Frost or Stevens can tolerate it. "Poem With Rhythms," like so much of Stevens, has a hidden origin in Whitman's "The Sleepers," particularly in a great passage apparently describing a woman's disappointment in love:

> I am she who adorn'd herself and folded her hair expectantly,
> My truant lover has come, and it is dark.
>
> Double yourself and receive me darkness,
> Receive me and my lover too, he will not let me go without him.

I roll myself upon you as upon a bed, I resign myself to the dusk.

He whom I call answers me and takes the place of my lover,
He rises with me silently from the bed.

Darkness, you are gentler than my lover, his flesh was sweaty and panting,
I feel the hot moisture yet that he left me.

My hands are spread forth, I pass them in all directions.
I would sound up the shadowy shore to which you are journeying.

Be careful, darkness! already, what was it touch'd me?
I thought my lover had gone, else darkness and he are one,
I hear the heart-beat, I follow, I fade away.

This juxtaposition of major Whitman to relatively minor Stevens is not altogether fair, but then I don't think I hurt Stevens by granting that Whitman, upon his heights, is likely to make his descendant seem only a dwarf of disintegration. Whitman-as-Woman invokes the darkness of birth, and blends himself into the mingled Sublimity of death and the Native Strain. Stevens-as-Interior-Paramour invokes only his mind's own figurations, but he sees himself cleansed in the vitalizing mirror of will as he could never hope to see himself in the mere outwardness of air. Whitman oddly but beautifully persuades us of a dramatic poignance that his actual solipsism does not earn, while Stevens rather less beautifully knows only the nondramatic truth of his own fine desperation.

What then is Stevens giving us? What do we celebrate with and in him when he leads us to celebrate? His vigorous affirmation, "The Well Dressed Man With a Beard," centers on "a speech / Of the self that must sustain itself on speech." Is eloquence enough? I turn again to the fountain of our will, Emerson, who had the courage to insist that eloquence was enough, because he identified eloquence with "something unlimited and boundless," in the manner of Cicero. Here is Stevens mounting through eloquence to his individual sense of "something unlimited and boundless," a "something" not beyond our apprehension:

Last night at the end of night his starry head,
Like the head of fate, looked out in darkness, part
Thereof and part desire and part the sense
Of what men are. The collective being knew
There were others like him safely under roof:

The captain squalid on his pillow, the great
Cardinal, saying the prayers of earliest day;
The stone, the categorical effigy;
And the mother, the music, the name; the scholar,
Whose green mind bulges with complicated hues:

> True transfigurers fetched out of the human mountain,
> True genii for the diminished, spheres,
> Gigantic embryos of populations,
> Blue friends in shadows, rich conspirators,
> Confiders and comforters and lofty kin.
>
> To say more than human things with human voice,
> That cannot be; to say human things with more
> Than human voice, that, also, cannot be;
> To speak humanly from the height or from the depth
> Of human things, that is acutest speech.

A critic who has learned, ruefully, to accept the reductive view that the imagination is only decaying sense, must ask himself: Why is he so moved by this transfiguration of language into acutest speech? He may remember, in this connection, the prose statement by Stevens that moves him most:

> Why should a poem not change in sense when there is a fluctuation of the whole of appearance? Or why should it not change when we realize that the indifferent experience of life is the unique experience, the item of ecstasy which we have been isolating and reserving for another time and place, loftier and more secluded. . . .

The doctrinal voice of Walter Pater, another unacknowledged ancestor, is heard in this passage, as perhaps it must be heard in any modern Epicureanism. Stevens, I suggest, is the Lucretius of our modern poetry, and like Lucretius seeks his truth in mere appearances, seeks his spirit in things of the weather. Both poets are beyond illusions, yet both invest their knowing of the way things are with a certain grim ecstasy. But an American Lucretius, coming after the double alienation of European Romanticism and domestic Transcendentalism, will have lost all sense of the communal in his ecstasy. Stevens fulfilled the unique enterprise of a specifically American poetry by exposing the essential solipsism of our Native Strain. No American feels free when he is not alone, and every American's passion for Yes affirms a hidden belief that his soul's substance is no part of the creation. We are mortal gods, the central strain in our poetry keeps saying, and our aboriginal selves are forbidden to find companionship in one another. Our ecstasy comes only from self-recognition, yet cannot be complete if we reduce wholly to "the evilly compounded, vital I . . . made . . . fresh in a world of white." We need "The Poems of Our Climate" because we are, happily, imperfect solipsists, unhappy in a happily imperfect and still external world—which is to say, we need Stevens:

There would still remain the never-resting mind,
So that one would want to escape, come back
To what had been so long composed.
The imperfect is our paradise.
Note that, in this bitterness, delight,
Since the imperfect is so hot in us,
Lies in flawed words and stubborn sounds.

HELEN VENDLER

The Sausage Maker

God of the sausage-makers, sacred guild.

"**M**y poems are like decorations in a nigger cemetery." This is Stevens' flagrant borrowed simile for a chain of poems, fifty of them, an experiment in poetry as epigram, or poetry as fossil bones: "Piece the world together, boys, but not with your hands" (*The Collected Poems of Wallace Stevens*. New York: Knopf, 1954. p. 192). The poem, a token of things to come, is, like many foretastes, perversely experimental. Though the poetry of disconnection is Stevens' most adequate form, and though the gaps from canto to canto in the long poems will always challenge the best efforts of critical articulation, still the discontinuity will never again be so arrogant as in this example. There are no bridges here for the magnifico; he must migrate from one "floral tribute" to another, some visionary, some cynical, some bitter, some prophetic, some comic. Each is a "nigger fragment, a *mystique* / For the spirit left helpless by the intelligence" (265). They are fragments of vision seen in the mirror of the mind refusing to reconstruct itself, refusing the attempt to make a whole from the ruses that were shattered by the large. *Harmonium* was by no means a harmony: all of Stevens is in it, and not in embryo either; but although its tonal spectrum is as diverse as the one we find in *Decorations*, it is less shocking because the tones are presented in separate units, not heaped together ruthlessly in one poem. In *Decorations*,

---

From *On Extended Wings: Wallace Stevens' Longer Poems*. Copyright © 1969 by Harvard University Press. Undesignated parenthetical page numbers refer to *The Collected Poems of Wallace Stevens*; *OP* designates *Opus Posthumous*, and *L*, *Letters of Wallace Stevens* (see Bibliography).

• 15 •

the work seems to be left to the reader, since he must do the ordering of impressions; these are haiku potentially articulable, like the *Adagia*. Whether *Decorations* is any more than fifty short pieces pretending to be one poem is debatable, but if we believe in Stevens' good faith we must assume he thought it a viable whole. His wholes were always melting into each other, of course; his work was all one poem to him, clearly, but yet he did divide it into parts.

The sense of death and fatal chill is the "subject" of *Decorations*, as it will be the subject of *The Auroras of Autumn*, but to read only physical death into Stevens' lines is to limit his range. To be dead is also not to live in a physical world, to "live a skeleton's life, / As a disbeliever in reality, / A countryman of all the bones in the world" (*Opus Posthumous: Poems, Plays, Prose by Wallace Stevens*. New York: Knopf, 1957. p. 117), and Stevens is afraid, in his fifty-sixth year, that he is already shriveling into that dwarf form. His depletion is his specter, and his wrestlings with it make up *Decorations*. The resources of man facing death compose the metaphorical range of the poem; from legacies left to heirs to the desire for heaven, from stoicism to cynicism, from hedonism to nostalgia, from self-delusion to a willed belief that life is as real as death. Stevens chooses to express no preference among these responses, except by the implicit preference accorded by convention to the beginning and end.

The mythologizing of Whitman-as-sun into a prophetic figure begins the poem boldly, in a partially tempered version of Stevens' boisterous tone. Instead of the ring of men chanting in orgy on a summer morn, we have the Whitman-sun chanting on the ruddy shore of an autumn day. He is a Jovian figure, moving with large-mannered motions, "A giant, on the horizon, glistening" (442), "rugged and luminous" (479), one of Stevens' many chanting figures:

> Nothing is final, he chants. No man shall see the end.
> His beard is of fire and his staff is a leaping flame.

Like the "new resemblance of the sun" in *An Ordinary Evening in New Haven*, this sun is "a mythological form, a festival sphere / A great bosom, beard and being, alive with age" (466), with all the equivocal sentimentality still attached to our images of Jehovah.

From this rather self-indulgent flame, the poem proceeds to its ending in snow, and the immortality of the chanting sun gives way, finally, to the stoic's revenge—lopping off his feet, as Blake said, so as not to want shoes. Human solidarity (advocated in the penultimate stanza) is no defense against decay, since there is no strength that can withstand process; only wisdom, by its slyness, anticipates destruction, slipping from the grip of winter by anticipating its clasp. What can winter do to one who has already forsaken casinos for igloos?

> . . . Can all men, together, avenge
> One of the leaves that have fallen in autumn?
> But the wise man avenges by building his city in snow.
>
> (i)

Neither sand nor rock, as in the Bible, but snow; and not a house but a city; and not "on," but "in," with its diffuseness of reference. This preventive avenging is stated as a proverb, and the suggested vengeance is reaffirmed by the telling dactyls of the last line. It is a remark, however, not an accomplishment; what it means to build a city in snow is to use this rhetoric of cunning, to put to bold use intimations of despair, to counter the erosions of process by one's own ice palace, not to regret autumn; to be the snow man, in short, and to decorate the cemetery.

To write of nothing that is not there is almost impossible to Stevens with his gift for nostalgic reminiscence, for the poetry of the vanished, but to write of the nothing that *is* there is more possible, and accounts for some of his most brilliant poems ("The Snow Man," "No Possum, No Sop, No Taters," "The Plain Sense of Things," "The Course of a Particular"). The full rhetoric of nostalgia and the taut rhetoric of the minimal are at war in him, profitably; sadness and stoicism contend, and forth the particulars of poetry come. There is a curiosity in Stevens' stoicism that redeems it from indifference or listlessness. As the joyless becomes the norm, the inveterate aesthetician's eye remarks the change:

> It was when the trees were leafless first in November
> And their blackness became apparent, that one first
> Knew the eccentric to be the base of design.
>
> (iii)

We scarcely have a name for a tone of this sort, verging, as it does, as close to irony as extreme dryness can bring it, grafting schoolmaster's language and impersonal detachment onto a sinister paradox of disorder, all to express a tragic intimation. It is the tone of the doctor investigating his own mortal disease and writing his report, embodying an intrinsic pathos as the clinician records his own decline.

Stevens is remarkable in his evasions of the first person singular, and the options of avoidance are many—"one" and "he" and "we" are Stevens' favorites, as well as the "I" of dramatic monologue. "We" is perhaps tarnished for us by its long use in "high sentence": it belongs to the rhetoric of sermons, of political oratory, of moral verse. Though Stevens is fond of its oracular potentialities ("We live in an old chaos of the sun") he uses it chiefly as a signal of an experience not peculiar to the poet, reserving for that special case the particularized "he." In the long poems, Stevens is uncomfortable with any pronoun after a while, and prefers (abandoning his practice in the *Comedian*) to change from first person to third person to second person at will. In this respect again, *Decorations* is the most eccentric of the long poems, as the speaker metamorphoses from detached aesthetician and scholar ("one") to one of us ("we") to a man alone ("Shall I grapple with my destroyers?") to a man having a dialogue with a servant (xxvi) to a commentator on someone else ("It needed the heavy nights of drenching weather / To make him return to people"). The extreme variation of speakers makes us, in defense, assume a single sensibility "behind" the scene, a puppet master of whom we can say only that he is a man revolving thoughts on middle age, death, and the compensations of creation. This temptation to impose order by a thematic statement explains the natural tendency to reduce Stevens to his subject matter, to look for consistency of some kind in such a welter of styles, even at the cost of making the manner disappear entirely.

The speaker of *Decorations* has a horror of dying "a parish death" (in which the cost of burial of a pauper is borne by the parish), because the irony is too great: Death the priest in his opulent purple and white vestments set against the pine coffin and maimed rites of the pauper. How to cheat death of that triumph, how to redeem our own ignominy, is the question of the poem, and the answer of course is both pitiful (we decorate the cemetery with grotesque poem-bouquets) and stern (we build our city in snow). The third "answer"—that the sun is eternal and so our death is fictitious—begins the poem, but never assumes any real importance in it, except in stanza xlvii, where the sun's indifference to the world, its self-sustenance ("It must create its colors out of itself"), is insisted upon. The stanzas explicitly about poetry both attempt to exalt it by Stevens' religious intonations (vii, xv, xxxvi, xlviii) and yet reduce it by revealing its carnality and its ineffectual "comedy of hollow sounds" (xiii, xxii). In the most ironic passage of all, Stevens visualizes his fifty stanzas as so many sausage links, presided over by the "god of the sausages" or possibly an even more insignificant Muse, a mere patron saint sanctifying himself by a complacent self-regard (xlii).

The oddest characteristic of *Decorations* is its abjuring of verbs. In at least a fifth of the poem the stanzas are syntactically incomplete, and verbs have been dispensed with. Partly, this yields a quality of epigram ("Out of sight, out of mind") which helps to give the poem its extraordinary aridity, and partly it strengthens the sense that these are jottings, *adagia*, epitaphs, the daily *pensées* of the inspector of gravestones. Usually, the verbs can be easily supplied, since Stevens is not interested in mystification for its own sake, but the absence of an opening clause impersonalizes the topic further:

[What we confront in death is]
[What I want to write about is]
[What we truly experience is]

Not the ocean of the virtuosi
But the ugly alien, the mask that
  speaks
Things unintelligible, yet understood.   (xxxix)

The stanza could imply any of the previous beginnings, but its strength lies in not needing them. The formula used in this stanza (not X but Y) is one of Stevens' commonest, and is frequently preceded elsewhere by "he wanted" or "he saw." The absence here of such a verb creates the phrase as an immediate object of perception to the reader, with no intervening subject, as Stevens achieves the poetry of no perceiver, the landscape poetry of the mind, so to speak. The personal voice, with its clamor of selfhood, is too desperately intrusive, and yet invented personae carry the immediate flavor of irony. One solution, adopted here, is to drop the subject voice entirely.

Another is to reproduce the interior musing of the mind, as the mind has no subject-relation to itself, needs no explanations to itself of its own hurdles, and can speak in ellipses:

The album of Corot is premature.
A little later when the sky is black.
Mist that is golden is not wholly most.
                    (xxxviii)

If we supply the missing links, the verse might read: "[Do not offer me] the album [of reproductions of paintings of summer] of Corot. [That] is premature [—to solace myself with art in the absence of the reality it reproduces, since something of summer is still left. Give me the album] a little later when the sky is black. [It is true that the mists of autumn are around me, but they are tinged with the gold of summer still, and] mist that is golden is not wholly mist." Or, as Stevens put it briefly to Hi Simons, "Do not show me Corot while it is still summer; do not show me pictures of summer while it is still summer; even the mist is golden; wait until a little later" (*Letters of Wallace Stevens*, edited by Holly Stevens. New York: Knopf, 1966. p. 349). My amplification of the original lines, and Stevens' paraphrase of them, both lose the dryness of the poem, where Stevens' truncated dismissal of art is flavored with epigram in the punning near-chiasmus of sound—mist, golden, wholly, mist—and where something like malice supervenes on the foreboding of the second line.

One of Stevens' continuing triumphs is his rapidity of change as he is flicked by various feelings. Despair overlaid by wry cynicism—"There is no such thing as innocence in autumn"—is succeeded immediately by a pallor of hope—"Yet, it may be, innocence is never lost" (xliv). The autonomy of the stanzas of *Decorations* suggests that all its exertions exist simultaneously rather than successively. Though Stevens can order his poems temporally, as his nostalgias, farewells, and prophecies attest, here, as in other long poems, the unity is radial, not linear. Stevens' true subject in *Decorations* becomes the complexity of mental response as he gives intimations, in these fifty stanzas, of almost all possible reactions to the decay that is the topic of the poem. If this is a poetry of meditation, it does not have the sustained progressive development that we know in other meditative poets; it is rather the staccato meditation of intimation and dismissal, of fits and starts, revulsions and shrugs, lightenings and sloughs, the play of the mind and sensibility over a topic.

Except for two sections (i and iv), the stanzas are of three or four lines, and depend almost entirely on very simple rhetorical figures for their form. Often the figure is antithesis, for instance, as in the dominating contrasts of summer and winter, rich and poor, the mechanical and the human, the social and the private:

> A bridge above the bright and blue of water
> And the same bridge when the river is frozen.
> Rich Tweedle-dum, poor Tweedle-dee.
>
> (xxiv)

Such antitheses stress the indistinguishability of the basic forms underlying the qualitative apparel. The decorations are a mediation between the living and the dead, and the speaker, not yet dead but no longer quite alive, stands between the systems of antitheses,

> Between farewell and the absence of farewell,
> The final mercy and the final loss,
> The wind and the sudden falling of the wind.
>
> (x)

Sometimes the rhetorical figure will come from logic, as in the deliberately trivial arithmetic by which one ascertains the density of life by dividing the number of legs one sees by two (xliii), or in the more enigmatic series of instances leading to an induction of stanza xxiii:

> The fish are in the fishman's window,
> The grain is in the baker's shop,
> The hunter shouts as the pheasant falls.
> Consider the odd morphology of regret.

Decorations is a poem of regret; placing decorations on graves is a gesture of regret; and yet these actions are reserved by the human world for its own members alone. No regret is expended on the deaths of the fish, the wheat, the pheasant. Rather, we buy, sell, and deal in death of all sorts without regret every day. But the compression of the verse forces us to leap from the three instances to the antithesis of the final ironic line without the explicit connectives of conventional logic.

The internal echoes of *Decorations* are casual, with certain spheres of metaphorical reference in the ascendant (sun and frost, wealth and poverty, vanished religion set against the new hymns sung by the various birds) but again, there is no particular consistency. There are, for instance, six poems about birds (I omit the pheasant, who does not sing, but only falls) and they vary in symbolic meaning. The birds "singing in the yellow patios, / Pecking at more lascivious rinds than ours, / From sheer Gemütlichkeit" (xiii) are both satirized and envied in their sensual and sentimental ease. To equate lasciviousness with bourgeois Gemütlichkeit is to dismiss it aesthetically rather than morally. The absence of possible lasciviousness is the deprivation of the next bird, the unmated leaden pigeon who, Stevens conjectures, must miss the symmetry of a female leaden mate. Imagining her, he makes her better than she would have been in reality, makes her not a leaden mortal pigeon but a silver ideal dove, and creates a transcendent ethereal bird who, like other Stevensian ideal figures, lives in a place of perpetual undulation:

> The leaden pigeon on the entrance gate
> Must miss the symmetry of a leaden mate,
> Must see her fans of silver undulate.
>
> (xiv)

Oriole and crow, the extremes of music in the natural world, form a simple opposition (xxv), and comment on the tendency of this declining decorator of cemeteries to distrust the beautiful and opulent. The sterile androgynous fowls of stanza xxx, one a day creature and one a night creature, are perhaps allied to the sun and moon, those two elements between which Crispin voyages. Singly, they are impotent, because creation requires the separation of genders.

> The hen-cock crows at midnight and lays no egg,
> The cock-hen crows all day. But cockerel shrieks,
> Hen shudders: the copious egg is made and laid.

The final fertility, Stevens might say in a less outrageous way, is in the journey back and forth between the antithetical states, not in any imagined confluence of opposites. Only with the interpenetration, but no identification, of the antithetical elements can the shrill vocalism of crowing become the copious egg, an exhibit scrutinized here at arm's length.

As for the rare and royal purple bird (xxxiii), he finds his rarity not exalting but boring; like the poet of abnormal sensibility, he has no company, and must sing to himself, if only to provide some fictitious company. Though purple is the color of royalty, it is also, in Stevens, the color of middle age, of the malady of the quotidian, leading "through all its purples to the final slate" (96) of some unimaginable bleakness. Finally, Stevens leaves us with an image of the impotence of poetry—though it may live radiantly beyond much lustier blurs, it lives uncertainly and not for long (xxxii). Time, not the song of the cuckoo (even though cuckoos, if any bird, might appeal to the mad clockmaker of this universe), is the regulative principle of this clanking mechanism, the world:

> Everything ticks like a clock. The cabinet
> Of a man gone mad, after all, for time, in spite
> Of the cuckoos, a man with a mania for clocks.
>   (xlvi)

All that Stevens expects of his reader, then, is a hazy notion, certainly traditional enough, that birds are a figure for poetry. It is understood that as the context differs, so will the bird. In a context of clock time, he will be a cuckoo; in a context of lonely regal rarity, he will be a purple bird; in a context of fertility and shrillness, cock and hen; in a context of the real and ideal, a pigeon-dove; in the context of beauty of song, oriole versus crow; and in the context of reality, in the yellow patios, an anonymous figure, a "meaningless, natural effigy" (xx), trite and uninteresting until given a "revealing aberration" by the observant eye. This flexibility of reference is necessary in invoking other image clusters in the poem—the theater, the weather, and so on. Stevens' metaphors are extremely provisional in their species, but quite permanent in their genus, and the vegetation still abounds in forms, as the Collected Poems declare.

The alternative to varying the species of bird is of course to vary the environment of the bird, as Stevens had done in Thirteen Ways of Looking at a Blackbird, an early poem that in its epigrammatic and elliptic form anticipates Decorations (just as its variational scheme resembles "Sea Surface Full of Clouds" or "Variations on a Summer Day," and as its theme is allied to "Domination of Black"). The Ananke or Necessity of Decorations appears in the Blackbird as the black principle, the eccentric which is the base of design, the strict, the final, the intrinsic, the limiting, the temporal. The blackbird is the only element in nature which is aesthetically compatible with bleak light and bare limbs: he is, we may say, a certain kind of language, opposed to euphony, to those "noble accents and lucid inescapable rhythms" which Stevens used so memorably elsewhere in *Harmonium*. To choose the blackbird over the pigeon is a possible aesthetic for Stevens, and it is different from the aesthetic of Crispin who chose arrant stinks, the anti-aesthetic. There are thirteen ways of looking at a blackbird because thirteen is the eccentric number; Stevens is almost medieval in his relish for external form. This poetry will be one of inflection and innuendo; the inflections are the heard melodies (the whistling of the blackbird) and the innuendos are what is left out (the silence just after the whistling):

> I do not know which to prefer,
> The beauty of inflections
> Or the beauty of innuendoes,
> The blackbird whistling
> Or just after.
>
> (v)

As a description of both *Blackbird* and *Decorations* this could hardly be bettered. Stevens himself called *Blackbird* a collection of sensations, rather than of epigrams or of ideas (*L*, 251), but the later remarks on it to Henry Church are intellectual ones: that the last section was intended to convey despair, that section xii existed to convey the "compulsion frequently back of the things that we do" (*L*, 240). We are not falsifying the poem entirely, then, if we ask how, by varying the blackbird's surroundings, Stevens conveys to us both the sensations and the ideas which exist with them.

The blackbird has perhaps something in common with Eliot's "shadow" that falls between potency and act, desire and consummation. But Stevens would deny that it is a remediable or accidental intrusion between two things that without it would be better off. It is, rather, of one substance with the things it relates:

> A man and a woman
> Are one.
> A man and a woman and a blackbird
> Are one.
>
> (iv)

Between the man and the woman is the blackbird, one with them; between the man's mood and his environment is the blackbird, the indecipherable cause of the mood which is man's response to nature (vi);

between the man of Haddam and their imagined golden birds is the blackbird, the real on which they construct their "artifice of eternity" (vii); between the haunted man and his protective glass coach is the terror of the blackbird (xi); it lies at the base even of our powerful verbal defenses, those beautiful glass coaches of euphony and lucidity. It is, finally, the principle of our final relation to the universe, our compulsions, first of all,

> The river is moving.
> The blackbird must be flying.
>   (xii)

and lastly, our despair at death:

> It was evening all afternoon.
> It was snowing
> And it was going to snow.
> The blackbird sat
> In the cedar-limbs.
>   (xiii)

But neurosis and death are only instances of a pervasive relational eccentricity. Our extent in space (as well as in time) goes only as far as the blackbird goes—the blackbird is our "line of vision" (ix), as it is our line of thought: when we are of two minds (or, as Stevens presses it, "of three minds"), it is not as if we had a blackbird, an oriole, and a pigeon in view, but only "a tree / In which there are three blackbirds" (ii). The blackbird is by no means all—it is surrounded by the vastness of twenty mountains, the autumn winds, the snow—but though only a small part, it is the determining focus of relation.

Blackbird is undoubtedly a more finished poem than Decorations, its fineness of structure making for remarkable strength, as Stevens pursues his single image for a single theme through several aspects. Its subject, the "new aesthetic" of the spare and the eccentric as it arises from flaw and mortality, prohibits the use of the oratorical mode of Sunday Morning, a mode which becomes a blemish in certain stanzas (notably viii and xlviii) of the usually tight-reined Decorations. Blackbird depends wholly on contraction, on the simple declarative sentence reduced almost to the infantile. Just as the declarative sentence is the simplest grammatical figure, so tautology is the simplest rhetorical form, and Stevens deliberately approaches it:

> A man and a woman
> Are one.
> A man and a woman and a blackbird
> Are one.
>   (iv)

It was snowing
And it was going to snow.
(xiii)

I know . . . accents . . .
But I know
That the blackbird is involved
In what I know.
(viii)

Like Stevens, *exotisme voulu,* this is simplicity *voulu,* calling flamboyant attention to itself in a way that the unobtrusive simplicity of colloquial language does not. As an instrument, it is brilliant but limited, and clearly will not do for much more than thirteen stanzas. The increased expanse of *Decorations* comes at the cost of high finish, but promises perfections still far away, in the greater long poems to come. Meanwhile, these two poems together represent Stevens' most remarkable compression of his naturally voluminous self, a new asperity of language over a long span, a daringly varied meditative form, and a willingness, in the case of the later poem, to sacrifice finish for experiment's sake.

J. HILLIS MILLER

Stevens' Rock
and Criticism as Cure

It is not enough to cover the rock with leaves.
We must be cured of it by a cure of the ground
Or a cure of ourselves, that is equal to a cure

Of the ground, a cure beyond forgetfulness.
—STEVENS, "The Rock"

A "cure of the ground"? What can this mean? "Progress," Stevens says in the "Adagia," "is a movement through changes of terminology." "Rock," "ground," and even "forgetfulness" readers of Stevens will be able to interpret from other poems by him, from works in his immediate tradition, the tradition of Whitman and Emerson, or from the common language of poetry and metaphysics. Such readers will remember, among other rocks in Stevens, "this tufted rock / Massively rising high and bare" in "How to Live. What to Do," the Leibnizian "thought-like Monadnocks" of "This Solitude of Cataracts," the rocky mountain of "Chocorua to Its Neighbor," the rock of "The Poem that Took the Place of a Mountain," "The exact rock where his inexactnesses / Would discover, at last, the view toward which they had edged," and that ecstatic meridian rock of "Credences of Summer":

> The rock cannot be broken: It is the truth.
> It rises from land and sea and covers them.
> It is a mountain half way green and then,

From *The Georgia Review* 30, no. 1, (Spring 1976). Copyright © 1976 by J. Hillis Miller.

> The other immeasurable half, such rock
> As placid air becomes

Forgetfulness, or its converse, memory, is also a motif found else-where in Stevens, inextricably entwined with the theme of time, as in "The Owl in the Sarcophagus," where the fleeting present moment, the presence of the present, "the mother of us all," cries in her vanishing, "Keep you, keep you, I am gone, oh keep you as / My memory."

"Ground" too is a common word in Stevens. To follow it through his poetry is to observe its modulation from the everyday use of it as the solid earth we stand on ("The jar was round upon the ground"), to ground as background upon which a figure appears, to the more "metaphysical" use of the term as meaning "foundation," "basis," "source," "mind," or "consciousness," "reason," "measure." The rock "is the habitation of the whole, / Its strength and measure," "the main of things, the mind," in short, a Monadnock. Ground and rock are apparently not the same, since a cure of the ground is necessary to cure us of the rock, though what the difference is between ground and rock remains, at this point, something still to be interrogated. The means of this interrogation, however, as of the investigation of "forgetfulness," would, it seems, be the familiar one of following these words in their interplay with other words as they gradually weave together in a single grand intertextual system, a polyphonic har-mony of many notes, "The Whole of Harmonium," as Stevens wanted to call his *Collected Poems*.

What, then, of "cure"? It has little resonance in philosophic or poetic tradition and, according to the *Concordance to the Poetry of Wallace Stevens*, the word is used only once, in a more or less unpregnant way, prior to its decidedly pregnant use in "The Poem as Icon," the middle of the three sections of "The Rock." "The Poem as Icon" is in fact partly a meditation on the multiple senses, "the new senses in the engenderings of sense," of the word "cure," in its relation to certain other terms and figures. The word thereafter disappears from the poetic canon, not even being used in the third poem of "The Rock," though it does appear in the "Adagia": "Poetry is a health"; "Poetry is a cure of the mind." In formula-tions of the workings of intertextuality—the weavings of word with word, of figure with figure, in the canon of a writer, or of that canon in relation to tradition—the theorist would need to allow for the emergence of a word which is played with, turned this way and that, mated or copulated with other words, used as an indispensable means of that progress which takes place through changes of terminology, and then dropped.

To think of the whole work of a writer as being based on a permanent ground in an underlying system or code of terms, conceptual, figurative, "symbolic," mythical, or narrative, is an error, just as it is an error to suggest, as I. A. Richards does in his admirable *How to Read a Page*, that there may be in our Western languages a finite set of key words of multiple sense whose mastery would give approximate mastery of Western thought and literature. The repertoire of such words, uncanny with antithetical and irreconcilable meanings, is very large, finite still (there are only so many words in the *OED*), but virtually inexhaustible. Any poet's vocabulary is to some degree irreducibly idiosyncratic. The most unexpected words, for example "cure," may become momentarily nodes, at once fixed rock and treacherous abyss of doubled and redoubled meanings, around or over which the thought of the poet momentarily swirls or weaves its web. Such words are not the equivalents or substitutes for other terms. Each has its own proper laws and so may not be made an example of some general law. Such words may not be translated, thereby made transparent, dispensed with, evaporated, sublimated. They remain stubbornly heterogeneous, unassimilable, impervious to dialectical elation (*Aufhebung*), rocks in the stream, though the rock is air. The vocabulary of a poet is not a gathering or a closed system, but a dispersal, a scattering.

What, then, of "cure"? The first section of "The Rock," "Seventy Years Later," is, at least until the last two stanzas, as bleak and cold a poem as any Stevens wrote. It is a poem about forgetting. The old man of seventy has forgotten not the illusions of his past but the affective warmth of those illusions, "the life these lived in the mind." When that warmth goes, the illusions come to be seen as illusions and so are undermined, annihilated. Not only are their validity and vitality rejected, their very existence is denied: "The sounds of the guitar / Were not and are not. Absurd. The words spoken / Were not and are not." "Absurd": from *ab*, away, an intensive here, and *surdus*, deaf, inaudible, insufferable to the ear. The sounds of the guitar, those for example played by Stevens' man with the blue guitar, were not only an inharmonious jangling masking as harmony, they did not even exist at the time, were inaudible when they most seemed audible. They did not exist because they were pure fiction, based on nothingness. A surd in mathematics is a sum containing one or more irrational roots of numbers. (The square root of two is an irrational number. There is a square root of two, but it is not a number that can be expressed as an integer or as a finite fraction, not a number that can be expressed "rationally.") A surd in phonetics is a voiceless sound in speech, that is to say, a sound with no base in the vibration of the vocal chords. The original root of the word surd, *swer*, means to buzz or whisper, as in "susurration" or "swirl." The Latin *surdus* was chosen in medieval mathematics to translate an Arabic term which was itself a translation of the Greek *alogos*, speechless, wordless, inexpressible, irrational, groundless.

The first six stanzas of "Seventy Years Later" record a radical act of forgetting. This disremembering annihilates everything that seemed most vital in the poet's past, most solidly grounded. It annihilates it by uprooting it, by seeing its roots as non-existent, "alogical." Then in the final three stanzas the dismantled illusion is put together again. Though the base may be "nothingness," this nothingness contains a "métier," a craftsmanlike power of working, "a vital assumption." It contains a desire for illusion so great that the leaves come and cover that high rock of air, as the lilacs bloom in the spring, cleansing blindness, bringing sight again to birth, and so starting the cycle of illusion over again. Blindness is parallel to the deafness of "absurd," and the power of seeing again is here replaced and implicitly figured by "a birth of sight." The lilacs satisfy sight. They fill the eye, as the sounds of the guitar filled the ear, saturated it, so hiding the "permanent cold" at the base, "the dominant blank, the unapproachable," as he calls it in "An Ordinary Evening in New Haven." A cure of ourselves equal to a cure of the ground would make us sound, heal us of our deafness, our absurdity. Then we could hear again the sounds of the guitar, as springtime makes us see again, like a blindness cured, or scoured.

The cure of the ground called for in the beginning of the second poem of "The Rock," "The Poem as Icon," must be a "cure beyond forgetfulness." It must be a cure not subject to the periodic cycles of annihilation revealing the illusion to be illusion and so negating it. Or, perhaps, it must be a cure which reaches beyond forgetfulness, that repression which disables present affirmations. Such repression has caused us to forget the something lacking in earlier satisfactions, something missing even when we "lived in the houses of mothers." To remove this repression would, perhaps, make it possible to get to something solid that lies beneath, or to make something solid beneath that is not based on a forgetting and so vulnerable to forgetting. After the cure we would live in a permanent state of illusion known as illusion, therefore "beyond forgetfulness." This illusion would be known in such a way that the abyss, the Abgrund, would appear as the truth of the ground, without undermining the illusion, so that the illusion might never be forgotten. Or does Stevens mean that the cure beyond forgetfulness would permanently cover or solidify the abyss? Then the illusion might never again be scoured away and the abyss never again be seen: "the poem makes meanings of the rock, / Of such mixed motion and such imagery / That its barrenness becomes a thousand things / And so exists no more." The undecidable oscillation among these alternatives is expressed in Stevens' often-cited adage: "The final belief is to believe in a fiction, which you know to be a fiction, there being nothing else."

A similar oscillation (but what is the status of similarity here?) is expressed in the relation between rock and ground. Ground and rock are each the base of the other. The rock is the truth, but the rock is air, nothingness, and so must be grounded on something solid beneath it. The ground, on the other hand, is itself not ground. It is an abyss, the groundless, while the rock remains visible in the air as "the gray particular of man's life / The stone from which he rises, up—and—ho, / The step to the bleaker depths of his descents. . . ." The rock is the solid of the ground, the ground the base of the rock, in a perpetual reversal, interchange, doubling, or abyssing, what Stevens elsewhere calls, "an insolid billowing of the solid" ("Reality Is an Activity of the Most August Imagination").

The cure of the ground would be a caring for the ground, a securing of it, making it solid, as one cures a fiberglass hull by drying it carefully. At the same time the cure of the ground must be an effacing of it, making it vanish as a medicine cures a man of a disease by taking it away, making him sound again, or as an infatuated man is cured of a dangerous illusion. "Cure" comes from Latin *cura*, care, as in "curate" or "a cure of souls." The word "scour," which I used above, has the same root. A cure of the ground would scour it clean, revealing the bedrock beneath. Such a curing would be at the same time—according to an obsolete meaning of the word, with a different root, Middle English *cuuve*, cover, conceal, protect—a caring for the ground by hiding it. Stevens might even have known (why should he not have known?) the word "curiologic," which means, according to the *OED*, "of or pertaining to that form of hieroglyphic writing in which objects are represented by pictures, and not by symbolic characters." The root here is neither *cura* nor *cuuve*, but the Greek *kuriologia*, the use of literal expressions, speaking literally, from *kurios*, as an adjective: regular, proper; as a noun: lord, master. A curiological cure of the ground would find proper names for that ground, make a mimetic icon of it, copy it exactly, appropriate it, master it. The cure of the ground proposed in the poem is the poem itself. The poem is an icon, at once a "copy of the sun" and a figure of the ground, though the relation of sun and ground remains to be established. The icon (image, figure, resemblance) at once creates the ground, names it "properly," reveals it, and covers it over. The poem annihilates the rock, takes the place of it, and replaces it with its own self-sufficient fiction, the leaves, blossom, and fruit which come to cover the high rock. At that point its barrenness has become a thousand things and so exists no more.

The multiple meanings of the word "cure," like the meaning of all the key words and figures in "The Rock," are incompatible, irreconcilable. They may not be organized into a logical or dialectical structure but remain stubbornly heterogeneous. They may not be followed etymologically, to a single root which will unify or explain them, explicate them by implicating them in a single source. They may not be folded together in a unified structure, as of leaves, blossom, and fruit from one stem. The origin rather is bifurcated, even trifurcated, a forking root which leads the searcher for the ground of the word into labyrinthine wanderings in the forest of words. The meaning of the passages in "The Rock" turning on the word "cure" oscillates painfully within the reader's mind. However hard he tries to fix the word in a single sense it remains indeterminable, uncannily resisting his attempts to end its movement. Cover the abyss, or open it up, or find the bottom, the ground of the rock, and make it a solid base on which to build—which is it? How could it be all three at once? Yet it is impossible to decide which one it is. To choose one is to be led to the others and so to be led by the words of the poem into a blind alley of thought.

Since it is a question here of the abyss of the absurd and of the grounding or filling of that abyss, one may borrow from the French an untranslatable name for this enigma of the nameless, this impasse of language: *mise en abyme*. *Abyme* is an older variant of modern French *abîme*, from late Latin *abyssus*, from Greek *abussos*, without bottom. The circumflexed î, an i deprived of its head or dot and given a hat or tent instead, indicates a dropped s. This is then dropped in turn to be replaced by a y, *i grec*, Greek i. In fact the late Latin y was an equivalent both for Greek u, *upsilon*, "bare u," and for the y, or u with a tail, that is, an i sound, as in French *ici*. The Greek u, which became Roman y, is only one of the two letters derived from the Phoenician *waw*, which itself was derived from v. The other descendant is f, Greek *digamma*, "double gamma." The *gamma* is of course also y-shaped. The word *abyme* is itself a *mise en abyme*, hiding and revealing the hollow of the u by the masculine addition of the tail, but leaving no sign of the absent s. The word contains dropped letter behind dropped letter, in a labyrinth of interchanges figured by the doubling shape of the y: a path leading to a fork. Hercules at the crossroads, or Theseus at one of the infinitely repeating branchings of the Daedalian labyrinth, to which I shall return.

Mise en abyme is a term in heraldry meaning a shield which has in its center (*abyme*) a smaller image of the same shield, and so, by implication, ad infinitum, with ever smaller and smaller shields receding toward the central point. The nearest equivalent in the English language of heraldry is the admirably suggestive term "escutcheon of pretense." The arms to which a knight pretends to have a claim are *mise en abyme* on his own shield. As in the case of a bend sinister, the implication is of a possible illegitimacy, some break in the genetic line of filiation. I have, in *The Form of Victorian Fiction,* called this structure "the Quaker Oats box effect." To name it or to give examples of it is not to create a concept, a general structure which all the examples illustrate, since it is precisely a question, in this case, of what has no concept, no literal name. Therefore it can only be "figured," each time differently, and by analogies which are not symmetrical with one another. What is the meaning of the terms "figure," "icon," "analogy" here if there is no literal name on which they are based? Here, in any case, from Michel Leiris's autobiography, *L'âge d'homme* (1939), is a splendid "example" of a *mise en abyme:*

> I owe my first precise contact with the notion of infinity to a box of cocoa of Dutch manufacture, raw material (*matière première*) for my breakfasts. One side of this box was decorated with an image representing a peasant girl with a lace headdress who held in her left hand an identical box decorated with the same image and, pink and fresh, offered it with a smile. I remained seized with a sort of vertigo in imagining that infinite series of an identical image reproducing a limitless number of times the same young Dutch girl, who, theoretically getting smaller and smaller without ever disappearing, looked at me with a mocking air and showed me her own effigy painted on a cocoa box identical to the one on which she herself was painted.

The paradox of the *mise en abyme* is the following: without the production of some schema, some "icon," there can be no glimpse of the abyss, no vertigo of the underlying nothingness. Any such schema, however, both opens the chasm, creates it or reveals it, and at the same time fills it up, covers it over by naming it, gives the groundless a ground, the bottomless a bottom. Any such schema almost instantaneously becomes a trivial mechanism, an artifice. It becomes something merely made, confected, therefore all-too-human and rational. Examples would include the Daedalian labyrinth, product, after all, of a human artificer, however "fabulous," and the Borgesian labyrinths of words, products of a visible manipulation of verbal effects. Another "example" is the cunning wordplay of Stevens' "The Rock," with its sagacious and somewhat covert use of the full etymological complexity of a word like "cure." If Stevens is right to say that "poetry must be irrational" and that "poetry must resist the intelligence almost successfully," then the moment when the intelligence triumphs over the poem, encompassing its *mise en abyme* with human reason, is the moment of the poem's failure, its resolution into a rational paradigm. The *mise en abyme* must constantly begin again. "The Rock" is, accordingly, a running *mise en abyme*. The poem repeatedly takes some apparently simple word, a word not noticeably technical or tricky ("found," "exclaiming," "ground," or "cure") and plays with each word in turn, placing it in a context of surrounding words so that it gives way beneath its multiplying contradictory meanings and reveals a chasm below, a chasm which the word, for example the word "cure," cures in all senses of the word.

There are other ways, however, in which "The Rock" is a *mise an abyme*. One is the sequence of phrases in apposition. This is a constant feature of Stevens' poetic procedure: "The blooming and the musk / Were being alive, an incessant being alive, / A particular of being, that gross universe"; "They bud the whitest eye, the pallidest sprout, / New senses in the engenderings of sense, / The desire to be at the end of distances, / The body quickened and the mind in root." The relation among the elements in such a series is undecidable, abyssed. Since the phrases often have the same synactical pattern and are objects of the same verb (most often the verb "to be"), it seems as if they must be equivalents of one another, or at least figures for one another, but can "eye," "sprout," "senses," "desire," "body," and "mind" really be equivalent? Perhaps the phrases form a progression, a gradual approximation through incremental repetition ("being alive, an incessant being alive"), reaching closer and closer to the desired meaning in what Stevens in "An Ordinary Evening in New Haven" calls "the edgings and inchings of final form"? Perhaps each new phrase cancels the previous one? Sometimes the parallel in syntax is misleading, as when the phrase "that gross universe" is placed in apposition with the subsidiary word "being" in the phrase before, rather than with the apparently parallel word "particular." The sequence plays with various incongruent senses and grammatical functions of the word "being." Sometimes the established syntactical pattern misleads the reader into interpreting the grammar incorrectly or at any rate leads him into a fork in the labyrinth where he cannot decide which path to take, as when the parallelism of "And yet the leaves, if they broke into bud, / If they broke into bloom, if they bore fruit, / And if we ate the incipient colorings / Of their fresh culls might be a cure of the ground" makes "colorings" appear to be simultaneously the object of "ate" and the subject of "might be," which it cannot, logically, be. The actual subject of "might be" is "leaves," three lines above. The phrase seems alogical, absurd, with no root in a single sense.

Such sequences, with their tantalizing half-parallelisms and asymmetrical analogies, with their suggestions that the series might continue indefinitely without exhausting itself or "getting it right," are *mises en abyme*. They are like those nursery rhymes which work by variation and incremental repetition, such as "The House That Jack Built." John Ruskin, in the twenty-third letter of *Fors Clavigera* (1872), compares "The House That Jack Built" to the Daedalian maze: "the gradual involution of the ballad, and the necessity of clear-mindedness as well as clear utterance on the part of its singer, is a pretty vocal imitation of the deepening labyrinth." Like Stevens' sequences of phrases in apposition, "The House That Jack Built" turns back on itself, a snake with its tail in its mouth, or a snake almost succeeding in getting its tail in its mouth. Just as "that gross universe" comments on or defines the word "being," which has been the theme varied in the sequence of phrases in Stevens' sentence until then, so the *mise en abyme* of the potentially endlessly mounting series in "The House That Jack Built" is broken when "the farmer sowing his corn" is reached, since that corn is presumably the source of the malt that lay in the house that Jack built. This takes the listener back to the second item in the sequence and so makes the infinitely receding series, the labyrinth within the house that Jack built, an infinitely rotating circle instead. In the same way the diminishing sequence described in the passage from Leiris quoted above is blocked by the end which turns back to remind the reader that the "first" girl is herself an image painted on a box. The series, moreover, is asymmetrically balanced by a second paragraph describing the multiplying of erotic reflections in facing mirrors: "I am not far from believing that there was mixed in this first notion of infinity, acquired at about the age of ten (?), an element of a distinctly disturbing sort: the hallucinatory and genuinely ungraspable character of the young Dutch girl, repeated to infinity as libertine visions can be indefinitely multiplied by means of a carefully constructed play of mirrors in a boudoir."

This structure of not quite congruent parallelism is characteristic of all forms of the *mise en abyme*. This is one of the ways it keeps open the chasm while filling it, resists the intelligence almost successfully. An admirable example of this asymmetry is that cartoon by Charles Addams showing the receding reflections in doubled mirrors of a man in a barber chair, facing frontwards, then backwards, then frontwards again, in endless recession. One figure in the midst of the sequence, five images back into the mirror's depths, is a wolfman with fangs and a hairy face. The wolfman is the terrifying item which is part of the series but does not fit it, though he is neither its beginning, nor its end, nor its base. Another more complex example of the mirror as *mise en abyme* is Thomas Hardy's admirable poem "The Pedigree." As Ruskin astutely saw, "Jack's ghostly labyrinth [meaning the mythical Daedalian maze, with its Charles Addams monster as inhabitant] has set the pattern of almost everything linear and complex, since."

Characteristic of such structures is some play with the figure of container and contained or with an inside / outside opposition which reverses itself. Inside becomes outside, outside inside, dissolving the polarity. The house that Jack built contains all the elements in the nursery rhyme, though they are mostly outside the house. As Ruskin suggests, the cunning artifice of the poem is the house itself, just as the Daedalian labyrinth is at once an enclosure and a place of endless wandering. A labyrinth is a desert turned inside out. In a similar way the passage from Leiris's autobiography turns on the cocoa box which is a container of the *matière première* of the child's breakfast, while the girl who offers the box is also offering herself, in a troubling erotic abyssing which is another characteristic of the *mise en abyme*. Eating and sex are interchanged, as also in "The Rock," which has in its first section an embrace at noon at the edge of a field and moves on to the image of curing the ground and curing ourselves by eating the fruit grown from the rock. That eating, with its disturbing Miltonic and Biblical echoes, is also a transgression, with erotic and Satanic overtones. These involve seeing and knowing, in various punning ways, knowledge of the whole and of the base of the whole by incorporation of a synecdochic part: "in the day ye eat thereof then your eyes shall be opened, and ye shall be as gods, knowing good and evil" (Genesis, 3:5); "They bear their fruit so that the year is known, / As if its understanding was brown skin, / The honey in its pulp, the final found, / The plenty of the year and of the world." Like the passage from Leiris, "The Rock" contains a complicated play on the figure of container and contained, a version of what Kenneth Burke calls "the paradox of substance." The rock is the base from which things rise up, therefore it is outside. At the same time it is the habitation of the whole, that in which space and all the contents of space are contained. This enigmatic structure is repeated by the houses of mothers, by the sun, the fruit, and by the poem itself. To read the poem or to eat the fruit is to incorporate the whole as it is contained in the part, to incorporate even the ground of that whole, and so to become oneself whole, sound, cured, knowing all in a final "found."

The *mise en abyme* is likely also to contain some puzzling play with the intertwined notions of representation, on the one hand, and, on the other, figure, metaphor. The girl on the cocoa box offers smilingly a picture of herself, an image, an effigy, but she is herself only an image. The image within an image tends both to affirm the literal reality of the outside image and to undermine it, as in another, more recent, *New*

Yorker cartoon showing a middle-aged couple watching on television a representation of themselves watching a televised picture of themselves watching television, and so on. In "The Rock" this aporia of representation enters by way of the contradictory meanings of the word "icon," as it has already entered more obscurely in the word "shadow" in the first section. The poem as icon is both curiological, a mimetic copy of the whole, and at the same time a figure, similitude, or metaphor of it. It is an icon in both senses, in an undecidable play between literal and figurative. This baffling interchange between proper and improper uses of language, in a bewildering multiplication of different chains of figurative terminology superimposed, juxtaposed, interwoven, is a final form of *mise en abyme* in the poem.

"The Rock" contains at least four distinct linguistic "scenes," repertoires of terms adding up to a distinct pattern. The poem is like one of those paintings by Tchelitchew that are simultaneous representations of several different objects, superimposed or interwoven, or it is like one of those children's puzzles in which the trick is to see the five monkeys hidden in the tree, or, more grotesquely, the sailboats in the vegetable garden. The poem contains a scene of love, even a love story: "the meeting at noon at the edge of the field. . . , an embrace between one desperate clod / And another"; "as a man loves, as he lives in love." The poem presents a geometrical diagram. This diagram is described and analyzed with appropriate mathematical and logical terminology: "absurd," "invention," "assertion," "a theorem proposed," "design," "assumption," "figuration," "predicate," "root," "point A / In a perspective that begins again / At B," "adduce." The poem presents in addition a natural scene, the rock which in the turn of the seasons and in the diurnal warmth of the rising and setting sun is covered with leaves, blossoms, and fruit. Man shares in this natural cycle as he eats of the fruit, or as he becomes himself a natural body rooted in the ground, his eye growing in power like the sprouting eye of a potato: "They bud the whitest eye, the pallidest sprout, / New senses in the engenderings of sense." "The Rock," finally, describes and analyzes itself. It presents a theory of poetry, with an appropriate terminology—"icon," "copy," "figuration," "imagery," and so on.

The question, it would seem, is which of these scenes is the literal subject of the poem, the real base of which the others are illustrative figures. This question is unanswerable. Each scene is both literal and metaphorical, both the ground of the poem and a figure on that ground, both that which the poem is centrally about and a resource of terminology used figuratively to describe something other than itself, in a fathomless *mise en abyme.* The structure of each scene separately and of all four in their relation is precisely a dramatization, or articulation, or iconic projection of the uncanny relation, neither polar opposition, nor hierarchy, nor genetic filiation, between figurative and literal.

In one sense the description of all four of the scenes is entirely literal. They are icons in the sense of being mimetic pictures of things which—for most practical purposes and for those living within the terminology of English or American communities—are supposed to exist as independent objects. There really are rocks, leaves, flowers, fruit, and the seasons of the year. A man and a woman have no doubt met in the "real world" at the edge of a field at noon to embrace. This may well be an autobiographical reference to some episode in the old poet's past. There really are geometrical diagrams with points A and B, theorems, and so on. A poem's self-referentiality is just that, a form of reference or mimesis, as "realistic" as a description of the weather.

On the other hand, no reader of "The Rock" can remain long under the illusion that it is a poem about the weather or indeed a poem about geometry or about love or about poetry. When the reader focuses on any one of these scenes, it emerges in full mimetic vividness, as the chain of words describing it is culled out of the mesh of other words in the poem, but at the same time the reader sees that it cannot be copied, made into an icon, without the use of terms drawn from the other scenes, as the embrace at noon at the edge of the field is, mathematically, "a theorem proposed between the two." Simultaneously, each scene, though it must borrow names from the others to name itself, becomes itself a resource of figurative language for the other scenes: the leaves bud, blossom, and fruit "as a man loves, as he lives in love." Each scene is both ground and design on that ground, both literal and figurative, icon in both senses of the word, in an oscillation which forms and reforms itself with each word, phrase, or image throughout the poem. As the reader tries to rest on each element in the poem or on a chain of elements forming a single scene, as he seeks a solid literal ground which is the curiological basis of the other figurative meanings, that element or chain gives way, becomes itself a verbal fiction, an illusion, an icon (in the sense of similitude and not in the sense of mimetic copy). The element becomes an *Abgrund,* not a *Grund.* The reader is forced then to shift sideways again seeking to find somewhere else in the poem the solid ground of that figure, seeking, and failing or falling, and seeking again.

Another way to put this is to say that the reader can make sense of the poem by assuming any one of the scenes to be the literal ground on the basis of which the others are defined as analogical, figurative, iconic.

By that definition, however, the base, when examined, must be defined as itself analogical. That which must necessarily be taken as literal in order to define the figurative is itself figurative, and so the distinction breaks down. In order for the fruit, man, lovers, poem, and geometric design to be defined as figurative, the leftover term, the sun in its turnings, must be taken as literal. If, however, fruit, man, poem, and so on are figurative, so is the sun, since it is, like the others, an icon of the ground. Analogy cannot be defined except with the use of analogies. The defined enters into and so contaminates the definer, annulling the validity of the definition. Figure must always be defined figuratively. There is always a remainder, something alogical left over which does not fit any logical scheme of interpretation. Something has to be left out, assumed to be marginal, in order to make a completely coherent interpretation. The word "cull" in the poem carries this ambiguity. A cull (from *colligere*, to gather) is a fruit chosen, collected, or separated out from the rest, but chosen because it does not fit. A cull is imperfect or inferior. The act of differentiation establishes the criteria of fitness or perfection. Without the culling out of the culls there can be no gathering of what is left as examples of a uniform grade. The figurative, as in the example I have just given, in fact defines the literal rather than the other way around. Whichever scene is taken as figurative implicitly defines some scene as literal, but that scene, when it is looked at directly, turns out to be itself clearly figurative. The reader must then seek the literal base elsewhere, in a constant lateral transfer with no resting place in the unequivocally literal, the mimetic, the "exact rock," cured at last.

Each of the scenes in "The Rock" is, as a "particular of being," the equivalent of all the others. Each holds an equivalent status as simultaneously both figure and ground, in a chain of chains which is articulated in the poem around the verb "to be": "The fiction of the leaves is the icon / of the poem, the figuration of blessedness, / And the icon is the man." "This is the cure / Of leaves and of the ground and of ourselves. / His words are both the icon and the man." Extending these chains of equivalence, or linking them together, one would get the following affirmation: the icon is the man is the poem is the fruit is the sun is a theorem or geometrical design is the relation of love is . . . the rock.

The structure of each of these scenes is the same. It is in fact the traditional metaphysical structure of *aletheia*, the appearance of something visible out of the abyss of truth. Truth is, for Stevens too, evasive, veiled, feminine, and dwells at the bottom of a well. The revelation or unveiling of what has been hidden brings the truth momentarily into the open, out of Lethean forgetfulness, and displays it. This revelation expands to become a container of the whole or means of appropriating the whole, and then instantaneously hides the abyss or ground. It quickly becomes a fiction, an illusion, something hollowed out, a mere "rind" or "cull," something that never was, and so vanishes. The lovers appear at noon and create a relation between one another, a theorem which makes them "Two figures in a nature of the sun, / In the sun's design of its own happiness." A geometrical design is an appropriation of space which appears in the open. Fruit grows out of the leaves and blossoms which come and cover the high rock. That fruit encompasses the whole year and becomes "the final found, / The plenty of the year and of the world." The fruit is a gathering of the whole, a cull. To eat the fruit would be to possess the whole and so to cure the ground. It would be to understand it, in the etymological sense of reaching the base and standing there, in a "final found," with a multiple pun on "found" as discovery, invention, and foundation. The man in turns grows like the fruit. His maturing is a birth and extension of sight, "new senses in the engenderings of sense." These allow him to encompass space. This equivalence of seeing and symbol making goes back, in Stevens' case, to Emerson, as in the formulation of Charles Sanders Pierce: "The symbol may, with Emerson's Sphynx, say to man, 'Of thine eye I am the eyebeam.' " All the symbols or icons of the poem are a means of seeing, an extension of sight, "like a blindness cleaned." The poem itself rises as an icon which is the equivalent of the leaves, blossom, and fruit, and so cures the ground.

The reader is tempted to arrange these items in some kind of hierarchy. Surely, he thinks, one item in the series is the base of the others, grounding the sequence and putting a stop to the discomfort of their oscillation. No doubt the prime candidate for such a base or head appears to be the self, the self of the poet or speaker, the self in general of each individual included in the collective "we" of the poem. One wants to find in the poem a personal voice and a personal drama, the voice and drama of Stevens himself in old age. The experience of reading the poem would then have the security and enclosure of an intersubjective relation. In such a relation my self as reader would respond through the words to the self of the poet and communicate with him, beyond the grave. After all, does not the poem assert that "a cure of ourselves" would be "equal to a cure / Of the ground, a cure beyond forgetfulness"? The affirmative substitutions and translations of "The Poem as Icon" seem to come to rest in the ecstatic certainty of a poem which would found and be founded on the solid rock of the self, the man's words being the man and rooting him:

> This is the cure
> Of leaves and of the ground and of ourselves.
> His words are both the icon and the man.

The poem's many echoes of its immediately preceding American tradition the Whitman of "Song of Myself," the Emerson of "Experience," would seem to confirm this priority of the self over the other icons of the poem. In Whitman there is the same return to the self as the base of all experience, and the same universalization of the self to enclose all events, things, and persons, as the reader is tempted to find in "The Rock." It is surely in honor of Whitman that Stevens chooses to have lilacs come and bloom, like a blindness cleaned, to cover the high rock. Stevens' leaves grow up from chthonic depths, as signs, like the inscribed leaves of a book, just as do Whitman's leaves of grass: "I bequeath myself to the dirt to grow from the grass I love"; "Or I guess the grass is itself a child, the produced babe of the vegetation, / Or I guess it is a uniform hieroglyphic." The equivalence, in Stevens' poem, between the leaves covering the rock, the man, and the poem as icon is sanctioned by Whitman. Whitman's pun on leaves as the leaves of a book surfaces most when Stevens says, "The fiction of the leaves is the icon / Of the poem." Whitman's "Song of Myself," moreover, like Stevens' "The Rock," is governed by the repeated movement of *aletheia*, the appearance from the dark ground of some "particular of being" which manifests itself in the sunlight. "I find," says Whitman, "I incorporate gneiss, coal, long-threaded moss, fruits, grains, esculent roots." Rocks and earth are part of these figures of descent and return in Whitman's song of himself: "the mica on the side of the rock," a shining from the depths, "the plutonic rocks" which "send in vain their old heat against [his] approach," "voluptuous cool-breath'd earth," "earth of departed sunset." There is even a striking anticipation of Stevens' embrace of two desperate clods at the edge of the field at noon in Whitman's: "I believe the soggy clods shall become lovers and lamps."

From Whitman the reader moves back one further step to Whitman's immediate precursor, Emerson. The sequence forms its own *mise en abyme* of successive influence and misinterpretation, from Emerson to Whitman to Stevens. For Emerson, in "Experience," the strong affirming self is the bedrock fiction beneath which one cannot and should not go. The self is the one power remaining when all else has been peeled off and cast away, like dead husks. Though the self is illusion too, it is an illusion which constantly reforms itself, however often it is expelled. It is the bleak truth which is the source of all power, as if nothingness contained a vital métier forming a base for all practical purposes as solid as the divine rock. Such a self would be a substance in the etymological sense, a ground on which all the experiences or affirmations of the self may be based. Once again the governing figure is that of descent and ascent again into solar prominence:

> The great and crescive self, rooted in absolute nature, supplants all relative existence and ruins the kingdom of mortal friendships and love. Marriage (in what is called the spiritual world) is impossible, because of the inequality between every subject and every object. The subject is the receiver of Godhead, and at every comparison must feel his being enhanced by that cryptic might. Though not in energy, yet by presence, this magazine of substance cannot be otherwise than felt; nor can any force of intellect attribute to the object the proper deity which sleeps or wakes forever in every subject. . . . We cannot say too little of our constitutional necessity of seeing things under private aspects or saturated with our humours. And yet is the God native of these bleak rocks. That need makes in morals the capital virtue of self-trust. We must hold hard to this poverty, however scandalous, and by more vigorous self-recoveries, after the sallies of action, possess our axis more firmly. The life of truth is cold and so far mournful; but it is not the slave of tears, contritions and perturbations. It does not attempt another's work, nor adopt another's facts. It is a main lesson of wisdom to know your own from another's. . . . [I]n the solitude to which every man is always returning, he has a sanity and revelations which in his passage into new worlds he will carry with him. Never mind the ridicule, never mind the defeat; up again old heart?—it seems to say—there is victory yet for all justice; and the true romance which the world exists to realize will be the transformation of genius into practical power.

This ringing affirmation, central in the American tradition of the strong self, makes the scandalous poverty of that self a radiating power and of its fictive and perspectival insubstantiality a godlike rock. Stevens' "The Rock," on the other hand, in spite of its discovery of a cure of the ground in the equivalence of self, leaves, ground, and rock, is a thorough deconstruction of the Emersonian bedrock self. Stevens' poem, in one of its aspects, is an interpretation of Emerson and Whitman which undermines their apparent affirmations (though of course both Emerson and Whitman had, each in his own way, already annihilated his own seemingly solid grounding). Stevens' poem, in any case, further hollows Emerson and Whitman out, gives their key figures and terms one final twist that shatters the structure based on them and shows it to have been baseless. For Stevens, Emerson's bleak rocks are no beginning below or before which one could not go. The self, for him, is deprived of its status as ground by being shown to be a figure on that ground. The self has the same status as the other elements with which it is equated. The self exists, but in the same fragile and groundless way as fruit, sun, poem, and geometrical diagram. It exists as icon, as image, as figure for the underlying nothing. The self is not the rock but an insubstantial substitute for the absent rock, something that was not, and is not, absurd. Moreover, the self is not the base of the sequence. It is only one link in a chain. This link has the same status as the others in the sense that it is inscribed in a horizontal series of displacements. In this series each item depends on the others for its definition and therefore for its existence. The self, for Stevens, is generated by this play of linguistic substitutions, vanishing itself if they vanish, depending for its illusory existence on figurative borrowings from them: "His *words* are both the icon and the man" (my italics).

Moreover, there is a significant difference between Stevens' use of the collective "we" and Emerson's. When Emerson says, "We must hold hard to this poverty," he means something not too different from Whitman's, "I incorporate gneiss, coal," or from his, "We also ascend dazzling and tremendous as the sun, / We found our own O my soul in the calm and cool of the daybreak." For both Emerson and Whitman, each self must affirm itself, if not in isolation, then as the axis of all, the incorporator of all: "I am large, I contain multitudes." One of the crucial moments of Emerson's "Experience" is his rejection of any confrontation of another, or equal relation to another, even in love. The other can only be an image or icon of the self and so not its equal. All doubling or imaging must be rejected as introducing chaos into the spherical and all-inclusive unity of the self. Subject can only marry object, that is, not something its equal or fellow but something which can be devoured, wholly mastered: "There will be the same gulf between every me and thee as between the original and the picture. The universe is the bride of the soul. . . . Life will be imaged, but cannot be divided nor doubled. Any invasion of its unity would be chaos. The soul is not twin-born but the only begotten, and though revealing itself as child in time, child in appearance, is of a fatal and universal power, admitting no co-life."

Who, in contrast, is the "we" of Stevens' "The Rock," the we of whom the first two lines say, "It is an illusion that we were ever alive, / Lived in the houses of mothers . . ."? Husband and wife? Poetic "we"? A general collective first person plural standing for all men and women together, all old folk of seventy? There is a bleak impersonality of tone and locution in Stevens' poem which forbids thinking of it or feeling it as the autobiographical statement of a recognizable person, the man Wallace Stevens, vice president of the Hartford Accident and Indemnity Company, author of *Harmonium*. This is thematized in the way the personal self in the poem dissolves into a plural self, all mankind and womankind, the "ourselves" of "a cure of ourselves," and that "ourselves" into a collective impersonal consciousness, "the main of things, the mind," "the starting point of the human and the end," and that mind, beyond any personality, into the rock, and the rock into nothingness. Self in the sense of individual personality is one of the major illusions dissolved by the poem. This dissolution, paradoxically, takes place not by a movement into a more and more vacuous solipsism, as is sometimes said to be Stevens' fate as a poet, but precisely by incorporating that doubling of self and other which Emerson so resolutely, and by the necessity of his genuinely solipsistic definition of the strong self, rejects. Stevens is more open to the existence of others, more in need of them, and so, in the end, vulnerable, as Emerson and Whitman are not, to an abyssing or dissolution of the self. This dissolution comes through the doubling of the self or through its attempt to found itself on a relation to another. For Stevens the self-enclosed sphere of the self is broken. It is thereby engulfed in the chasm of its own bifurcation. This conflict between an attempted self-subsistent enclosure and the doubling, breaking apart, and abyssing of that enclosure may be seen in all the chief scenes of "The Rock."

All four scenes take the form, or attempt to take the form, of a rounded, unified whole which is soundly based. Poem, fruit, sun, geometrical diagram or logical system, single man rooted in the earth, child enclosed in the house of his mother, lovers embraced at noon—all strive to take that form. Each of these figures, however, divides itself by a scission both horizontal and vertical and so becomes not an enclosed finite figure but a *mise en abyme*. The geometrical design appears at first to be a closed logical system based on solid predicates which may secure the proposition of theorems generating figures in the sun's design of its own happiness. Such figures would satisfy the desire to be at the end of distances. This closed figure, alas, turns into an infinitely repeating series, like that cartoon by Charles Addams, with the rock, "that which is near," functioning not as a base but as "point A / In a perspective that begins again / At B." Starting at A, motivated by the desire to be at the end of distances, one reaches on a line toward the horizon point B. At B the receding perspective begins again, and so on, ad infinitum, without ever reaching the end of distances. No solid starting place exists, but only an arbitrary beginning which constantly begins again at points B, C, D, and so on, and there is no reaching the horizon. This endlessly receding geometrical figure is asymmetrically balanced, in "Forms of the Rock in a Night-Hymn," by the figure of the rock as "The starting point of the human and the end, / That in which space itself is contained, the gate / To the enclosure." Which figure can be built on the rock? The question is unanswerable. The circumscribed design constantly turns into the labyrin-thine *mise en abyme*, as the enclosure of the last lines is abyssed by their opening into the alternations of day and night, night with its midnight-minting fragrances exhaling or coining chasms of darkness.

The same transformation deconstructs the human scene of the poem. To "live in the houses of mothers" rather than in the masculine labyrinth of the house that Jack built was to dwell in a warm embracing enclosure which at the same time allowed an idyllic openness and freedom of movement. In the houses of mothers, says Stevens, we children "arranged ourselves / By our own motions in a freedom of air." The doubling of that relation in the meeting of lovers at noon at the edge of the field produced a schism which in retrospect undermines both scenes and makes them like a perspective starting at A that begins again at B. If the *mise en abyme* has something uncanny about it, one can also often detect in it, as in the passage cited above from Leiris or in the present poem, a shadowy psychodrama involving the differences of the sexes and of generations, the prohibition against incest, and narcissistic mirroring. In one version of the myth of Narcissus he is in love with his twin sister, who dies, and who is searched for, vainly and fatally, in the mirror image. The doubling of brother and sister or of any man and woman of the same generation is the embrace of two desperate clods, detached bits of the substantial earth beneath, trying to recover a lost unity, trying to make a global whole which would encompass space in a theorem proposed between the two. This theorem would generate a finite diagram, a closed logical system, in a warm house: "Ah, love, let us be true / To one another!" Let us recover together what we had in the houses of mothers but have lost. Once the division has occurred, however, and it has always already occurred, the chasm between self and other remains unfilled.

The desire to be at the end of distances can never be satisfied. The division perpetuates itself in whatever expedients are chosen to close or cure the wound. In "a fantastic consciousness" I face my sister self, that other desperate clod. I see in her a substitute for the lost mother, but the failure of that substitution reminds me that the mother was herself the abyss I have forgotten. The warmth in the mother's house was an illusion, something that never was. Her house stands "rigid in rigid emptiness." My narcissistic relation to my double of the other sex is an affective move-ment seeking to find a bedrock for the self or in the self. It discovers only a perspective that begins again at B, a perpetually receding horizon. Stevens dismantles Emerson by insisting on the doubling or imaging of the self in the other, by making the self, against Emerson's prohibition, twin-born, a schismatic or schizoid "we." The relation to my mirror image doubles my relation, across a generation gap, to my mother and reveals that relation too to have been an empty image, an icon of nothing. Though it seemed an enclosure, solidly based, it was already the abyss, since there was something missing which was suppressed or veiled. This absence has now been revealed in the annihilating, after the fact, both of that warm enclosure and of the security of its repetition in the embrace at noon at the edge of the field. Both the relation to the mother and the relation to the beloved are the experience of a perpetual distance, desire, dissatisfaction, an "emptiness that would be filled" ("An Ordinary Evening in New Haven"). They are figures, not realities, "Two figures in a nature of the sun, / In the sun's design of its own happiness."

Perhaps, then, if the self, for Stevens, is no Emersonian or Whitmanian rock, a solid foundation may be found in that which is imaged by the self in its doublings, that is, in the sun's rising and setting, in the sequence of the seasons, in that universal manifestation of permanence in change of which Whitman said, "there are millions of suns left." Poem, man, lovers, fruit, geometric figure are all heliotropic, "copies of the sun," "figures" or "shadows" cast by the sun. The poem is the sun. The fruit is a little sun, a mango. Both the man alone and the man in relation to his beloved are suns or figures in the sun. The poem is governed, like so many of Stevens' poems, by the annual and diurnal movements of the sun, as it shifts with the seasons, causing them, and as it rises and sets each day, appearing like man from the ground and disappearing into the rock, that "stone from which he rises, up—and—ho, / The step to the bleaker depths of his descents."

Is the sun, then, the literal, of which all the other icons are figures, the bedrock which supports and validates them? No, the sun is the figure par excellence, both in Western tradition generally and in Stevens' work as a whole. The sun is that which cannot be looked at directly but is the source of all seeing, the designer of the figures of its happiness. The sun is the visible, invisible figure for the invisible and unnameable, for the base of the intelligible, "the main of things, the mind." The sun is the traditional icon for being, for the good, for the real, in short, for the rock. The rock in turn is a figure for the ground, and vice versa, in a perpetual displacement.

If the structure of the various scenes in "The Rock" is a repetition of the act of manifestation, it is also a deconstruction of that structure. The rhetorical name for this is catachresis. Catachresis is the violent, forced, or abusive use of a word to name something which has no literal name. The word also means, in music, a harsh or unconventional dissonance, a surd. Examples of catachresis are table "leg" and mother "tongue." Such a word is neither literal, since a table leg is not truly a leg, nor speech a tongue, nor figurative, since it is not a substitute for some proper word. (The Romance word for tongue, *lingua, lengua, langue*, is folded into the apparently literal word "language.") Catachresis explodes the distinction between literal and figurative on which the analysis of tropes is based and so leads the "science" of rhetoric to destroy itself as science, as clear and distinct knowledge of truth. (See Jacques Derrida's "La mythologie blanche," *Marges*, for the best discussion of catachresis, including an identification of its relation to the solar trajectory.)

"The Rock" seems to be based on the notion of a name which would be an icon for the hidden truth, the figure for a covert literal. All the terms in the poem, however, are at once literal and figurative. Each is a catachresis. According to the logic of a theory of language which bases meaning on the solid referentiality of literal names for visible physical objects, open to the light of the sun, the referent of a catachresis does not exist, was not, and is not, absurd. Each term in "The Rock," including "rock" and "ground," is a catachresis for something which has not, cannot have, a proper name. That something is the abyss, the *Abgrund* or *Ungrund*, the chasm, the blank, the unapproachable, of which the poem, in all the ways I have identified, is a *mise en abyme*. The cure of the ground in a curiological picturing, which Stevens says we *must* have, remains necessarily a future imperative. This imperative can never be fulfilled. To name the abyss is to cover it, to make a fiction or icon of it, a likeness which is no likeness. What is a likeness of the sun? Of what is the sun a likeness?

All the catachreses in the poem reform the fiction of the referential, the illusion that the terms of the poem refer literally to something that exists, some physical rock or ground, some psychological entity, even some metaphysically existing nothing, the "nothing that is." In fact they refer to the blind spot, the perpetually absent, the sun when it is below the horizon, "grounded." For this invisible sun, as Aristotle said, there is no name and therefore no substance, no *logos*. The sun in its risings and settings is alogical, the father of all *mises en abyme*. The word "sun" itself is deprived thereby of full propriety. It is a catachresis, since the word cannot be based on a full perception by the senses of what it names. Since all referentiality in language is a fiction, the aboriginal trope or turning away from the abyss, the blind spot, the referentiality of language is its fall, its unconquerable penchant toward fiction. All words are initially catachreses. The distinction between literal and figurative is an alogical deduction or bifurcation from that primal misnaming. The fiction of the literal or proper is therefore the supreme fiction. All poetry and all language are *mises en abyme,* since all language is based on catachresis. The continuity of Western thought on this point and Stevens' congruity with that tradition in his use of the rising and setting sun as the prime "example" of the iconic structure which disarticulates itself is indicated by the applicability to "The Rock" of a passage in Aristotle's *Topics:* "he who has stated that it is a property of the sun to be 'the brightest star that moves above the earth' has employed in the property something of a kind which is comprehensible only by sensation, namely 'moving above the earth'; and so the property of the sun would not have been correctly assigned, for it will not be manifest, when the sun sets, whether it is still moving above the earth, because sensation then fails us" (V, 3, 131B).

Where is the sun after it sets, disappears into the ground? It becomes the ground, vanishes into the rock, where sensation fails us and where blindness is substituted once more for sight and insight. Of that blind spot nothing "true" or "proper" can be said, and so we must be silent, deaf and dumb, absurd. The end of Stevens' poem is a brilliant illustration or expression (darkness made visible, silence given speech) of this doubleness of the sun, its visibility and invisibility as the *mise en abyme* of the rock. Like the poem, the man, and the fruit, the sun rises from the rock as its visible embodiment or icon, while the rock is a night-sun, shining with its fragrant black light on what "night illumines." The rock as "the habitation of the whole" encloses the sun and all things under the sun. The rock, though it may appear to be the literal of which all else is a figure, is itself another catachresis. At the farthest or deepest point of the *mise en abyme,* at the end of the poem, the perspective begins again with a further glimpse, a seeing which is no seeing, into the chasm of night. The rock is

> The starting point of the human and the end,
> That in which space itself is contained, the gate
> To the enclosure, day, the things illumined
>
> By day, night and that which night illumines,
> Night and its midnight-minting fragrances,
> Night's hymn of the rock, as in a vivid sleep.

"As in a vivid sleep"! The final quiet displacement by way of the "as" to another figure expresses once more and for the last time the cadence which has governed the poem. Like a voice of the voiceless, or like an ability to hear the soundless, the absurd, or the mute, or like a seeing, with "blindness cleaned," of what can be only illusion, a vivid sleep is an oxymoron. It is a sleep which is yet acutely conscious, though a consciousness not grounded in sensation. A vivid sleep is a clear consciousness of nothing, as night's hymn of the rock is darkness visible. That hymn is the final icon or figuration of blessedness, the last appearance of religious terminology in the poem. These terms, like the other chains of terms, are another, perhaps even the most powerful or violent, catachresis. This hymn creates what it praises in the very act of naming it. It creates what it worships in the abusive displacements that figure forth that which has no proper name, and so has only a figurative or poetical existence. "After one has abandoned a belief in God, poetry is that essence which takes its place as life's redemption"; "God and the imagination are one" ("Adagia").

Beginning with the word "cure" in "The Rock" the interpreter is led further and further into a labyrinth of branching connections going back through Whitman and Emerson to Milton, to the Bible, to Aristotle, and behind him into the forking pathways of our Indo-European family of languages. Stevens' poem is an abyss and the filling of the abyss, a chasm and a chasmy production of icons of the chasm, inexhaustible to interpretation. Its textual richness opens abyss beneath abyss, beneath each deep a deeper deep, as the reader interrogates its elements and lets each question generate an answer which is another question in its turn. Each question opens another distance, a perspective begun at A which begins again at B, without ever reaching any closer to the constantly receding horizon. Such a poem is incapable of being encompassed in a single logical formulation. It calls forth potentially endless commentaries, each one of which, like this essay, can only formulate and reformulate its *mise en abyme*.

HELEN REGUEIRO

The Rejection of Metaphor

Multiplicity and particularity must still be achieved through the poetic word. In "By Broad Potomac's Shore" Whitman offers a prayer to reality, for reality, asking that the poetic creation be infused with a reality outside itself. Stevens, too, speaks of "conceiving words, / As the night conceives the sea-sounds in silence" (*The Collected Poems of Wallace Stevens*. New York: Knopf, 1954. p. 86). The use of the same verb for the poetic creation and for the natural process suggests that the imaginative conception may indeed be an organic act, that the words may be conceived as epiphanic manifestations rather than conscious creations. But words conceived in the mode of being of the natural object are conceived "in silence." The attempted creation of reality ends in a silencing of the word in face of a reality it cannot name, order, or "conceive." Stevens wants to jump the zone of consciousness, passing "from that which was conceived to that / Which was realized" (CP, 354), turning the individual act of consciousness into a universal act of reality. "Not the symbol but that for which the symbol stands" (CP, 238), the poetic creation would be a creation *of* reality. But to achieve this coincidence the poet would have to create with "letters of rock and water, words / Of the visible elements and of ours" (CP, 232).

Time and again Stevens contends that such creation is possible: "the world / Goes round in the climates of the mind / And bears its floraisons of imagery" (*Opus Posthumous: Poems, Plays, Prose by Wallace Stevens*. New York: Knopf, 1957. p. 102). The images here are no longer alienating entities, springing from consciousness and stylizing reality. They

From *The Limits of Imagination*. Copyright © 1976 by Cornell University Press. Undesignated parenthetical page numbers refer to *The Collected Poems of Wallace Stevens*, OP designates *Opus Posthumous*, and NA, *The Necessary Angel* (see Bibiography).

are emerging as naturally as the flower, and the alien world that comes into contact with the mind "bears" the flowers that bespeak the union of both. The mind, in fact, is no longer subject to moods but to climates: mental processes have become "naturalized."

If words and images are objects-in-reality, then the natural objects no longer close their meaning within themselves. The word-thing is "a sign of meaning in the meaningless" (CP, 529), a symbol that is not a stylization of reality but a revelation of it—"the presence of the intelligible / In that which is created as its symbol" (CP, 529). Creation is revelation, and the image does not usurp reality but lays bare the essence of the real: "as in images we awake, / Within the very object that we seek, / Participants of its being" (CP, 463). Consciousness and reality would seem to merge in this reading of the image as a pathway into the object.

But Stevens begins to meditate, even before "The Blue Guitar," on the incapacity of the word, the image, the poem, to name the object in its essence or capture it in its immediacy. That "it is a world of words to the end of it" (CP, 345) is the problem rather than the solution: "The words of things entangle and confuse. / The plum survives its poems" (CP, 41). In "Extracts from Addresses to the Academy of Fine Ideas" he compares "the silent rose of the sun" with "this paper, this dust." To the natural flower he opposes the rose of paper, the rose of words on paper, and then goes on to suggest that the sun, the sky, the natural world, are rendered artificial through the written word. The natural rose is a "silent rose," beyond the power of the word to alter or experience it. It lives "in its smell," complete in itself, and defies the poet to penetrate the circle of perfection of its being. The metaphor, on the other hand, is an artifice that cannot take hold in reality. It is "never the thing but the version of the thing" (CP, 332), never the immediate object but the conscious image that the natural world rejects. Each version is a projection a little different from reality and ultimately a diversion from the object it projects. Instead of finding in metaphor a generation of reality, that poet sees "metaphor as degeneration" (CP, 444), always altering the object and undermining the possible experience.

In "The Motive for Metaphor," for example, the poet refuses to arrive at a metaphor and remains with the motive of a metaphor still unformed. The poem opens with the blowing of the wind, blowing words without meaning in a reality itself devoid of meaning. In the half-deadness of autumn and the half-colors of spring, happiness and a single bird seem to foreshadow "Of Mere Being." But this is no golden, bronzed decor. An obscure moon lights an obscure world, suggesting the incapacity of the object to be expressed and to become itself in a passage from silence to speech. Yet to express things, to light the obscure world of reality, the metaphor must usurp the "thingness" of the object, casting it into a shape that is not its own. Stevens stops short of the metaphor here and ends the poem on the dominant X. X is the enigma of reality not contained in metaphor, and the "dominant" quality of X underlines the presence of this enigma by implying, beyond the idea of domination, a sense of something unresolved. The motive rather than the metaphor, the enigmatic X rather than the clarified reality, become the valid subjects of poetry. The way toward decreation of the poem and the sudden experience of reality begin with this acceptance of motive over metaphor, the enigma over the resolution. "How many poems he denied himself / In his observant progress, lesser things / Than the relentless contact he desired" (CP, 34). Crispin never arrives at the relentless contact, but by rejecting the total reconstruction of reality Stevens attempts to reach the unmediated experience.

The rejection of totality begins, as we have seen, by a rejection of metaphor. In "Metaphors of a Magnifico"

> Twenty men crossing a bridge,
> Into a village,
> Are twenty men crossing twenty bridges,
> Into twenty villages,
> Or one man
> Crossing a single bridge into a village.

The individual consciousnesses of twenty men make reality different for each, and the single bridge and village turn into twenty bridges and villages. Or else there is a singleness of perception by which the twenty men become one man crossing the bridge into the village. The assumption of sameness or difference, of course, takes place in the mind of the perceiver, who refuses to make a choice. "This is old song / That will not declare itself." The song introduced into the poem would create a framework within the framework, except that the song does not declare itself, it is not enacted. The poet's quest is to go beyond the various metaphors to the origin of song. But the song remains silent, and in a sense uncreated.

> Twenty men crossing a bridge,
> Into a village,
> Are
> Twenty men crossing a bridge
> Into a village.

Stevens rejects here the infinite possibilities of metaphor, two of which he had presented in the first stanza—that the twenty men were twenty men crossing twenty bridges into twenty villages, or one man crossing a bridge into a village. Here the verb "to be" links two equal statements—twenty men crossing a bridge into a village are twenty men crossing a bridge into a village—suggesting that there is no possible metaphor to express the variations of reality. The second stanza thus rejects even the simple correlations of the first and makes the poem move toward the simplicity and silence of song. The old song will not declare itself, it is as silent as the sounds of reality. In rejecting the metaphoric posing of the object or even the variations of the first stanza, the second stanza begins to adopt the undeclared quality of the song and leads the poem to decreate itself. To reach reality, it has to silence itself. "That will not declare itself / Yet is certain as meaning": the untold reality is meaningful precisely because it is untold. It is "certain" because it is not ordered by the distinctive individual consciousness which makes poetry possible. Poetry, in this sense, is always a destructive force, a force that re-creates and destroys the real: "She searched / The touch of springs, / And found / Concealed imaginings" (CP, 90). There is no contact, only divergings from reality. Later Stevens will seek the immediate aspect of objects which makes "imaginings of them lesser things" (CP, 430). In "Metaphors of a Magnifico" the essential meaning of reality and the certainty of meaning of the unsung song elude thought: "Of what was it I was thinking? / So the meaning escapes."

In "The Idea of Order at Key West" Stevens contends that the song masters reality even after it ends. In "Metaphors of a Magnifico" the unsung song attracts the poet to reality. In "Key West" the song is alluded to in the poem but never introduced verbally into its structure. In "Metaphors of a Magnifico" it is not clear whether the poem *is* the song, whether the partial refrain is an irruption of the song into the poem or a destruction of the poem in commenting on the song. In rejecting metaphor, in approximating the simplicity of song, the poem slowly becomes the song that is undeclared. The comments on the song are comments on itself: "This is old song . . . / That will not declare itself / Yet is certain as meaning." Finally, the comment on the song takes off from the third stanza, and the repetition of the white wall and the fruit trees in the apparently formless refrain suggests that the poem, in the measure in which it has become the song, is open-ended. The poet cannot recollect the experience or round it off into the perfect structure of "Domination of Black." But precisely because the poem is "imperfect," because it fades into the undeclared song and rejects the posing of metaphor, it draws closer to reality. The meaning of the scene escapes and, as it does, the poem seems to melt into the scene. The poet pursues the meaning into the last refrain, but the unfinished sentences taken from the third stanza suggest an increasing distance between meaning and reality. As the meaning eludes the poem, the poem paradoxically moves closer to the certainty of reality. The rejection of metaphor, the irruption of song—the refrain that breaks the continuity—and finally the sense of open-endedness and the deliberate diffusion of the song in space turn the poem itself into a bridge leading into the reality of white walls and fruit trees.

In "Of the Surface of Things" the subject of the poem is again the impossibility of the enactment of song within the poem:

> In my room, the world is beyond my understanding;
> But when I walk I see that it consists of three or four hills and a cloud.

The first line establishes the dichotomy between the inner enclosed space and the outside world. In undercutting that space, the protagonist moves outward and begins to see.

In the second stanza he returns to a simile he had written about that outside world—"The spring is like a belle undressing"—and implicitly rejects the simile. What is particularly interesting about this poem is how much is implied, successfully, about the protagonist's inability to say anything about reality. The poem rejects what the poet has written. The deliberately trite simile seems at the same time to spread out into the poem and invalidate it, and to become the point at which the poem rejects itself.

The third stanza consists of three separate statements in which reality is woven into a song that, as in "Key West," is never sung, or, as in "Metaphors of a Magnifico," does not declare itself.

A similar use of song occurs in "Country Words": "It was an old rebellious song, / An edge of song that never clears." Again the poet cannot reach the song, as he cannot reach reality. The song is "rebellious" because, like the objects in reality, it does not yield to us its meaning. It is an edge of song, a partial creation that does not reveal its structure, that eludes, rather, the conscious structuring of the imagination. Country words are not enough to turn poetry into song.

Again in "Poem Written at Morning" the poetic metaphors are the divisive elements between the poet and reality. Through the metaphor the object is posed into "this" or "that"—always into something that violates its "thingness." "It is this or that / And it is not. / By metaphor you paint / A thing." The painting of metaphor is ultimately a faking of reality, not a valid means of experiencing it: "The strawberries once in the Apennines . . . / They seem a little painted, now. / The mountains are scratched and used, clear fakes" (CP, 226).

Stevens returns to this idea in "The Common Life": "The paper is whiter / For these black lines." In a first reading, reality is made more "acute" by the poetic image. But if the paper is reality, the black lines fail to impose a pattern, and instead make the blank paper glare in defiance. Whiteness and colorlessness finally engulf the poetic imagination. And the ink remains to make the unordered reality glare against the imposed pattern. "The paper is whiter," but "the men have no shadows / And the women have only one side." The creative act does not give of bird or bush, and the metaphoric posing is as one dimensional as a painting by Seurat. Without shadow and without volume, the poetic image serves only to make more "acute" its unreality and to allow the whiteness of the paper to cover the possible design.

This preoccupation with the image as lifeless painting is discussed further in "So-And-So Reclining on Her Couch." There is a sense of anonymity in the title, or perhaps a sense of the unimportance, or even the impossibility, of identity. So-And-So is anybody, and what is important is that it does not matter who it is. She is anybody, but she cannot become somebody, for as the poem progresses it is evident that she cannot "become."

> On her side, reclining on her elbow.
> This mechanism, this apparition,
> Suppose we call it Projection A.

It is not certain at what point the reader realizes that the object in question is a sculpture (though the argument could also be made that it is a painting). But there is from the first line a sense of something contrived, forced into a pose. Perhaps because the pose is so unnatural it may be taken as a symbol of the posing of metaphor. The work of art is a "mechanism" lacking the vital, organic aspects of reality. It is a projection in a series of projections. If the work of art is a conscious structure "vitally deprived" of reality, the consciousness of intentionality is carried further by the poet who speaks of this work in terms of a series of projections. The cold detachment of the sculpture is matched by the cold detachment of the poet. In speaking of art, the poem speaks about itself, and Projections A, B, C, are ways in which it attacks its own "mechanism," its own intentional posing. Though there is a feeling of nonchalance in the first stanza—"suppose we call it . . ."—the seriousness of the poet's rejection of the intentional structure is unquestionable.

> She floats in air at the level of
> The eye, completely anonymous,
> Born, as she was, at twenty-one,
>
> Without lineage or language, only
> The curving of her lip, as motionless gesture.

That she floats in air underlines her rootlessness in reality, the fact that she was never conceived naturally but created intentionally, mechanically, "at twenty-one." The intentional construct denies natural processes. The "birth" of the figure is an *ex-nihilo* conception, "anonymous" because she has no identity other than the artist's intention. Identity and intention, for the creator as well as the creation, are mutually exclusive. The creator seeks to become himself through his creation and finds that he has created an image of himself. And the creation is "without lineage or language," without past or future, and without means of expression. Raised out of the temporal, like the bird of Byzantium it cannot sing into reality, and it cannot be. The "motionless gesture" suggests a movement forever about to take place, caught like Keats's urn in the deadening eternity of its pose. The pose, like the metaphor, is incapable of thrusting itself into the "now" of reality.

> If just above her head there hung,
> Suspended in air, the slightest crown
> Of Gothic prong and practick bright,

> The suspension, as in solid space,
> The suspending hand withdrawn, would be
> An invisible gesture. Let this be called

> Projection B.

In the first three stanzas the sculpture was presented in its anonymity and its inability to become. Here the "invisible gesture" introduces into the sculpture, and consequently into the poem, the process of creation. The artist hypothetically suspends "the slightest crown." But the "invisible gesture" inevitably becomes the "motionless gesture" of Projection A, and Projection B shares with Projection A the inability to actualize itself in "solid space." "The suspending hand [is] withdrawn," and the creation closes in upon itself.

There is, however, a progression from projection to projection. In Projection A the sculpture was anonymous, the artist ostensibly absent. In Projection B the artist introduces himself into the sculpture and withdraws, underlining the intentional aspect of his creation. In Projection C we are told that the woman in the sculpture "is half who made her."

> She is half who made her.
> This is the final Projection, C.

The artist, deliberately absent in Projection A (since the woman was anonymous), entering and withdrawing in Projection B, becomes the definite creator in Projection C. The sculpture is an intentional structure, created in an act of consciousness, not of reality. It is not reality that the artist reveals in his creation, but himself. Yet he is also denied access to it. Precisely because he is present in it, because it is an image of himself, it lacks the reality of what has not been intentionally created. When he enters, as in Projection B, to add an invisible gesture, it is only to underline its intentional quality. He is caught, like the sculpture, between "the thing as idea and / The idea as thing," between the conceptualization of reality inherent in artistic creation and the impossible actualization of an intentional construct. The act of consciousness never becomes an act of reality, and from the anonymity of Projection A to the assertion of the creator in Projection C So-And-So remains a further projection that cannot be, a projection that is never projected into reality.

> The arrangement contains the desire of
> The artist. But one confides in what has no
> Concealed creator. One walks easily
> The unpainted shore, accepts the world
> As anything but sculpture. Good-bye,
> Mrs. Pappadopoulos, and thanks.

Through the series of projections and hypothetical ways of seeing a work of art, Stevens arrives once again at the rejection of the intentional structure. The intentional posing, the deliberate arrangement, at the same time alienate the artist from his creation and imprison him in it. In "So-And-So Reclining on Her Couch" Stevens comes back to the un-painted shore, the unordered world. In rejecting metaphor he accepts the gratuitousness of experience, accepts the world "as anything but sculp-ture." The last words, "Good-bye, Mrs. Pappadopoulos, and thanks," act out this rejection of intentional constructs by suggesting that the poem itself was a series of possible projections, a series of musings on an art-object and thus, like "The Man with the Blue Guitar," a series of diversions from reality.

The problem of artistic creation is thus not solved by the structure within the structure. The ballad and the porcelain of "Three Travelers Watch a Sunrise" and the sculpture of "So-And-So Reclining on Her Couch" are imagined structures in a world that the imagination has not humanized, has not rendered "habitable." "The statue is the sculptor, not the stone" (OP, 64). For Stevens the sculpture bears the mark of the artist, and it rejects and is rejected by reality: "But could the statue stand in Africa? / The marble was imagined in the cold" (OP, 56). The marble consciously created opposes itself to the unimaginable world. And to the enclosed space and the intentional creation is added a sense of coldness, a physical experience of desolation. But it is a physical experience that tends to deny all physical experience. The coldness of the imagined structure is the deathlike coldness of the art-object, raised out of the temporal, like Keats's "cold pastoral," and out of the realm of experience.

In rejecting metaphor Stevens begins to seek an experience that cannot be imagined, a simplicity beyond all the "intricate evasions" of structure. "Thought is false happiness," he begins in "Crude Foyer." It is false to think "that there lies at the end of thought / A foyer of the spirit in a landscape / Of the mind." For even though the foyer is to be found "at the end of thought," it is still placed "in a landscape of the mind." The poet will have to find a foyer not only "at the end of thought" but also "at the end of the mind," one which will deny the validity of mental constructs. "The mind / Is the eye, and . . . this landscape of the mind / Is a landscape only of the eye." The inner eye is caught in the landscape it has created. But as in Wordsworth's poetry, the inner vision does not coincide with the outer world. Elsewhere Stevens argues that "the mind is smaller than the eye" (CP, 161). "We live in a place / That is not our own and, much more, not ourselves" (CP, 383), and every attempt to make the world "home" ends in deeper alienation:

> We are ignorant men incapable
> Of the least, minor, vital metaphor, content,
> At last, there, when it turns out to be here.

The metaphor is not "vital" but "vitally deprived." It is always a "there," for it creates a temporal and spatial distance between the poet and the object. The alien place may become "our own" and the crude foyer a hearth of being only if the "thereness" of the mental landscape gives way to the presence of reality.

The arrival at the "hereness" of reality remains essentially unexplained, particularly since Stevens is still dealing with the possible revelation of language, a revelation which does not take place. Even as he rejects the paper rose, he believes that "the innermost good of their [the philosophers'] seeking / Might come in the simplest of speech" (CP, 27), "as if the language suddenly, with ease, / Said things it had laboriously spoken" (CP, 387). The quest for simplicity begins with the word. To say what is unspeakable, the word must reach the essence of the object it names. But the "simplest of speech" is a movement toward silence: "Is there a poem that never reaches words?" (CP 396). Stevens speaks of "immaculate syllables" (CP, 188), an "immaculate imagery" (CP, 250), suggesting that there is a point at which the word and the object meet.

But he cannot utter the syllable or create the imagery that might "secrete us in reality" (CP, 310).

Sight, like speech, is an impediment to poetic vision. "You must become an ignorant man again / And see the sun again with an ignorant eye" (CP, 380). But "something of the trouble of the mind / Remains in the sight" (OP, 97). The eye in Stevens *creates* a landscape of the mind and shares the mind's inability to penetrate the natural world. There is always a film of consciousness that turns reality into a mental landscape. For a moment, Stevens closes his eyes, refusing to see a reality that has been mediated by his conscious perception: "nothing has been lost, / Sight least, but metaphysical blindness gained, / The blindness in which seeing would be false" (OP, 94–95). The metaphysical blindness is a refusal to accept a mediated reality, a perception that is not "immaculate." But there can be no unmediated perception, as there can be no "immaculate" speech. "The sun / Must bear no name, gold flourisher, but be / In the difficulty of what it is to be" (CP, 381). "Things as they are" are changed not only by the poet's imaginative perception of them but by any verbal utterance that hinges on their reality. "Phoebus is dead, ephebe. But Phoebus was / A name for something that never could be named" (CP, 381). The poet's voice names only the absence of things, and his remembrance of their presence is a further testimony of his loss. His quest is thus for a word that is uttered and not uttered, for a voice that is speechless in its speech: "A sunken voice, both of remembering / And of forgetfulness, in alternate strain" (CP, 29). The forgetfulness of self would be a remembrance of reality, but a reality in which the creating self would be forgotten. The sunken voice would be unable to create, unable to pluck the strings of the blue guitar. Only a dual act of remembrance and forgetfulness, of assertion and denial of the conscious self "in alternate strain," could make the creative act suffice. But Stevens finds, like Rousseau, that artistic creation asserts the creative consciousness by opposing it to the natural world it tries to reach. There is always a reaching out toward reality, but never an experience, never a fulfillment: "A color that moved us with forgetfulness. / When was it that we heard the voice of union?" (CP, 494). Again in this passage forgetfulness is a means of integration to reality. But the voice of union is also a voice of silence, a "sunken voice" that suggests the dissolution of the self in the natural world.

HAROLD BLOOM

"An Ordinary Evening in New Haven"

The poet who writes *An Ordinary Evening in New Haven* is about to turn seventy, but as a poet he is never less desiccated or leafless. Nothing else by Stevens is more exuberant or extravagant than this second longest and most indirect of all his poems. Yet even the indirection is Whitmanian and exhibits a passion for yes that could not be broken.

Stevens sanctioned the shorter, eleven-section original version of *An Ordinary Evening* by including it in his carefully chosen British *Selected Poems*. I will take as text here the definitive, thirty-one-section poem, which scrambles the continuity of the final three sections with poetically happy results, and I will introduce comparisons with the original sequence when I approach the poem's conclusion. But I will note which sections were part of the original as I go, for structural reasons which should become apparent.

I am going to assert more for *An Ordinary Evening* than criticism as yet allows it, and so I will begin by giving something of the contrary case. By this, I do not intend the merely ignorant hostility of many negative critics of the poem, but rather its very best expositor, Helen Vendler, for whom the poem is strong only where she judges it to be a portrayal of desiccation, of an old man's most deliberately minimal visions. The critic, though I judge her to be mistaken here, is formidably eloquent:

From *Wallace Stevens: The Poems of Our Climate.* Copyright © 1977 by Cornell University Press.

In this, the harshest of all his experiments, Stevens deprives his poetry of all that the flesh, the sun, the earth, and the moon can offer, and, himself a skeleton, examines the bare possibilities of a skeletal life. . . . It is, humanly speaking, the saddest of all Stevens' poems. One wants it to have succeeded totally, to have proved that Stevens could find, in life's most minimal offering, something which would suffice. . . . *An Ordinary Evening* is, in short, almost unremittingly minimal, and over and over again threatens to die of its own starvation.

I myself, as I read *An Ordinary Evening,* encounter a very different poem from the one just described. There is much harshness, yes, but a great deal also that is rather more genial than is usual in Stevens. There is some deprivation, and yet the flesh, the sun, the earth, and the moon are all there, and so are a surprising vigor and joy. The poem I read is threatened not by its own starvation but by its own copiousness, its abundance of invention that varies the one theme, which is the problematic Stevensian image that he unhelpfully always called "reality." Critics can diverge absolutely on this poem because the text is almost impossible to read, that is, the text keeps seeking "reality" while continually putting into question its own apotheosis of "reality." Stevens said of the poem: "Here my interest is to try to get as close to the ordinary, the commonplace and the ugly as it is possible for a poet to get. It is not a question of grim reality but of plain reality." We can observe that this intention is wholly Whitmanian, and on that basis we might doubt Vendler's judgment that the celebrated title is polemic. "Ordinary" here seems to mean "true" or at least "not false," but true in the root sense of "ordinary," *ar* or "fitted together." New Haven is simply any city that is not home, a city that unsettles the self just enough so that it is startled into meditation, but close enough to home so that the meditation keeps contact always with the commonplace.

Kermode usefully points to the prose first section of *Three Academic Pieces* for a sentence that illuminates Stevens' intentions: "What our eyes behold may well be the text of life but one's meditations on the text and the disclosures of these meditations are no less a part of the structure of reality." But that leaves us with the word "reality" in Stevens, a word I wish Stevens had renounced, since it takes away more meaning than it tends to give. He was addicted to it in prose; he used some form of it well over a hundred times in his poetry, and it appears in thirteen different sections of *An Ordinary Evening.* The best attempt to reduce it to order is made by Frank Doggett in his useful book, *Stevens' Poetry of Thought:*

> *Reality,* in Stevens' use of the word, may be the world supposed to be antecedent in itself or the world created in the specific occurrence of

thought, including the thinker himself and his mind forming the thought. Often the term offers the assumption that if the self is the central point of a circle of infinite radius, then reality is the not-self, including all except the abstract subjective center. Sometimes *reality* is used in the context of the nominalist position—then the word denotes that which is actual and stands as a phenomenal identity, the existent as opposed to the merely fancied. Stevens usually means by *reality* an undetermined base on which a mind constructs its personal sense of the world. Occasionally he will use the word *real* as a term of approval, as a substitute for the word *true,* and, therefore, no more than an expression of confidence.

All of these meanings of "reality" occur in *An Ordinary Evening.* The commonest is the Emersonian one in which reality is the not-self, or as Emerson said, Nature or the Not-Me, including one's own body, other selves, the external world, and the anteriority of art. That leaves only one's own mind or imagination to set against a reality that comprehends all otherness, in a dialectical struggle without a victory.

An Ordinary Evening begins, "The eye's plain version is a thing apart" and ends with the premise that reality, rather than being a solid, "may be a shade that traverses / A dust, a force that traverses a shade." The eye's plain version is the First Idea as an imagined thing, abstracted, "a thing apart," and like reality this plain version is force, shade, dust, and so a palpable crossing into an impalpable. "Crossing" is of the essence, because "traverses" means "crosses." Force or a trope of Power crosses shade or the residuum of the Freedom of meaning, and shade crosses dust or a trope of Fate. Reality or the eye's plain version thus turns out to be only a crossing between turnings, a continual troping in, through, and with the eye. Haunting *An Ordinary Evening,* as Vendler demonstrates, are three ancestral versions of the eye. Keats's bright star, Milton's universal blank, and Emerson's transparent eyeball. All these return us ultimately to the *res* or thing that is close to the root of reality, that root being *rei,* meaning "possession." "Plain" for Stevens also goes to the root, to flat, clear vision of what is spread out before us, as in the 1952 poem *The Plain Sense of Things:*

> After the leaves have fallen, we return
> To a plain sense of things. It is as if
> We had come to an end of the imagination,
> Inanimate in an inert savoir.
>
> It is difficult even to choose the adjective
> For this blank cold, this sadness without cause.
> The great structure has become a minor house.
> No turban walks across the lessened floors.

The greenhouse never so badly needed paint.
The chimney is fifty years old and slants to one side.
A fantastic effort has failed, a repetition
In a repetitiousness of men and flies.

Yet the absence of the imagination had
Itself to be imagined. The great pond,
The plain sense of it, without reflections, leaves,
Mud, water like dirty glass, expressing silence

Of a sort, silence of a rat come out to see,
The great pond and its waste of the lilies, all this
Had to be imagined as an inevitable knowledge,
Required, as a necessity requires.

A total leaflessness returns us to a plain sense of things, yet at first
this plainness is not ordinary. That is, it does not help fit things together.
The "blank cold" seems to defy imagination, and yet is shown to be itself
an imagining, though not yet a reimagining. That "a fantastic effort has
failed" hardly can be an indictment of nature, but refers back to *Blue
Guitar*, XI, where repetition is a nightmare: "The fields entrap the children, brick / Is a weed and all the flies are caught."

The difference is in the vision of Ananke, if not quite of a
Beautiful Necessity, since Stevens considers his reduction to a First Idea as
an inevitable knowledge: "Yet the absence of the imagination had / Itself
to be imagined." What *The Plain Sense of Things* omits is a reimagining; for
Stevens in his early seventies, to live with the First Idea alone was no
longer wholly dehumanizing.

An Ordinary Evening opens with a five-canto meditation upon just
such a plain sense of things, culminating in canto V with an Emersonian
vision of the fall of the self. Cantos II through V are all organized as
commentaries upon canto I, which suggests the curious, genetic principle
of structure in the longer, thirty-one-canto version of *An Ordinary Evening*.
All of the twenty cantos added to the later version are in support of, or in
apposition to, the eleven cantos of the shorter version. Since the shorter
version itself followed the characteristic image patterns of the post-
Wordsworthian crisis-poem, the two can be mapped together, with some
revealing emphasis. Here are the poem's divisions, in the longer version,
with the first canto in each group occupying also its position in the
original sequence, except at the end:

1	I–V
2	VI–VIII
3	IX–X
4	XI

5	XII–XV
6	XVI–XXI
7	XXII–XXVII
8	XXVIII
9	XXX
10	XXXI
11	XXIX

In the original eleven-canto poem, cantos V–VII are a unit, and VII–XI are another. Indeed, the same division prevails in the longer version, which thus falls into the familiar patterns of the post-Romantic crisis-poem:

Clinamen	I–V
Tessera	VI–VIII
Kenosis	IX–X
Daemonization	XI
Askesis	XII–XXVII
Apophrades	XXVIII–XXXI

It will be observed that, in the poem's amplification, its movement of metaphoric sublimation, the *askesis* of the original cantos V–VII, was elaborated into cantos XII–XXVII; or sixteen out of thirty-one cantos, more than half the poem. This accounts for that curious impression of "total leaflessness," as Stevens endlessly elaborates, usually by apposition, a brilliant series of images that substitute for his poem's central trope, "the eye's plain version" that begins it, in a swerve initially away from Emerson. The epigraph to *An Ordinary Evening* might well have been from the first paragraph of Emerson's *Circles*, an essay that could have been called *Freedom* or *Wildness*:

> The eye is the first circle; the horizon which it forms is the second; and throughout nature this primary figure is repeated without end. . . . Our life is an apprenticeship to the truth that around every circle another can be drawn; that there is no end in nature, but every end is a beginning; that there is always another dawn risen on mid-noon, and under every deep a lower deep opens.

Emerson genially undoes, in that closing trope, the Miltonic, tragic moral of Satan's self-realization on Mt. Niphates. An American Satan merely discovers, "There are no fixtures in nature. The universe is fluid and volatile." Emerson's nature is, as we will see, Stevens' "reality," and the fitting together on an ordinary evening in an ordinary city of the different degrees of reality will expose a volatile interplay of ocular circles. So, at the start, the thing apart or abstracted is again the First Idea as an imagined thing, the perceptual language of experience. "Experience" is as central and as precise a term here as it is in Emerson. The root of "experience," *per,* means "risk," and Stevens like Emerson had used "experience" as a mode opposed to the higher activity of perception. *Poem Written at Morning,* in *Parts of a World,* insists, "The truth must be / That you do not see, you experience, you feel," and *Description without Place* had set description as a revelation by seeing against "the experience of sun / And moon." The late poem *Recitation after Dinner* was to venture a final definition of experience:

> Is it experience, say, the final form
> To which all other forms, at last, return,
> The frame of a repeated effect, is it that?

An Ordinary Evening labors to bring experience and seeing together, but inevitably they keep parting, and Stevens will opt for the priority and necessity of seeing even what you cannot hope to feel, whether ever or ever again. But he knows his own preferences from the start, and these are the "an and yet, and yet, and yet" that parodistically start off his poem, genially mocking his own incessant self-qualifications. Where "experience" risks the beginnings of thought as an activity of testing, "description" attempts an image-thinking that cannot be bounded by the otherness of "reality." Freud had remarked that it was an error to apply the standards of "reality" to repressed psychical structures, and we can note that everything Stevens sees in *An Ordinary Evening* inhabits the same universe as such structures. This means that "the never-ending meditation" is not "experience" but rather the process of Stevens' writing, which asks the question that reduces to the First Idea and its thinker, the giant; the question being how to begin perceiving the inconceivable idea of the sun. The second giant that kills the first is once again the reimagining of any single First Idea, and the similitude suggested by that idea invokes a familiar compound ghost in Stevens' poetry:

> Much like a new resemblance of the sun,
> Down-pouring, up-springing and inevitable,
> A larger poem for a larger audience,
>
> As if the crude collops came together as one,
> A mythological form, a festival sphere,
> A great bosom, beard and being, alive with age.

It was Whitman's ambitious dream, in particular, to write "a larger poem for a larger audience," and the "festival sphere" or eye as first circle is Whitman-as-Jehovah, the paternal, affirming, farewell-saying figure throughout Stevens. Yet this is not Whitman or any man, because the collops or crude rolls of flesh are being fitted together as myth, and

Stevens' own ambivalence is conveyed by the adjective "festival," though the Transcendental image of spheral man or human globe is scarcely qualified by Stevensian anxiety. Nor are anxieties emphasized in the cantos of commentary that follow the originary text of this canto. In canto II, Stevens internalizes New Haven as a visionary city, impalpable as we are impalpable, because we live in the mind. New Haven too is half sun, half mind, as much poem or trope as it is anything else, if only imagined but imagined well. So dialectical is this canto that the reader can judge no longer whether New Haven is an image of total presence or of total absence, and a curiously complex irony is developed as Stevens exploits a synesthesia of the spirit: "impalpable town," "impalpable bells," "transparencies of sound," "transparent dwellings," "impalpable habitations," "seem to move," "obscure," "uncertain," "indefinite, confused illuminations and sonorities," "cannot tell apart." Presumably, these all are part of "the hum of thoughts evaded in the mind," part of a dilemma that is "so much ourselves." The dilemma is neither philosophic nor psychological, though it can be mistaken for both. Most simply, it is a need for poetry that cannot be satisfied by poetry, whether written or to-be-written. This is Stevensian "poverty" or "misery," too rich in desire to be gratified by fulfillment, too imaginative in need to be redressed by imagination. No attitude toward poetry could be more American or more Emersonian, more hopeful or more frustrating. "The misery of man is to be balked of the sight of essence and stuffed with conjectures," said Emerson cheerfully, as he proceeded to deplore "the coldness and poverty of our view of heaven," while dialectically humming, "Dependence is the only poverty." Stevens put his earlier version of this best in *Poetry Is a Destructive Force:* "That's what misery is, / Nothing to have at heart. / It is to have or nothing." His definitive meditation upon "misery" and "poverty" is *In a Bad Time*, written the year after *The Auroras of Autumn*, and a year before *An Ordinary Evening*, and constituting a powerful commentary upon both major long poems:

> How mad would he have to be to say, "He beheld
> An order and thereafter he belonged
> To it"? He beheld the order of the northern sky.
>
> But the beggar gazes on calamity
> And thereafter he belongs to it, to bread
> Hard found, and water tasting of misery.
>
> For him cold's glacial beauty is his fate.
> Without understanding, he belongs to it
> And the night, and midnight, and after, where it is.

What has he? What he has he has. But what?
It is not a question of captious repartee.
What has he that becomes his heart's strong core?

He has his poverty and nothing more.
His poverty becomes his heart's strong core—
A forgetfulness of summer at the pole.

Sordid Melpomene, why strut bare boards,
Without scenery or lights, in the theatre's bricks,
Dressed high in heliotrope's inconstant hue,

The muse of misery? Speak loftier lines.
Cry out, "I am the purple muse." Make sure
The audience beholds you, not your gown.

The order of the northern sky initially was Sublime terror and then
was transformed into innocence in *The Auroras of Autumn*, an innocence
close to a poverty that "becomes his heart's strong core." Theatre, for
Stevens always a negative image, belongs here to a sordid muse of tragedy,
akin to Coleridge's wind in *Dejection: An Ode*, which is addressed as an
actor rather too close to perfection in all tragic sounds. Stevens ends *In a
Bad Time* by advising Melpomene to be more like Hoon, which means
that she too must find herself more truly and more strange. This attitude
informs the difficult canto III of *An Ordinary Evening*, which returns
"desire" to its root meaning of "longing for by shining forth," *sweid*, and
so can locate it "deep in the eye, / Behind all actual seeing." This is desire
transcending the world of Keats's Grecian Urn, for this emptiness and
denial are only potentially a porcelain, being still in the state of the bats
or lumps of clay out of which the artifact is to be formed.

A crucial image of voice, the savage cry of a savage assuagement,
rises in canto IV, as another commentary upon the plainness of plain
things or the achieved abstraction of a First Idea. Like so many fierce cries
in Stevens, this goes back to Whitman's ocean crying for its castaways and
suggests something of the cost of poetic incarnation. Canto IV begins
as ironic comedy, with Stevens himself as the "man who has fought /
Against illusion and was." "Illusion" here is the pathetic fallacy, and
"was" is time's "it was" against which Nietzsche urged the will's revenge.
The cry, as a "mating of surprised accords," undoes the pain of the
seasonal cycle, rendering the reduction of cold into a similitude of "a
sheen of heat romanticized." Again, we have an argument against illusion
conveyed in the *illusio* of irony, as the supposedly plain version of the eye
turns out to be a wholly visionary or Transcendental circle. This irony
emerges overtly in canto V, to conclude the poem's first movement.

Reality or the Not-Me is itself found to be "inescapable romance, inescapable choice / Of dreams." Stevens resumes the self-mockery of *Auroras*, V, when he brings his chant of the inauthentic to its pitch by declaiming, "Everything as unreal as real can be, / In the inexquisite eye," a long fall from having been the nomad exquisite of *Harmonium*. A precisely Emersonian fall of the self is then recorded, albeit with considerable gusto:

> Why, then, inquire
> Who has divided the world, what entrepreneur?
> No man. The self, the chrysalis of all men
>
> Became divided in the leisure of blue day
> And more, in branchings after day. One part
> Held fast tenaciously in common earth
>
> And one from central earth to central sky
> And in moonlit extensions of them in the mind
> Searched out such majesty as it could find.

There is no better description in Stevens' poetry of his characteristic dualism and of his precise variety of self-consciousness. The poetry of earth is only one part of him; the Transcendental searcher is after all the more dominant part. What has the eye's plain version to do with this questing after majesty, with these moonlit extensions? I read Stevens as answering such a question himself, by the disjunction between cantos I-V and VI-VIII. Canto VI, the second section of the poem's original, short version, presents a fable of naked Alpha, the ever-early candor, and the hierophant Omega, the late plural. When we pass from "searched out such majesty as it could find" to "Reality is the beginning not the end," we negotiate, with Stevens, a Crossing of Election, another testing of his poethood. Canto VI shows a fresh triumph in such a crossing:

> Reality is the beginning not the end,
> Naked Alpha, not the hierophant Omega,
> Of dense investiture, with luminous vassals.
>
> It is the infant A standing on infant legs,
> Not twisted, stooping, polymathic Z,
> He that kneels always on the edge of space
>
> In the pallid perceptions of its distances.
> Alpha fears men or else Omega's men
> Or else his prolongations of the human.
>
> These characters are around us in the scene.
> For one it is enough; for one it is not;
> For neither is it profound absentia,

Since both alike appoint themselves the choice
Custodians of the glory of the scene,
The immaculate interpreters of life.

But that's the difference: in the end and the way
To the end. Alpha continues to begin.
Omega is refreshed at every end.

So inspired is this synecdochal representation that at first we may miss the sense in which Stevens turns against himself here, though the two cantos VII and VIII, added as commentary, clarify the compensating sorrows that pay for this poetic election. Naked Alpha or the infant A is the reduction of the Not-Me, of reality as an otherness. The aged Z occupies the position that the palm at the end of the mind holds in Stevens' death-poem *Of Mere Being*, at the edge of space, beyond the last thought, and therefore can be called the final reimagining of all First Ideas. We live with both "characters," beginnings and ends of alphabets, and we depend upon both, and though Stevens seems to insist upon the difference between them there now seems less distinction between abstraction or Alpha and reimagining or Omega than ever before. To continue to begin is to be refreshed at every end, which means that reality as Alpha does the same work for us that the finished fiction of the self does as Omega. A variation occurs in canto VII, where the chapels and schools of New Haven, the visible towers of Yale, play the role of Omega, redressing the poverty or imaginative need of their makers but also of Stevens as spectator, the poet as Alpha or representative of reality. New Haven as vision of Omega or the incredible ends by becoming again the credible day of the eye's plain version.

More interesting is the variation of canto VIII, where Stevens descends out of his hotel onto the streets of New Haven, and finds his love of the real leading him to "the syllable / Of recognition, avowal, impassioned cry, / The cry that contains its converse in itself." This cry is a recognition of origins, here "the origin of a mother tongue," and should arouse in the reader a recognition of how prevalent and central in Stevens such a cry is, taking him back to Whitman's fierce old mother, the sea, crying out in the night for her sons, the poets, who have been cast away from her, who have fallen down into the occasions that are the cries of their poems.

A new moment, this time of undoing or emptying out of the poetic self, begins in canto IX and receives its commentary in canto X. In IX, the third canto of the original poem, Stevens returns to the hotel as the real to seek "the poem of pure reality, untouched / By trope or deviation," which is necessarily not a poem at all but rather New Haven as seen through the Emersonian transparent eyeball, "the eye made clear of uncertainty, with the sight / Of simple seeing, without reflection." Where the Emersonian epiphany is invoked, we can expect high vision to follow:

>   We seek
> Nothing beyond reality. Within it
>
> Everything, the spirit's alchemicana
> Included, the spirit that goes roundabout
> And through included, not merely the visible,
>
> The solid, but the movable, the moment,
> The coming on of feasts and the habits of saints,
> The pattern of the heavens and high, night air.

Some critics have deplored this vision as not being Stevens' own, or at least as not being the authentic speech of his own self. Yet the passage is the purest Stevens, though this is the central Whitmanian strain in Stevens. It is the poet of *Song of Myself* who keeps going "roundabout / And through," and who is likely to see visions in the high, night air. Stevens qualifies as elsewhere, by stressing the moment-to-moment glimpsing nature of his vision, and also by stressing that what he seeks is part of "the coming on" and not part of what already is. But, most of all, this is not poetry, not "of the hymns / That fall upon it out of the wind." By going "straight to the transfixing object," Stevens is destroying the only language in which poems can be written. The commentary on this metonymic rejection of poetry comes in canto X, where the drive "straight . . . to the object / At the exactest point at which it is itself" is severely qualified by the admission "We do not know what is real and what is not." But this is then shown to be a saving ignorance, part of living in change, which is repetition as the fulfillment of expectations, spoken of as "this faithfulness of reality." The rejection of a poetry of language for the poem of pure reality is itself partly undone by Stevens' praise for a mode of being, the joyous acceptance of change, that makes "gay the hallucinations in surfaces." It does not matter if they are hallucinations, particularly since the crossing to the poem's next movement juxtaposes "Make gay the hallucinations in surfaces" with "In the metaphysical streets of the physical town." This is a disjunction that does the work of a Crossing of Solipsism, as Stevens mounts into a very Emersonian version of the American Sublime:

> In the metaphysical streets of the physical town
> We remember the lion of Juda and we save
> The phrase . . . Say of each lion of the spirit

It is a cat of sleek transparency
That shines with a nocturnal shine alone.
The great cat must stand potent in the sun.

The phrase grows weak. The fact takes up the strength
Of the phrase. It contrives the self-same evocations
And Juda becomes New Haven or else must.

In the metaphysical streets, the profoundest forms
Go with the walker subtly walking there.
These he destroys with wafts of wakening,

Free from their majesty and yet in need
Of majesty, of an invincible clou,
A minimum of making in the mind,

A verity of the most veracious men,
The propounding of four seasons and twelve months,
The brilliancy at the central of the earth.

Except for the poem's final four cantos, this fourth canto of the shorter version is the only one upon which Stevens wrote no commentary in the form of interpolated cantos. No qualification or expansion seemed possible because of the strength of this lyric. The lion, here as elsewhere in Stevens an emblem of the power and menace of poetry, enters as the traditional phrase "the lion of Juda" and is then converted into each or any lion of the spirit, Transcendentalist in its imagery:

Say of each lion of the spirit

It is a cat of a sleek transparency
That shines with a nocturnal shine alone.

Though this is metaphysical, high and bright, it is in the physical town that mere being centers itself: "the great cat must stand potent in the sun." The fact takes up the phrase's strength, or rather the phrase alters itself to "the lion of New Haven," so that the lion of the spirit participates also in the being of fact. Stevens, the subtle walker in New Haven's metaphysical streets, is accompanied by the profoundest forms of lions as he goes. Any waft of wakening can destroy these irrealities, and yet Stevens needs them as evidences of the majesty of poetry. The invincible clou, the peg or point of greatest interest for Stevens, is still a point of brightest origin in a logocentric universe of discourse. Stevens acquires daemonic or Sublime force as he mounts into the hyperboles he insists are for him the given: a Gnostic, Emersonian uncreated element or "minimum of making in the mind" and an attendant truth founded upon the seasonal cycle and the earth's central splendor. The strength of repression in Stevens here is awesome, yet it is the menace of the lions that is being repressed when the poet too easily says that he is free from their majesty.

It is vital to any interpretation of *An Ordinary Evening* that the reader consider how extraordinary an elaboration Stevens made of cantos V–VII of the original version, which in the final text become cantos XII, XV, and XXII. With the cantos written as commentary upon them, these form now the long movement XII through XXVII. This dominant movement is the most protracted and ambitious development, in all of Stevens' poetry, of the revisionary ratio I have called *askesis*. The huge curtailment or limitation of meanings centers upon two Shelleyan metaphors: the fiction of the leaves in cantos XII and XVI, and the image of the evening star in canto XXII. The movement is through three phases of an ascetic reduction of the image-making power, from "leaves . . . resembling the presence of thought" on to "the total leaflessness" and then at last to the internalization of the star so that, like desire, "it shines / From the sleepy bosom of the real."

Stevens begins this movement of self-deconstruction with one of his major triumphs or central poems, another revision of the *Ode to the West Wind*, the eloquent cry of canto XII.

> The poem is the cry of its occasion,
> Part of the res itself and not about it.
> The poet speaks the poem as it is,
>
> Not as it was: part of the reverberation
> Of a windy night as it is, when the marble statues
> Are like newspapers blown by the wind. He speaks
>
> By sight and insight as they are. There is no
> Tomorrow for him. The wind will have passed by,
> The statues will have gone back to be things about.
>
> The mobile and the immobile flickering
> In the area between is and was are leaves,
> Leaves burnished in autumnal burnished trees
>
> And leaves in whirlings in the gutters, whirlings
> Around and away, resembling the presence of thought,
> Resembling the presences of thoughts, as if,
>
> In the end, in the whole psychology, the self,
> The town, the weather, in a casual litter,
> Together, said words of the world are the life of the world.

An occasion is an event or happening, but its etymological meaning is a falling down, and its Indo-European root means falling *or* dying.

To be the cry of fallen leaves is to be a cry in the etymological sense of crying out or imploring the aid of one's fellow citizens ("cry" is from the Latin *quiritare*, in turn from *quiris* for a Roman citizen). A poem is a cadence, and so etymologically a dying fall, as when in *Credences of Summer*, VIII, the poem's "resounding cry / Is like ten thousand tumblers tumbling down." In what had been the next canto of the shorter version, now canto XVI, Stevens associates himself as his poem's speaker with the occasion as a falling into or near death: "The venerable mask, / In this perfection, occasionally speaks / And something of death's poverty is heard." Here, in canto XII, the poem as deathly cry is "part of the res itself and not about it," which means that the thing itself is death or the reality principle. Speaking the poem as it is, not as it was, is to speak the poem as part of the reverberation of a night when the wind, more even than in *The Auroras of Autumn*, is blowing one toward destruction, as indeed it did in Shelley's *Ode*. "Reverberation" is a peculiarly rich word for and in Stevens, meaning not only a re-echoing or resounding (etymologically a relashing, as of a whip) but also a rewording or reverbalization, here of Shelley, but also of earlier Stevens. *Man and Bottle* had featured the realization that "the poem lashes more fiercely than the wind," that is, the poem reverberated more in the fierce mode of the maternal sea than even the Shelleyan wind rebounded against Stevens' precursor. Two cantos on, in XIV, "reverberation" receives Stevens' own commentary when "the point of reverberation" is identified as "not grim / Reality but reality grimly seen / And spoken in paradisal parlance new." Reverberation that is a grim seeing of the reality principle is now precisely the Stevensian *askesis*, but by no means the final resting point of his vision, even in canto XII of this poem.

In the present that is more absence than presence, Stevens locates his poem or fiction of the leaves "in the area between is and was." The trope is exactly Shelley's "my dead thoughts . . . like withered leaves," and the occasion is not wholly dissimilar: "What if my leaves are falling like its own!" Nor are the conclusions fundamentally different, though Shelley even in despair is a prophet, and Stevens merely meditates upon loss and gain. Shelley also "said words of the world are the life of the world," though the Shelleyan hope for "a new birth" was not to be Stevens' until the final phase, when it emerges in *A Discovery of Thought* and some related lyrics.

Cantos XIII–XV scarcely come near the achievement of XII, but they do illuminate it, as is their function. Stevens himself is the solitary ephebe of XIII, defining his enterprise in terms taken from his anti-Eliotic lyric, *The Creations of Sound*. Professor Eucalyptus, the Canon Aspirin of

New Haven, makes his first entrance in XIV as a parody of Stevens, not so much mocking the quest for reality as repeating it in a coarser tone. But canto XV raises Eucalyptus to a first glory and implicitly reveals why the Yale Professor of Metaphysics has received the name of so aromatic a tree. The flowering leaf of the eucalyptus is a well-covered flower until it opens, hence the tree's name from the Greek for "covered" or "hidden." One of Stevens' early *Primordia* poems thirty years before had spoken of a

> Compilation of the effects
> Of magenta blooming in the Judas-tree
> And of purple blooming in the eucalyptus—
> Map of yesterday's earth
> And of tomorrow's heaven.

Professor Eucalyptus is himself a mapper of yesterday's earth and tomorrow's heaven:

> The instinct for heaven had its counterpart:
> The instinct for earth, for New Haven, for his room,
> The gay tournamonde as of a single world
>
> In which he is and as and is are one.

Either Stevens remembered *Primordia* across thirty years, or else we have yet another instance of the uncanny persistence of his work. "Tournamonde" is his own coinage, of which he said, "For me it creates an image of a world in which things revolve and the word is therefore appropriate in the collocation of is and as." We can say that "tournamonde" is an economical equivalent of the Nietzschean motive for metaphor: "The desire to be different, to be elsewhere." Professor Eucalyptus merges into Stevens as the meditation attains a majesty of fresh desire, as much a part of this poem as is any vision of a reality principle:

> The hibernal dark that hung
> In primavera, the shadow of bare rock,
>
> Becomes the rock of autumn, glittering,
> Ponderable source of each imponderable,
> The weight we lift with the finger of a dream,
>
> The heaviness we lighten by light will,
> By the hand of desire, faint, sensitive, the soft
> Touch and trouble of the touch of the actual hand.

This hushed eros, so little credited to Stevens, is wholly characteristic of him. Though the image here is of a world in which things revolve, Stevens subtly sublimates the summer of that revolution, as the passage goes from wintry dark hanging in early spring, or bare rock, to glittering rock of autumn. Summer would be too imponderable a source, as *Credences of Summer* had shown its poet, who nevertheless remained uniquely grateful for that poem and who echoes it again in canto XVII. Too large for the somewhat sublimated desires of this poem, summer by its absence qualifies this final commentary upon the ways in which "words of the world are the life of the world."

Canto XVI, originally VI, begins another submovement of Stevens' triple *askesis*, setting the image of "the total leaflessness" against the fiction of the leaves. Though I will dispute an aspect of Helen Vendler's interpretation of canto XVI, like her I am moved by its expressive power, astonishing even for Stevens:

> Among time's images, there is not one
> Of this present, the venerable mask above
> The dilapidation of dilapidations.
>
> The oldest-newest day is the newest alone.
> The oldest-newest night does not creak by,
> With lanterns, like a celestial ancientness.
>
> Silently it heaves its youthful sleep from the sea—
> The Oklahoman—the Italian blue
> Beyond the horizon with its masculine,
>
> Their eyes closed, in a young palaver of lips.
> And yet the wind whimpers oldly of old age
> In the western night. The venerable mask,
>
> In this perfection, occasionally speaks
> And something of death's poverty is heard.
> This should be tragedy's most moving face.
>
> It is a bough in the electric light
> And exhalations in the eaves, so little
> To indicate the total leaflessness.

This, to Vendler, is "desiccation itself," and "the venerable mask" is hieratic, hiding, "with its stiff grandeur, the unimaginable ruin which has befallen the lapidary rock." The issue between interpretations here turns upon tone, so frequently uncanny in the later Stevens. I take "venerable mask" as ironic metaphor, since "venerable" and "mask" both have an ironic anteriority in Stevens' poetry. Stevens had played upon the venery in "veneration" in *Le Monocle de Mon Oncle*: "Most venerable heart, the lustiest conceit / Is not too lusty for your broadening"; and he had ended the paternal canto IV of *The Auroras of Autumn* with the bitter rhetorical question "What company, / In masks, can choir it with the naked wind?" As "the wind whimpers oldly of old age / In the western night," Stevens assumes the mask of the most venerable of hearts, in the double sense of age and of a barren desire, "above / The dilapidation of dilapidations," his decayed body, but more significantly and particularly his sexual power. A "dilapidation" is what has fallen into a state of ruin, but etymologically it means to throw the stones apart, and it is like Stevens to play at so elegant a sexual bitterness. Reality or the Not-Me comprises for him, as it did for Emerson, four sundries: nature, art, other persons, and one's own body. Art here is represented by "time's images," nature by night, day, and the night wind, other persons by the obscure contrast between the Oklahoman and Italian blue skies, evidently standing for feminine and masculine meeting: "Their eyes closed, in a young palaver of lips." Like the decayed body, all this is estrangement for Stevens, an otherness, ironically "this perfection," that he cannot address, because reality seems complete without him. His stance approximates that of Yeats in the first stanza of Sailing to Byzantium and recalls also The Poems of Our Climate, where "the imperfect is our paradise" because the perfect, being finished or done completely, does not allow for the delight that "lies in flawed words and stubborn sounds." The mask of aged desire, speaking as the cry of its occasion, speaks the poem of death's poverty, which fails to be "tragedy's most moving face," because it is still only a mask that we hear speaking.

But what does it mean that Stevens compares his own poem to "a bough in the electric light" or to "exhalations in the eaves"? Are those analogues of what is "altogether drier and more brittle," as Vendler says? A bough in artificial light makes a very different and doubtless more qualified impression than a bough in sunlight, yet it is a bough. Exhalations in the eaves are spookily out of context, yet remain exhalations. An Ordinary Evening in New Haven is an index, a forefinger indicating much by little, and here at the close of canto XVI it does show the total leaflessness of Stevens' still poignant desire. Yet this is only the start of the middle movement of the Stevensian askesis, and from the deliberate nadir at his poem's midpoint we will watch Stevens slowly, steadily, and as deliberately rise to "an alteration / Of words that was a change of nature."

Cantos XVII through XXI, the commentary upon XVI, adumbrate the total leaflessness and in every instance mitigate it. In XVII, the Arnoldian high seriousness is saluted, with the effect of dismissing comedy and tragedy alike in the name of commonplace reflection, or a mirroring of reality by that "dominant blank" that Stevens had seen, in The Auroras of Autumn, as Emerson saw it, but now sees as the true mode, the eye's plain version. This is severely said, but its rhetoric is uneasy, as when Stevens too insistently deprecates his usual repressed combination of Jehovah and Whitman:

> Like blessed beams from out a blessed bush
>
> Or the wasted figurations of the wastes
> Of night, time and the imagination.

The repetitions of "blessed," and "wasted" and "wastes," are an index of Stevensian anxiety.

More persuasive is the fable of the carpenter in XVIII, where the "clear water in a brilliant bowl, / Pink and white carnations" of *The Poems of Our Climate* are reduced to "a fuchsia in a can." The eye's plain version being a thing apart, not of the mere present, and life and death being at least as much metaphysical as physical, even so "this carpenter," Stevens, lives and dies in perceiving the poems, "a carpenter's iridescences," of his own climate. New Haven, "slapped up like a chest of tools," rises in the poet's mind as an iridescence of purged thought, a sublimation of reality. The sublimating force is personified in the less vital canto XIX as "a figure like Ecclesiast," whose chant presumably would be the traditional "all is vanity."

Another of Stevens' fierce reductions dominates canto XX, with a characteristic reimagining coming on as fiercely in XXI. Both of these cantos again are uncannily Emersonian if we think of the Emerson of *The Conduct of Life* rather than of *Nature*. Stevens begins canto XX by apprehending the cloudiness for him, now, of his past poems and his memories of his own past feelings. New Haven, juxtaposed with such an estrangement, is "a neuter shedding shapes in an absolute," not even an auroral serpent of a change. Yet it remains "a residuum," reminding us of the positive coloration that word has elsewhere in Stevens, the sense it conveys of a reduced substance in us that nevertheless prevails. In canto XIX, thinking back to the nineteenth century and to the celebration of great and central men, Stevens had invoked the personage who was the axis of vision for his time, Emerson, as "an image that begot its infantines." Here in XX, Stevens deliberately becomes a bitter version of the transparent eyeball, an infant of solipsism:

> In this chamber the pure sphere escapes the impure,
>
> Because the thinker himself escapes. And yet
> To have evaded clouds and men leaves him
> A naked being with a naked will
>
> And everything to make. He may evade
> Even his own will and in his nakedness
> Inhabit the hypnosis of that sphere.

But this Emersonian reduction becomes Emerson again, at the opening of canto XXI, in what could be the epigraph to *The Conduct of Life*:

> But he may not. He may not evade his will,
> Nor the wills of other men; and he cannot evade
> The will of necessity, the will of wills.

The power of necessity restitutes every ascetic movement of the spirit, though it be a power at last of death's necessity. Cythera, island of Venus, appears as Baudelaire's isle of Cythère, and yet Stevens' "black shepherd's isle" is secondary here in comparison to "another isle," where the senses give without taking, an island of a more sympathetic imagination:

> The opposite of Cythère, an isolation
> At the centre, the object of the will, this place,
> The things around—the alternate romanza
>
> Out of the surfaces, the windows, the walls,
> The bricks grown brittle in time's poverty,
> The clear. A celestial mode is paramount,
>
> If only in the branches sweeping in the rain:
> The two romanzas, the distant and the near,
> Are a single voice in the boo-ha of the wind.

The "romanza out of the black shepherd's isle" joins with Stevens' "alternate romanza" in the single voice of the wind, yet Stevens' kind of poetry is near, "this place, / The things around." Such a finding cannot alter the interpretation of the wind of section XVI; it still "whimpers oldly of old age / In the western night," yet those "branches sweeping in the rain" have more life in them than their status as commentary upon "the total leaflessness" might indicate.

With the re-entrance of Professor Eucalyptus in canto XXII (originally VII), Stevens begins the final phase of his threefold *askesis*, this one comprising six cantos, XXII–XXVII. As before, Eucalyptus parodies Stevens, and the high pomposity scarcely conceals the intensity of Stevens' own quest: "The search / For reality is as momentous as / The search for god." The inside / outside jugglings between philosopher and poet betray the obsessiveness of Stevens' lifelong anxieties concerning the rival authorities of philosophy and poetry. More impressive is Stevens' conscious palinode in the matter of the First Idea, "the inhalations of original cold / And of original earliness." The First Idea is no longer seen as a reduction, "the predicate of bright origin," but simply as the eye's plain version, the daily sense of cold and earliness. Returning to Crispin, and to Crispin's precursor in the Poet of *Alastor*, Stevens now dismisses the romance of the solitary quester: "Creation is not renewed by images / Of lone wanderers." Reimagining from the eye's plain version is still praised, though Stevens' example of such re-creating is beautifully equivocal:

> Likewise to say of the evening star,
> The most ancient light in the most ancient sky,

> That it is wholly an inner light, that it shines
> From the sleepy bosom of the real, re-creates,
> Searches a possible for its possibleness.

This is primarily the evening star of *Adonais* and of many other Shelleyan texts, but "the sleepy bosom of the real" may be an allusion to Keats's sonnet *Bright Star*, where the poet wants to be at once the star "in lone splendour" but also pillowed upon the sleepy bosom of the real, which for him is "my fair love's ripening breast." The evening star is one of time's images, ancient in its anteriority. By saying that it is an inner light and then calling its home the real, Stevens has introjected reality even as he tries to draw the star out of the Not-Me into the me. Re-creating the High Romantic metaphor of the star as the endurance and immortality of poetry involves a troping from metaphor to metalepsis, to the Power or *pathos* of possibleness or *potentia*. The evening star remains, in part, a sublimating metaphor, but rather less so than the fictions of the leaves or of leaflessness.

Canto XXIII, which begins the commentary upon the evening-star canto, is one of my special favorites. Having written of it elsewhere at length, particularly in *Poetry and Repression*, I will note here only the link between its repressed Whitmanian desire for the "cozening and coaxing sound" of the maternal sea of night and the Shelleyan and Keatsian use of the evening star as an emblem of the persistence of desire. After this strength, canto XXIV disappoints in its rhetorical execution, though its importance for Stevens is clear. The "escape from repetition," at the edge between afternoon and evening, hints at the difficult theme of the last of Stevens, after *The Rock*, the topography of a new birth into Transcendental perceptiveness. As New Haven poises at the horizon's dip, Stevens prepares for the visions that will begin for him a year later, in 1950, with *A Discovery of Thought*.

There is a sudden onslaught of Stevens' uncanny power again in canto XXV, with its obsessive imagery of eyes, looks, watched, stared, as the poet confronts man with the blue guitar, earlier form of his own vocation and identity, and so his Whitmanian *daimon*, akin to the figure who mocks Whitman on the beach in *As I Ebb'd*. The demands made upon Stevens by the hidalgo are necessarily too stern, reminding us that "hidalgo" means "son of something" where "something" is substance or property. There may be a memory here of the bitter *Thought Revolved*, IV, published with the *Blue Guitar*:

> Behold the moralist hidalgo
> Whose whore is Morning Star.

Description without Place, VII, spoke of how "the hard hidalgo / Lives in the mountainous character of his speech." The hidalgo of *An Ordinary Evening* is both a moralist and a hard looker, "a hatching that stared and demanded," the egg of the eye never quite hatched. Though "permanent, abstract," the hidalgo is hardly a muse but more nearly a superego, whose scrutiny withers every privileged moment. This withering extends into canto XXVI, which is a kind of late revision of *Sea Surface Full of Clouds*. Stevens would like to indulge in the perspectives of distance and so to see the earth as inamorata. But with the attentive eyes of his own hidalgo-aspect upon him, he regards the earth in a plainer version in canto XXVII:

> Again, "The sibilance of phrases is his
> Or partly his. His voice is audible,
> As the fore-meaning in music is." Again,
>
> "This man abolishes by being himself
> That which is not ourselves: the regalia,
> The attributions, the plume and helmet-ho."

As so many times, elsewhere, Stevens is at his most tender, even Whitmanian, when he accepts a self-imposed poverty of vision. The whole of this most extensive of all his sublimations ends in this flamboyant canto, the fable of the Ruler of Reality and his spouse, the Queen of Fact. If reality is the otherness beheld by the eye, then the unreal self is the peculiar kingdom ruled by the Queen of Fact. The scholar's Segmenta are Stevens' own notes for an unwritten poem, and they celebrate a major man precisely like the MacCullough of *Notes toward a Supreme Fiction*. Like the MacCullough or like the Whitman of *Sea-Drift*, the Ruler of Reality lies lounging by the sea, doubtless "reading in the sound, / About the thinker of the first idea." Yet the later fable is fuller, because of the presence of the Queen of Fact, or theorist of death, the true muse of Stevens' poetry.

In the transition from "and, with the Queen / Of fact, lies at his ease beside the sea" to the final four cantos, we move with Stevens through the most complex of all his Crossings of Identification, because

on the other shore of this disjunction he makes a truly central defense of
his own poetry, a defense that turns against his worthiest opponent,
himself:

> If it should be true that reality exists
> In the mind: the tin plate, the loaf of bread on it,
> The long-bladed knife, the little to drink and her
>
> Misericordia, it follows that
> Real and unreal are two in one: New Haven
> Before and after one arrives or, say,
>
> Bergamo on a postcard, Rome after dark,
> Sweden described, Salzburg with shaded eyes
> Or Paris in conversation at a café.
>
> This endlessly elaborating poem
> Displays the theory of poetry,
> As the life of poetry. A more severe,
>
> More harassing master would extemporize
> Subtler, more urgent proof that the theory
> Of poetry is the theory of life,
>
> As it is, in the intricate evasions of as,
> In things seen and unseen, created from nothingness,
> The heavens, the hells, the worlds, the longed-for lands.

This, the eighth of the original eleven cantos, is the most famous
and I think the best, surpassing even "The poem is the cry of its occasion." The key word is "misericordia," a dispensation from the ordinance
of fasting and, in this context, a release from the necessities of reduction
and from the anxieties of seeking to determine the divisions between real
and unreal. On the premise that reality has been taken up into the mind,
that the First Ideas of nature, other persons, art, and one's own body have
been reimagined fully, then it follows at last that real and unreal, reduction and expansion, are two in one; both of them are synecdoches for the
desire to be elsewhere, the desire to be different, to be anywhere in the
world except New Haven, or anywhere out of the world except the poem
of An Ordinary Evening in New Haven. The rocking cradle that endlessly
vexed Yeats's rough beast to nightmare, or that earlier first stirred Whitman to the life of poetry, has become in Stevens his variational appositional stance. Stevens elaborates precisely as the Whitmanian maternal
ocean rocks, because he too is calling home his castaway, whose name is
reality.

Always precise about language, Stevens does not deprecate his poem by describing it as "endlessly elaborating." To elaborate is to exe-cute with truly painstaking detail, to pay attention so that every part is in place, to work the poem out. Yet Stevens says "elaborating" and not "elaborated," which means not that his is a process-poem but that it demands active reading even as it actively reads. "Theory" etymologically means a "viewing," as at a theatre, and "life" goes back to a root meaning "to adhere or stick," or charmingly enough, "fat." To "display" is to "exhibit" yet goes back through a word meaning "scatter" to a root meaning "plait" or "weave." Endlessly working itself out, *An Ordinary Evening in New Haven* scatters and weaves a vision of poetry as being that which sticks or adheres in poetry, the fat of poetry as it is of life. We have met this viewing throughout the poem's theatre, and we now can name it for what it is, the attempt to see earliest, the Emersonian and American doomed attempt to establish a priority in seeing, as though Europe had seen nothing before us. Stevens knows himself to be a great elaborator of this program, but he cannot extemporize as subtly and as urgently as the greatest of all poetic extemporizers, Whitman.

Whitman's art, far more than Stevens', is to give the effect of an impromptu, to deceive us into the confidence that we listen to an orator who can function without a prepared text. Stevens cannot harass us as Whitman can; his poem is not as severe as *Song of Myself* or *The Sleepers*, because "severe" in its root means "true" and Stevens is too Nietzschean to assert that his poem can give truth. "Life, as it is, in the intricate evasions of as" is the enormous, the truly supreme fiction of Whitman, not of Stevens, who knows that what he believes in cannot be true. Yet Stevens is never more moving than when he affirms the Transcendental nostalgia by negating it. Out of the nothingness of his fictive self, Whit-man, no snow man, created "the heavens, the hells, the worlds, the longed-for lands." Stevens is not, cannot be, such a master, but no proclamation of his poverty, and of ours, is more poignant than this great canto that concludes by singing so passionately what Stevens says he cannot sing.

When we reach the final three cantos of *An Ordinary Evening*, we confront the complexity of Stevens' self-revisionism, since cantos IX, X, XI of the shorter version appear in the definitive poem as XXX, XXXI, XXIX. Since I am following here the sequence of the later, longer version, I pass now to canto XXIX, yet it remains important to remember that this had been the original closure of the poem. Canto XXIX is as brilliant a fable as Stevens wrote, yet it may be a fable impossible to interpret, a text too problematic to read fully or at least for the reader to persuade himself or others that he has read severely enough:

In the land of the lemon trees, yellow and yellow were
Yellow-blue, yellow-green, pungent with citron-sap,
Dangling and spangling, the mic-mac of mocking birds.

In the land of the elm trees, wandering mariners
Looked on big women, whose ruddy-ripe images
Wreathed round and round the round wreath of autumn.

They rolled their r's, there, in the land of the citrons.
In the land of big mariners, the words they spoke
Were mere brown clods, mere catching weeds of talk.

When the mariners came to the land of the lemon trees,
At last, in that blond atmosphere, bronzed hard,
They said, "We are back once more in the land of the elm trees,

But folded over, turned round." It was the same,
Except for the adjectives, an alteration
Of words that was a change of nature, more

Than the difference that clouds make over a town.
The countrymen were changed and each constant thing.
Their dark-colored words had redescribed the citrons.

There are two lands in this fable, or rather there is only one land, since the real land of the elm trees, New Haven, and the unreal, Goethean paradise or Stevensian Florida of the citrons are two in one. The mariners desire to be elsewhere, to be different, to forsake the fulfillments of reality for an Eden of language or simply to be poets. But they take New Haven with them, and neither they nor Stevens (since they *are* Stevens) can decide whether this means that nothing can change or whether it means that there is nothing except change.

In the *Harmonium* world of "dangling and spangling, the mic-mac of mocking birds," the yellow of the lemons was both blue and green, pungencies alike of mind and of earth. In New Haven, traditionally the land of the elm trees (Stevens writes just before the major elm blight of the 1950's), wandering, big mariners (or Odysseus assimilated to Stevens) stare at autumnal women, women more of the earth and its ripeness than of the mind's desires. Language also is gaudy, in the *Harmonium* world, but the language of New Haven is again too much of the earth our mother. Presumably, it is in search of a language "to roll / On the expressive tongue, the finding fang" that the mariner Stevens comes to the land of citrons. But his representatives, arriving at last in their Eden, proclaim, "We are back once more in the land of the elm trees, / But folded over, turned round." I know of nothing else in Stevens so problematic in tone; is this a lament, a defiance, or simply a kind of statement as to that which is? Vendler, with a most acute ear, reads the third possibility:

> This possibly depressing recognition is certainly anticlimactic, but Stevens expresses it without tone, as though he wished the moment to be neutral. The repetitiveness of experience is no new theme in Stevens, but here he refuses to speak of it either as pleasurable or as diminishing. Instead, it is factual; and he has it both ways.

The recognition, as I read it, is not depressing or toneless, but positive, even a touch truculent and defiant. An adjective is an addition, something thrown on to something else, so that to say, "It was the same, / Except for the adjectives" is more self-contradictory than dialectical. The mariners have been troped in being "folded over, turned round"; they have been recolored, and so the mariner Stevens is not just a permanently dark-colored self. He is not within the difference, but beyond the difference, in the faith that "an alteration / Of words that was a change of nature" may be an authentic alteration in the fiction of the self.

What was the force of the original close of the poem, when it ended that "Their dark-colored words had redescribed the citrons"? Too hopeful an earliness, is surely part of the answer. After so many sublimations, so ever-early a candor would not have been appropriate. With marvelous judgment, Stevens took the original cantos IX and X and placed them after the fable of the mariners as cantos XXX and XXXI. It is not a total leaflessness that is observed in XXX, but what nevertheless presents itself as a barrenness:

> The last leaf that is going to fall has fallen.
> The robins are là-bas, the squirrels, in tree-caves,
> Huddle together in the knowledge of squirrels.
>
> The wind has blown the silence of summer away.
> It buzzes beyond the horizon or in the ground:
> In mud under ponds, where the sky used to be reflected.
>
> The barrenness that appears is an exposing.
> It is not part of what is absent, a halt
> For farewells, a sad hanging on for remembrances.
>
> It is a coming on and a coming forth.
> The pines that were fans and fragrances emerge,
> Staked solidly in a gusty grappling with rocks.
>
> The glass of the air becomes an element—
> It was something imagined that has been washed away.
> A clearness has returned. It stands restored.

It is not an empty clearness, a bottomless sight.
It is a visibility of thought,
In which hundreds of eyes, in one mind, see at once.

After so many dominant blanks, so many staring eyes hatching like
an egg, so many parodied transparent eyeballs, as well as eyes' plain
versions, inexquisite eyes, and assorted reflections, we experience a profound sense of liberation when we are told: "A clearness has returned. It
stands restored." Truly, the clarity has its menace; it is the moment poised
just before winter. But though those hundreds of eyes may belong to the
animal kingdom, to the huddled squirrels sensing the imminence of
winter, they suggest also Shakespeare's play upon a bottomless dream,
and more directly the American Transcendentalist dream of open vision,
of seeing as Whitman hoped to see, with the eyes of a multitude. Something strange begins to come on and come forth in Stevens, that "visibility of thought" which will be the discovery of the final phase, when the
course of all the particulars of vision and visionary sound is finally tracked.
Summer was imagined well but has been washed away, and what remains
is no longer an abstraction or reduction to a First Idea. This is revelation
without description, tentative and yet definitive, and rhetorically a troping
upon all the earlier undoings and sublimations in the poem. There is no
finer example in Stevens of a scheme of transumption or metaleptic
reversal, the far-fetching of an antipodal creature, worthy of birth.

Stevens does not end the poem upon this introjection of a fresh
earliness that huddles expectantly, waiting for the blasts of winter. He
goes back to the central Paterian trope of *Harmonium*, the apprehension
of reality as the solipsistic recognition of privileged moments, sudden
perfections of sense, flakes of fire, fluttering things having distinct
shapes:

The less legible meanings of sounds, the little reds
Not often realized, the lighter words
In the heavy drum of speech, the inner men

Behind the outer shields, the sheets of music
In the strokes of thunder, dead candles at the window
When day comes, fire-foams in the motions of the sea,

Flickings from finikin to find finikin
And the general fidget from busts of Constantine
To photographs of the late president, Mr. Blank,

These are the edgings and inchings of final form,
The swarming activities of the formulae
Of statement, directly and indirectly getting at,

> Like an evening evoking the spectrum of violet,
> A philosopher practicing scales on his piano,
> A woman writing a note and tearing it up.
>
> It is not in the premise that reality
> Is a solid. It may be a shade that traverses
> A dust, a force that traverses a shade.

The first six lines refine *Harmonium,* but the next three genially mock the Hoonian vision. "Flickings from finikin to fine finikin" transumes earlier Stevensian intimations as to the high fastidiousness of poetry and of poetic perception, of which the crucial instance is *Like Decorations,* XXXII:

> Poetry is a finikin thing of air
> That lives uncertainly and not for long
> Yet radiantly beyond much lustier blurs.

The mockery in that early passage is overbalanced by the praise of poetry, and so it is here in the final canto of *An Ordinary Evening.* Even "the general fidget," the nervous decline of representation "from busts of Constantine" to the aptly named Mr. Blank, perhaps a departed insurance executive, is redeemed as one of "the edgings and inchings of final form," of history getting at getting it right. There is no full stop in the canto until evening evokes, the metaphysician plays, and the woman makes up and unmakes her mind, presumably upon an issue of erotic choice. What are all these but variant versions, analogues, of Stevens' own appositional method in *An Ordinary Evening?* They share Stevens' achieved premise, that reality, whether it be nature, art, others, or one's body is a crossing or transition, a disjunctive versing of force, shade, dust. "Dead candles at the window" may be only a poignant emblem of ineffectual inchings toward final form, when the sun comes up, yet they are part of the emblematic reality of poet or scholar, the solitary outward form of his internalization of the evening star. Stevens ends his great poem on "shade," but the final emphasis is upon a force crossing a shade, and so freshly breaking a form, writing another canto on an ordinary evening in New Haven.

MARIE BORROFF

An Always
Incipient Cosmos

The exact repetition in the present of
the verbal and other forms of behavior used on ceremonial occasions in
the past has always been an important means of inducing or perpetuating
reverence for authority. Despite Wallace Stevens's insistent and sometimes
rude repudiations of the cultural establishment, including the academies
and their old descriptions of the world, the first thing to be noted here is
his consistent and thorough exploitation of the inherited resources of high
formal language. These of course include elevated diction (sporadically
undercut, as we have observed, by eccentric word combinations); they
also, less obviously, include a repertoire of grammatical constructions,
ways of putting together and connecting phrases, clauses, and sentences
whose expressive power consists in our conscious or unconscious identification of them with certain kinds of formal context. Two areas of culture
and the literary genres connected with them are of especial importance for
Stevens. We find them reflected in a scholarly or discursive and a sacred or
hierophantic strain, respectively, in his idiosyncratic version of the high
style.

The scholar in Stevens's poetry (more narrowly, the philosopher)
expounds and excogitates in a language whose forms and patterns suggest
the treatise, the textbook, or the classroom lecture. This discursive voice
sounds sporadically in single lines and short line sequences; it is most
conspicuously audible in whole poems or sections of poems explicitly

From *Language and the Poet*. Copyright © 1979 by The University of Chicago Press. Undesignated parenthetical page numbers refer to *The Collected Poems of Wallace Stevens*;
OP designates *Opus Posthumous* (see Bibliography).

dramatized as philosophic essays—for example, "Study of Two Pears" (an "opusculum paedagogum"), "The Glass of Water," "Connoisseur of Chaos," "Description without Place," and parts of "Notes toward a Supreme Fiction" and "An Ordinary Evening in New Haven."

In such passages and poems, terminology and syntax are characterized by the preponderance of nominal over verbal and adjectival elements; abstract nouns of course occur frequently, as does the verb *to be* in its role of copula.

> If seeming is description without place,
> The spirit's universe, then a summer's day,
>
> Even the seeming of a summer's day,
> Is description without place;
> The freshness of transformation is
>
> The freshness of a world. It is our own,
> It is ourselves, the freshness of ourselves,
> And that necessity and that presentation
>
> Are rubbings of a glass in which we peer.
>
> (p. 398)

> The poem is the cry of its occasion,
> Part of the res itself and not about it.
>
> (p. 473)

Another feature of importance in these examples is the reiteration of key words and phrases. The effect is didactic; the pace of exposition seems to be deliberately held back while thought is elaborated and qualified, as if by a careful teacher. With regard to larger grammatical structures, Stevens's poetry of course presents us with a host of examples of the patterns traditionally used in formal discourse and excluded, by and large, from spontaneous utterance—multiple subordinations, compoundings of subordinate and independent clauses, participial or infinitive constructions where everyday speech would prefer a finite verb. But sentence structure in Stevens's discursive language may go to the opposite extreme, with a brevity and simplicity as remote from ordinary speech as the conventional elaborations and complications of formal syntax.

> The pears are not viols,
> Nudes or bottles.
> They resemble nothing else . . .
>
> The shadows of the pears
> Are blobs on the green cloth.

> The pears are not seen
> As the observer wills.

(pp. 196–97)

> Ideas are men. The mass of meaning and
> The mass of men are one. Chaos is not
>
> The mass of meaning. It is three or four
> Ideas or, say, five men or, possibly, six.

(p. 255)

Again we note the reiteration of key words and phrases; again there is an effect of didactic emphasis and retardation of pace. A minor feature of similar import is the sequence of numbers or letters conventionally serving to mark off the divisions of a text or the points of an argument—the Roman numerals preceding the stanzas of "Study of Two Pears," and "A" and "B" propositions and "Projections" of "Connoisseur of Chaos" and "So-and-So Reclining on Her Couch," the numbered descriptive "exfolia-tions" of "Someone Puts a Pineapple Together," part III.

A second important realm from which Stevens draws traditionally formal features of language is the sacred or hierophantic, and, in looking to this source, we must recognize that the formal language of religion cannot be fully distinguished from that of poetry itself. Much of the most important poetry of the earlier periods of English, as of other European literatures, is explicitly Christian. And those later poets who found Christianity inadequate or rejected it entirely have themselves tended to assume the role of nondenominational or secular priest, proselytizing in the very accents of religious authority. Stevens himself is a notable case in point. Though he is capable of lashing out ironically against major articles of the Christian faith, of calling the resurrected Jesus a "three-days' personage" (p. 97) and the crucifixion a "glamorous hanging" (p. 192), his poetry from first to last uses Christian imagery for its own purposes with utmost seriousness, having its "dove, alighting" (p. 357), its "communion" (p. 253), its "Candle a Saint" (p. 223), its "chants" of "final peace" (p. 258), its "pastoral nun" whose final vision identifies poetry with apotheosis (p. 378), even its "sudarium" (p. 188) and "wounds" transfigured into roses (p. 318). Genres and modes of discourse associated with the sacred— invocation, prayer, prophecy, hymn, litany, parable—frequently give form to single lines and short passages and, on a larger scale, to poems and sections of long poems; "To the One of Fictive Music," "The Idea of Order at Key West," "Chocorua to Its Neighbor," "The Owl in the Sarcophagus," and parts of "Esthetique du Mal," "Notes," and "An Ordinary Evening" are important examples.

Terminology and syntax are here characterized by the predominance of nominal *and* adjectival over verbal elements, with heavy reliance on qualitative terms of solemnizing or celebratory import, some venerable, some innovative:

> The brilliant height
> And hollow of him by its brilliance calmed,
> Its brightness burned the way good solace seethes.
>
> This was peace after death, the brother of sleep, . . .
>
> Adorned with cryptic stones and sliding shines,
> An immaculate personage in nothingness.
>
> (p. 434)

We find inversions of word order of the time-honored poetic sort ("Green is the night" [p. 223], "In his poems we find peace" [p. 251], "By one caterpillar is great Africa devoured" [p. 456]); the negative qualifications and logical connections among clauses characteristic of the discursive mode give way to appositives and series of nouns and adjectives (also, strikingly, of finite verbs). These may accumulate with a rhythmic continuity furthered by the use of linking conjunctions that eliminate pauses and with an intensity enhanced by traditionally "rhetorical" repetitions of meanings, words, and sounds:

> There was
> Only the great height of the rock
> And the two of them standing still to rest.
>
> There was the cold wind and the sound
> It made, away from the muck of the land
> That they had left, heroic sound
> Joyous and jubilant and sure.
>
> (p. 126)

> And I walked and talked
> Again, and lived and was again, and breathed again
> And moved again and flashed again, time flashed again.
>
> (p. 238)

When the discursive content itself of Stevens's poetry takes on a solemn aura, as it frequently does, the propounding and sanctifying voices merge. Thus the sixth section of "Description without Place" moves from its expository opening,

> Description is revelation. It is not
> The thing described, nor false facsimile,

to a climax in which definition and distinctions give way to celebratory variations on the symbolic theme of a "text we should be born that we might read,"

> the book of reconciliation,
> Book of a concept only possible
>
> In description, canon central in itself,
> The thesis of the plentifullest John.
> (p. 345)

We see the abstract concept of revelation turning into the Book of Revelation as philosophic statement becomes colored by Christian allusion.

The inherited language of the formal modes of discourse in English is, as we know, associated with elevated diction of the sort tending to give rise to statistically high percentiles of words of Romance and Latinate origin. It is thus to be expected that successive Romance-Latinate percentiles of 20 and over will be found in poems like "Credences of Summer" and others in which the discursive and hierophantic modes predominate. The diction of this and other similar poems is to some degree bound to the subject matters or areas of culture associated with these two modes, as is apparent in the passages quoted above in words like *description, presentation, res, state, concept,* and *thesis,* on the one hand; and *peace, immaculate, revelation, reconciliation,* and *canon,* on the other. But subject matter cannot fully account for the presence in these same passages of other words of Romance and Latinate origin such as *cry, resemble, brilliant, adorned, cryptic, personage, facsimile,* and *central.* These latter must be recognized as symptoms of the pervasive bias in Stevens's language we noted earlier, its persistent exploitation, for all its flamboyant originality, of the inherited features of high formal style. An abundance of such features may even make his most opaque passages *rhetorically* intelligible, directly conveying such qualities as discursive seriousness or visionary exaltation:

> This is the mirror of the high serious:
> Blue verdured into a damask's lofty symbol,
>
> Gold easings and ouncings and fluctuations of thread
> And beetling of belts and lights of general stones,
> Like blessed beams from out a blessed bush
>
> Or the wasted figurations of the wastes
> Of night, time and the imagination,
> Saved and beholden, in a robe of rays.
> (p. 477)

Here the words themselves dazzle not only in the intricacies of their sounds and rhythms and their qualities as diction but in their unaccustomed combinations and applications as well, whether or not we grasp their meanings as metaphorical and symbolic description. The reader of such a passage may well feel that in it rhetoric has shouldered meaning aside to an extent verging on self-indulgent display—a vice of style that is perhaps inevitable, given so tremendous a virtuosity.

Stevens's pervasive formal bias, then, manifests itself on the level of diction not only in learned and allusive language but also in the frequent occurrence of distinctively formal words of Romance and Latinate origin, tied neither to any particular area of meaning nor to any particular genre or set of genres, for which native synonyms belonging to the common level of diction are available. Examples of such "free formal" tags are *desire* versus *want*, *distant* versus *far*, *edifice* versus *building*, *interior* versus *inner/inside*, *labor* versus *work*, *possess* versus *own*, *regard* in the meaning it shares with *look (at)*, and *respond/response* versus *answer*. Another such symptom is the use of full, in preference to contracted, forms of the verb: "Let *us* make hymns" (p. 151), "I *cannot* bring a world quite round" (p. 165), "*We are* conceived in your conceits" (p. 195), "*It is* how he gives his light. *It is* how he shines" (p. 205), "It *has not* always had/To find" (p. 239), "We *do not* say ourselves like that in poems" (p. 311).

While fully exploiting the inherited repertoire of formal Romance and Latinate diction, Stevens by no means neglects that other traditional means of elevation in English, which involves the use of simple words mostly of native origin, associated since early modern times with poetry and the Bible. Except in the case of archaisms and archaic forms (e.g., *begat*, *spake*), our recognition of such associations and our response to the stylistic qualities generated by them are dependent on the contexts in which the words appear—on relationships among the ideas expressed and on the cooperative presence of other words of similar potential. In this respect, poetic-biblical diction differs from from diction of the ornate, elevated variety. The word *argentine*, for instance (used memorably by Stevens in the third part of "Notes"), has its distinctively formal quality regardless of context; the word *silver* belongs to the common level of diction but has certain biblical associations (most notably in connection with the thirty pieces of silver paid to Judas) which might or might not be evoked and form part of its expressive value in a literary work.

To follow this allusive process in operation, let us look at what happens to the word *know*, among others, in "The Hand as a Being." The poem is written in the form of a parable or simple allegorical narrative; its story is located at the outset "in the first canto of the final canticle" and is thereby linked in significance to the similarly allegorical (or at least traditionally allegorized) Song of Songs, also known as Canticles. Like the Song of Songs, "The Hand as a Being" has an ostensibly sexual theme. In it, the beneficent seduction of the central figure by a mythic feminine being symbolizes a change within the mind from confusion to order. Having been "too conscious of too many things at once," "our man" becomes "composed," with a play on the meanings "serene" and "put into form." At the end of the poem, diction modulates to the extreme of simplicity and Romance and Latinate elements all but disappear:

> Her hand took his and drew him near to her.
> Her hair fell on him and the mi-bird flew
>
> To the ruddier bushes at the garden's end.
> Of her, of her alone, at last he knew
> And lay beside her underneath the tree.
> (p. 271)

Of the preceding forty-four words, only *garden* is non-native (Romance). (I consider *mi* to be a sound-symbolic coinage, as it is also in "the thinnest *mi* of falsetto" in "Parochial Theme" [p. 191], and not the Latinate name of the third note of the musical scale.) In context, the potential biblical suggestiveness of the words *garden* and *tree* and, retrospectively, of *naked* in the first stanza of the poem, is realized with specific reference to the fall of man, and "the hand appeared" of stanza 5 may be seen as alluding to the story of Belshazzar's feast. The verb *drew* in the passage quoted has archaic-poetic status in the sense of "pulled," and *lay beside* is reminiscent of the archaic expression *lie with*, designating sexual intercourse. The prediction of the materializing hand, unlike that of the Old Testament story, is favorable; enlightenment does not bring perdition but comes as a saving grace. The play on the modern and biblical senses of *know*, bringing together the concepts of intellectual enlightenment and sexual consummation, epitomizes the basic symbolic equation of the poem.

So far, we have considered formality in Stevens as a means of associating his poetry with the inherited forms, and thus imputing to it the inherited values of literary and cultural tradition. But it serves other purposes as well, and these should at least be mentioned briefly. First, the solemnity of tone reinforced by formal language in much of the poetry is consonant with Stevens's often-expressed belief in the importance and dignity of the imaginative enterprise, in the poet's public role of helping people to lead their lives (*The Necessary Angel: Essays on Reality and the*

Imagination. New York: Knopf. p. 29). Second, learned diction and other features of elevated language serve here as elsewhere (the point is so obvious that we tend to overlook it) as a kind of accreditation, investing the user with a believable authority. Entirely apart from the significance of each in its context, the foreign words and wide-ranging references to persons and places which appear throughout Stevens's poetry are impressive in general as "verbal credentials." We respect the desire to repudiate the past in the man who proves himself thoroughly conversant with it. And there is a heightening of dramatic intensity in the longing of such a man to divest himself of his knowledge, his melancholy conviction that mental nakedness is a condition of imaginative vitality.

> It may be that the ignorant man, alone,
> Has any chance to mate his life with life
> That is the sensual, pearly spouse, the life
> That is fluent in even the wintriest bronze.
>   (p. 222)

Such lines, paradoxically redolent of erudition, bring to mind the speaker of Yeats's "The Dawn," whose longing to be "ignorant" is tacitly frustrated by the knowledge displayed in the very poem in which the longing is expressed. Third and last, formality in the sense in which I have been using the word is consonant with formality in the different but related sense of dignity or aloofness of manner. The "central man" of Stevens's poetry is not only an erudite scholar and polyglot but also an austere personage who keeps his distance from us and confides nothing, seeming to dismiss as trivial all personal griefs and joys, if not all personal relationships whatsoever. A symptom of his loftiness of tone is his preference for the impersonal pronoun *one* over a possible *I* or *you*: "One has a malady here" (p. 63); "Among the dogs and dung, / One would continue to contend with one's ideas" (p. 198).

To recognize the pervasive formality of Stevens's poetic language is not to say that that formality is unremittingly sustained. Colloquial phraseology was, in fact, exemplified by one of the passages cited at the beginning of the preceding chapter. But such passages are hard to come by in Stevens, and it is surely significant that statements of major importance in his poetry do not sound like anything anyone would actually say. It is instructive to compare him in this respect with Frost, setting such lines as "Home is the place where, when you have to go there, they have to take you in"; "Something has to be left to God"; "We have ideas yet we haven't tried"; and "It's knowing what to do with things that counts" side by side with "The gaiety of language is our seigneur"; "Life consists / Of propositions about life"; "The reason can give nothing at all / Like the response to desire"; and "The sentiment of the fatal is a part / Of filial love." (Though I cannot resist citing a delightful counterinstance, from "Parochial Theme": "Piece the world together, boys, but not with your hands.") Colloquial phrases may appear in the immediate neighborhood of important pronouncements ("That's it: the more than rational distortion, / The fiction that results from feeling. Yes, that" [p. 406]), but they serve as intensifiers of tone rather than as content carriers, conveying the urgency and excitement attendant upon insight rather than insight itself:

> That's it. The lover writes, the believer hears,
> The poet mumbles and the painter sees,
> Each one, his fated eccentricity.
>
> (p. 443)

More typically, the colloquial note is sounded when all is not well—to express a failure of inner vitality ("My old boat goes round on a crutch / And doesn't get under way" [p. 120]) or the speaker's sense of a stale past or an inane present ("Panoramas are not what they used to be" [p. 131], "The solar chariot is junk" [p. 332]; "All sorts of flowers. That's the sentimentalist" [p. 316]). Beyond this, it serves in a few poems to give a deceptively casual air to symbolic or mythic narration ("Sure enough, the thunder became men" [p. 220]; "So you're home again, Redwood Roamer, and ready / To feast" [pp. 286–87]).

A particularly interesting and significant aspect of Stevens's poetic language, considered in conjunction with its prevailingly formal tenor, is his vocabulary of sound-symbolic words, including frequentatives and iteratives. This vocabulary bulks large in both number of items and frequencies of occurrence; some of the words in it are used a dozen times or more; for example, *flash* (21), *hum* (20), *boom* (13), and the frequentatives *glitter* (31), *dazzle* (14), *flutter* (14), *sparkle* (12), and *tumble* (12). *Flick* and *flicker* (13 total) and *glisten* (16) should also be listed here; the latter, though labeled sound symbolic neither by the *Oxford Dictionary of Etymology* (1966) nor by the *Shorter Oxford English Dictionary* (3d ed., 1973), has obvious affinities of phonetic shape and meaning with *glitter* and the archaic word *glister*. Such words are inherently sensory and specific, with an immediacy that can animate scenic description (the more so in that many of them literally designate some sort of rapid motion or change), or, in startling metaphorical translation, relieve the dryness of abstract discourse:

> Air is air.
> Its vacancy glitters round us everywhere.
>
> (p. 137)

> The banners of the nation flutter, burst
> On the flag-poles in a red-blue dazzle, whack
> At the halyards.
>
> (p. 390)

> Then Ozymandias said the spouse, the bride
> Is never naked. A fictive covering
> Weaves always glistening from the heart and mind.
>
> (p. 396)

> The satisfaction underneath the sense,
> The conception sparkling in still obstinate thought.
>
> (p. 448)

Substitution of either a simpler or a more elevated word for any of the sound-symbolic words in the passages above (*brightness* or *glory* for *dazzle*, *shining* or *luminous* for *glistening* or *sparkling*) throws into relief the latter's peculiar expressive force.

Many, if not most, of the sound-symbolic words in Stevens are in fact assigned metaphorical roles. Reviewing the examples amassed in chapter 3 in relation to the topics of laughing and crying, we find that, of the sound-symbolic words listed there, Stevens has *chuckle*, *guffaw*, *titter*, *blubber*, and *sob*. *Guffaw* and *sob* occur once each in their literal meanings (pp. 15, 317), but *blubber*, *chuckle*, and *titter*, each used once, refer to sounds made by tom-toms, birds, and locusts, respectively (p. 41; *Opus Posthumous: Poems, Plays, Prose by Wallace Stevens*. New York: Knopf, 1957. pp. 28, 71), while *sob* denotes the cooing of the turtledove, called "turtle" in biblical fashion (*O.P.*, p. 71), and, with bitter paradoxical force, the sharp intake of breath in "the laughter of evil" (p. 253). The dramatic qualities deriving from the affinities of such words with the spoken language are retained in metaphorical application, while any suggestion of triviality vanishes in strangeness. The shift of reference may be from one physical agency to another, as when frogs boom (p. 17), water makes a blather (p. 22), the blue guitar chatters or buzzes (p. 167), thunder straggles (p. 208), grass dithers (p. 234), roses tinkle (p. 252), fire fidgets (p. 352), wind whimpers (p. 477), and crickets babble (p. 523). A more radical shift is that from the sensory to the abstract, as in "the pitter-patter of archaic freedom" (p. 292), "the hullabaloo of health and have" (p. 292), a "flick" of feeling (p. 407) or "false flick, false form" (p. 385), "a strength that tumbles everywhere" (p. 354), and "form gulping after formlessness" (p. 411). Words are said to make "glistening reference to what is real" (p. 309), and in "apparition" there are "delicate clinkings not explained" (p. 340). Perhaps most characteristically of all, such metaphors figure in an interpenetration of substance and thought, as, for example, in "The Bouquet":

> The bouquet stands in a jar, as metaphor, . . .
>
> [as] a growth
> Of the reality of the eye, an artifice,
> Nothing much, a flitter that reflects itself, . . .
>
> The bouquet is part of a dithering:
> Cloud's gold, of a whole appearance that stands and is.
>
> (pp. 448, 452)

An especially remarkable metaphorical operation is performed on certain sound-symbolic words which, as normally used, designate partly audible or intelligible speech and have some degree of derogatory force, but which in Stevens are applied to fully articulate speech, including the language of poetry itself. In "The Reader," the statement

> Everything
> Falls back to coldness,
> Even the musky muscadines,
> The melons, the vermilion pears
> Of the leafless garden,

emanates from a disembodied voice described as "mumbling" (p. 147), while in "Examination of the Hero in Time of War" the hero is said to glide

> to his meeting like a lover
> Mumbling a secret, passionate message.
>
> (p. 276)

In "A Primitive like an Orb," the speaker concludes that

> the lover writes, the believer hears,
> The poet mumbles and the painter sees,
> Each one, his fated eccentricity.
>
> (p. 443)

In "An Ordinary Evening in New Haven," cosmic "actors . . . walk in a twilight muttering lines" (p. 497), and "milky [Stevens-ese for "spiritually nourishing"] lines" are muttered by "the philosophers' man" of "Asides on the Oboe" (p. 250). Elsewhere, Stevens refers to hymns that buzz (p. 65), "a crackling of voices" (p. 292), a lecturer who hems and haws a disquisition on "This Beautiful World of Ours" (p. 429), "the tragic prattle of the fates" (O.P., p. 34), and "the poet's hum" (O.P., p. 71).

By all odds, the most significant instance of this sort of metaphorical use is the word *gibberish* in its three occurrences toward the end of the second section, "It Must Change," of "Notes toward a Supreme Fiction":

> The poem goes from the poet's gibberish to
> The gibberish of the vulgate and back again,

and "It is the gibberish of the vulgate that [the poet] seeks" (pp. 396–97). I shall return to this important passage later. Here the point is that *gibberish*, like other sound-symbolic words similarly translated, dramatizes Stevens's paradoxical insistence that poetic language remain partly inarticulate, partly inhuman, that it incorporate within itself something of "the incommunicable mass" (p. 328) of external reality. The "necessary angel of earth," speaking to the countrymen who have welcomed him, tells them and us that

> in my sight, you see the earth again,
>
> Cleared of its stiff and stubborn, man-locked set,
> And, in my hearing, you hear its tragic drone
>
> Rise liquidly in liquid lingerings,
> Like watery words awash; like meanings said
>
> By repetitions of half-meanings.
>
> (p. 497)

The expressive powers of the sound-symbolic word, half meaning, half echo, fit this description with uncanny aptness.

It is now time to return to our starting point: the perceptible diversity of Stevens's poetic language and particularly his use of many different kinds of words. In terms of the variables included in the spectrum of diction, we can now say that, on a scale of levels of formality, his vocabulary runs from common to elevated, while on a scale of frequencies of use it runs from common to rare, transcending the established boundaries of the language with a profusion of innovative borrowings and formations of both learned and popular types. Colloquial elements, save for a sprinkling of contracted verb forms, are almost wholly lacking. Sound-symbolic words are an important expressive resource for Stevens, but the colloquial tendencies of these are modified by their use in metaphorical meanings. As one element of a prevailingly formal style, diction figures in the production of a variety of effects, from a studied simplicity (with or without biblical allusiveness) to elaboration and exoticism. Odd verbal combinations were identified at the beginning of chapter 3 as a hallmark of his style; among these, we can single out one type as especially worthy of note: that in which Latinate (*L*), and sound-symbolic (*s-s*) words appear side by side.

The examples "A syllable [L], / Out of these gawky [s-s] flitterings [s-s], / Intones [L] its single emptiness"; "addicts [L] / To blotches [s-s], angular [L] anonymids [L], Gulping [s-s] for shape"; and "the honky-tonk [s-s] out of the somnolent [L] grasses," which were cited earlier, may now be supplemented by "the irised [L] hunks [s-s]" (p. 227); "sprinklings [s-s] of bright particulars [L] from the sky" (p. 344); "delicate [L] clinkings [s-s]" (p. 340); "the dazzle [s-s] / Of mica [L], the dithering [s-s] of grass, / The Arachne [L] integument [L] of dead trees" (p. 234) and "Alive with an enigma's [L] flittering [s-s]" (O.P., p. 105). Iterative coinages appear in "A shiddow-shaddow [s-s] of lights revolving [L]" (p. 279) and "a destroying spiritual [L] that digs-a-dog [s-s]" (p. 332). Such sequences become the more conspicuous as one's ear is alerted to their peculiar timbre; they are dramatically significant in that they blend abstraction with sense perception, solemnity with familiarity, embodying on the level of diction one kind of "choice [not] / Between, but of" (p. 403).

To understand how diversity of diction in Stevens is dramatically motivated, we need to think of it in terms not of static patterns of contrast but of temporal unfolding. From this point of view, diversity is change, perceived as we read a number of poems or a single long poem—as we pass, say, from "The Idea of Order at Key West" to "The American Sublime" in the Collected Poems, or from "Chocorua to Its Neighbor" to "So-and-So Reclining on Her Couch" in The Palm at the End of the Mind, or from section IV to section V of "The Bouquet," or from section III to section IV of "Esthetique du Mal." Within such lines as "addicts / To blotches, angular anonymids / Gulping for shape" or "alive with an enigma's flittering," change is kaleidoscopic, the hand of the poet all but deceiving the eye. We may be aware of a pleasant strangeness in the proportion, without knowing exactly wherein that strangeness consists.

What the reader perceives as change, a diversity enacted in successive periods or instants of time, may also be described in terms of the activity of the poet. As everyone knows, the basic concerns and preoccupations of Stevens's poetry remained the same from first to last. His essential theme, the interplay of imagination and reality, may be defined, in terms of the plots dramatized in the poems themselves, as the relationship of a central consciousness to its perceived world. From this relationship real people and the real events and circumstances of the poet's life are almost wholly excluded (an important exception is "To an Old Philosopher in Rome"). Such autobiography as there is remains implicit in the seasonal movement, to summer and then to autumn, of the titles of the successive volumes, and in the long backward perspective of the last poems, as, for example, in the opening of "Long and Sluggish Lines," "It makes so little difference, at so much more / Than seventy, where one looks, one has been there before," and the first section, entitled "Seventy Years Later," of "The Rock." Good and bad fortune consist wholly in the success or failure of the mind in its lifelong attempt to achieve, and simultaneously to find words for, a satisfying apprehension of reality. This activity and the writing of poetry are one and the same; thus Stevens can say that "Poetry is the subject of the poem. / From this the poem issues and / To this returns" (p. 176) and that "Life consists / Of propositions about life" (p. 355). The poems may be seen in their entirety as the record of a "never-ending meditation" (p. 465), so defined, as "makings of [the] self" which are "no less makings of the sun" (p. 532). But vitality is change, "life is motion" (p. 83), no less for the mind than for the world which is the mind's necessary complement. And herein we detect a paradox as dramatically fruitful as it is logically insoluble. Poetic statement is language set into form, sequences of words which are and must remain fixed, so that the mind's attempt to give definitive expression to its sense of an "always incipient cosmos" (O.P., p. 115), is doubly self-defeating. "It must be abstract"; "it must change"; these two equally important dicta regarding the supreme fiction meet each other head-on. The very word *abstract*, it should be noted, is in origin a past participle, designating the result of an action that has already taken place; it properly applies neither to natural nor to mental process. Thus

> There's no such thing as life; or if there is,
>
> It is faster than the weather, faster than
> Any character. It is more than any scene.
>   (p. 192)

(*Character* here may well mean "written letter" as well as *dramatis persona;* "written in character" [p. 257].) The vital formulation loses vitality in the very moment of utterance, as the iridescent scented rushes gathered by Alice from the boat in *Through the Looking-Glass* became instantly dull. We see language in Stevens straining through time to express instantaneity:

> The breadth of an accelerando moves,
> Captives the being, widens—and was there.
>   (p. 440)

So too the giant conjured up in the present tense in "Poem Written at Morning" immediately reverts to the past: "Green were the curls upon that head." The mind must constantly discard its own representations. "Goodby, Mrs. Pappadopoulos, and thanks" (p. 296), or, in the more solemn accents of "The Auroras of Autumn," "Farewell to an idea."

Just as we see the Stevens of the *Collected Poems* turning from one metaphor, one analogy, one symbolic setting, person, or event to another, so also we see him turning from one expressive means to another, trying out now this kind of language, now that, now this kind of word, now that, in the incessant attempt to express what remains perpetually "beyond the rhetorician's touch" (p. 431). And in this same restlessness of mind, these same rejections not only of the past but also of the present which has already become the past, we can see a motive for his ransacking of the lexicon, his borrowings from foreign languages, his creation of new metaphorical meanings, the coinages and innovative formations that mark his diction. "It is never the thing but the version of the thing" (p. 332); Stevens's poetic language is diverse, versatile, full of *divertissements*, in the root sense of all those words, knowing that "what it has is what is not" and turning from it "as morning throws off stale moonlight and shabby sleep" (p. 382). These turnings or shiftings at the verbal level are analogous to the changes with which the poems are concerned in their subject matter and descriptive detail—the cycles of day and night and the seasons, the rising and falling of waves or, on a geological time scale, of mountains, the endless transformations of the weather. The world of Stevens's poems may well be described, adopting one of his happiest coinages, as a *tournamonde* (p. 476) in large and in little, from the grandiose "shiddow-shaddow of lights revolving" at the climax of "Examination of the Hero in Time of War" to the single leaf "spinning its eccentric measure" toward the end of "Notes." Cyclical change, despite Stevens's cynical treatment of the theme in "Le Monocle de Mon Oncle," is for him most characteristically a source of pleasure—not the fateful intersecting gyres of a Yeats or the monotonous "birth, copulation, and death" of an Eliot but "The Pleasures of Merely Circulating," repetition felt as "beginning, not resuming" (p. 391), necessity accepted without tragic posturing as "final . . . and therefore, good,"

> the going round
>
> And round and round, the merely going round,
> Until merely going round is a final good,
> The way wine comes at a table in a wood.
>
> (p. 405)

The last line of this passage, to my mind one of the finest touches in "Notes," deserves further comment. From the point of view of the reader, it both signifies and accomplishes the giving of pleasure and so accords with the title of the last section of the poem, to which it belongs. Unanticipated by anything that precedes it and no sooner introduced than dropped, it typifies the prodigality of Stevens's inventiveness, an ever-accruing wealth which need never hoard itself but can be spent at once. As an event in the mind of the speaker of the poem, it represents a refreshment of life following the acceptance of finality, an ending giving way to a new beginning. Such freshness and spontaneity are thematic. If the moment of imaginative satisfaction, resulting as it does from an encounter between two changing entities, is fleeting, it is by that same token unpredictable. "One looks at the sea / As one improvises, on the piano" (p. 233). A poem entitled "The Sense of the Sleight-of-Hand Man" opens with a statement of this theme, leading off characteristically with a series of three alternative images:

> One's grand flights, one's Sunday baths,
> One's tootings at the weddings of the soul
> Occur as they occur.
>
> (p. 222)

The speaker now asks rhetorically, introducing yet another image, "Could you have said the bluejay suddenly / Would swoop to earth?" He continues,

> It is a wheel, the rays
> Around the sun. The wheel survives the myths.
> The fire eye in the clouds survives the gods.
> To think of a dove with an eye of grenadine
> And pines that are cornets, so it occurs.

These lines make clear that what are called "occurrences" belong both to the external world (the sun with its rays, the red eye of the dove, the sound of wind in the pine trees) and the world within (the metaphors of wheel, eye, grenadine and cornets). To the day-by-day vagaries of wind, weather, and cloud within the framework of seasonal change, the mind responds in accordance with its own fluctuations of vitality and mood, constantly rising to unforeseen occasions. Reality "occurs" independently of our expectations; we say of it what it "occurs" to us to say.

As in the opening lines of "The Sense of the Sleight-of-Hand Man," the grammatical device of the series—whether of words, phrases, or similarly constructed clauses or sentences—lends itself in Stevens to the expression of alternative and equally valid apprehensions. Such sequences dramatize the rapid "play" of thought upon object or idea, and the mind appears in them as "playful" in that its activity is self-sufficing, intrinsically pleasurable without regard to what it accomplishes.

> The wind is like a dog that runs away.
> But it is like a horse. It is like motion

> That lives in space. It is a person at night,
> A member of the family, a tie,
> An ethereal cousin, another milleman.
>
> (p. 352)

Some of the poems, indeed, consist largely or wholly of lists of appellations amounting to so many descriptive "hypotheses" among which no choice need be made—or, rather, all of which must be chosen. In "Jumbo," for example, the figure named in the title is a tempest, plucking the trees like the "iron bars" of a huge stringed instrument, or as a captive elephant might pluck apart the iron bars of his cage. The speaker's question to himself, "Who was the musician . . . wildly free," is answered in the last three stanzas of the poem:

> The companion in nothingness,
> Loud, general, large, fat, soft
> And wild and free, the secondary man,
>
> Cloud-clown, blue painter, sun as horn,
> Hill-scholar, man that never is,
> The bad-Leopoken lacker,
>
> Ancestor of Narcissus, prince
> Of the secondary men. There are no rocks
> And stones, only this imager.
>
> (p. 269)

Another grammatical device, the appositive, may similarly express an unanticipated turn of thought, as in the famous manifesto of "Notes":

> the sun
> Must bear no name, gold flourisher, but be.
>
> (p. 381)

"Gold flourisher" is of course a name for the sun, but in appositive use it strikes us as a designation that occurs to the speaker at this moment, as he thinks about the necessity of freeing the sun from the designations of the past. The same effect of a mental occurrence or event is similarly produced in "Two Versions of the Same Poem," which opens with the lines

> Once more he turned to that which could not be fixed,
> By the sea, insolid rock, stentor.
>
> (p. 353)

Later, the sea is addressed as "Lascar, and water-carcass never named."

If there is something both "shifty" and "makeshift" about the imagination's endlessly self-destructing output, there is also something tentative. Again and again, the poet-speaker speaks of what he has achieved so far as "Segmenta" (p. 485), "fragments found in the grass" (p. 515), "patches and pitches" (O.P., p. 114), "edgings and inchings of final form" (p. 488). We remember in this connection that Stevens thought of calling *Harmonium*, his first book, *The Grand Poem: Preliminary Minutiae* and of calling the *Collected Poems* in turn *The Whole of Harmonium*. If the full experience of reality resists even momentary expression, how much more unlikely of accomplishment is the grand poem itself, the supreme fiction in which being will come true and the structure of ideas will be one with the structure of things. We hear, in Stevens's poems, of total edifices, compositions of the whole, summaria in excelsis, but these projects remain forever "possible"; we do not see them realized. The most important of the long poems, "Notes toward a Supreme Fiction," "The Auroras of Autumn," and "An Ordinary Evening in New Haven," lack the architectonic unity, the linear movement toward culmination and resolution or systems of complementary relationships among parts, of "When Lilacs Last in the Dooryard Bloomed," "The Tower," *Four Quartets*, or even "The Waste Land"—though each has its own emotional climate, its dramatic succession of moods and modes, its risings and fallings off of intensity, its thematic repetitions. In a sense, each is a collection of shorter poems, a set of variations rather than a symphonic movement. When Stevens does develop a single fictional concept at length, as in "Examination of the Hero in Time of War," "Chocorua to Its Neighbor," and "The Owl in the Sarcophagus," he is not at his most compelling. Something in him did not love the building of massive monolithic structures.

At the end of "The Owl in the Sarcophagus," Stevens's solemn "mythology of modern death" gives way to a simple and self-deprecatory image:

> It is a child that sings itself to sleep,
> The mind, among the creatures that it makes,
> The people, those by which it lives and dies.
>
> (p. 436)

This conception of the imagination's lifework as child's play is a sign of another happy paradox: the presence, in so austere and abstruse a poet and one who took the poetic vocation so seriously, of so much that does not take itself seriously. Our pleasure in Stevens has its source in the picnics as well as the parades and processions, the clowns as well as the rabbis, the ithy oonts and long-haired plomets as well as the lions and swans, the banjo's twang as well as the reverberations of choirs and bells, the beating of the lard pail as well as the blows of the lyre, the hair ribbons of the child as well as the glittering belts and flashing cloaks of the stars. And then there is the irrepressible gaiety and glitter of the language itself, the embellishments of its verbal music "lol-lolling the endlessness of poetry" (p. 458), its flashes of immediacy amid the most abstract or solemn statements, its "tootings at the weddings of the soul" (p. 222). This strain of unpretentiousness and playfulness finds expression in the *Letters* as well as the poems. "People ought to like poetry," Stevens wrote, "the way a child likes snow" (p. 349); and "Many lines exist because I enjoy their clickety-clack in contrast with the more decorous pom-pom-pom that people expect" (p. 485). From the *Letters*, too, we learn that for a long time Stevens thought of adding other sections to "Notes Toward a Supreme Fiction" and "one in particular: *It Must Be Human*" (pp. 863–64).

Toward the end of the second section of "Notes," "It Must Change," there occurs a statement that I quoted earlier in another connection: "The poem goes from the poet's gibberish to / The gibberish of the vulgate and back again." The description of imaginative activity as a dialectic in process leads to a series of questions:

> Does it move to and fro or is it of both
>
> At once? Is it a luminous flittering
> Or the concentration of a cloudy day?
> Is there a poem that never reaches words
>
> And one that chaffers the time away?
> Is the poem both peculiar and general?

As is usually the case in Stevens when the nature of poetry is in question, all these pairs of alternatives apply, even, or rather especially, when they contradict each other (so too, later in the poem, with the Canon Aspirin's mutually exclusive alternatives, thought as thought and fact as fact, both of which must be chosen [p. 403]). This is made clear by the definitive statement at the end of the passage, where it is said of the poet that

> He tries by a peculiar speech to speak
>
> The peculiar potency of the general,
> To compound the imagination's Latin with
> The lingua franca et jocundissima.

Lingua franca, that is, "a mixed language or jargon," is an apt metaphor for the element of "gaiety" in Stevens's diction—his borrowings from modern foreign languages, his sound-symbolic vocabulary, his playful alterations and coinages. Nor is it surprising that the words used in this passage themselves exemplify the opposite extremes which must be fused into a single voice—*flittering* and *chaffers* belonging to the *lingua franca;* *luminous, concentration,* and others, to the imagination's Latin.

The power to bring about such compoundings remained undiminished in Stevens's last years, and the late poems collected in "The Rock" and *Opus Posthumous* make manifest his continuing delight in "reality as an activity of the most august imagination" (*O.P.*, p. 110). As a final emblem of delight and renewal, we may take the description of the chapel rising from "Terre Ensevelie" beside the ruins of the church in "St. Armorer's Church from the Outside." The church is replaced by the chapel as the past, for him who chooses to remain on the "outside," is perpetually replaced by the present:

> The chapel rises, his own, his period,
> A civilization formed from the outward blank,
> A sacred syllable rising from sacked speech, . . .
>
> Time's given perfections made to seem like less
> Than the need of each generation to be itself,
> The need to be actual and as it is.
>
> St. Armorer's has nothing of this present,
> This *vif*, this dizzle-dazzle of being new
> And of becoming, for which the chapel spreads out
> Its arches in its vivid element,
>
> In the air of newness of that element,
> In an air of freshness, clearness, greenness, blueness,
> That which is always beginning because it is part
> Of that which is always beginning, over and over.
>
> The chapel underneath St. Armorer's walls,
> Stands in a light, its natural light and day,
> The origin and keep of its health and his own.
> And there he walks and does as he lives and likes.

With its high-style rhetoric, its mixture of common native words with elements of the imagination's Latin and of the *lingua franca* (foreign borrowing, sound-symbolic coinage, and all), its play on the ordinary and archaic poetic meanings of *keep*, its succession of equally valid descriptive formulations, its protracted series of nouns and nominal phrases giving way in the last line to a flurry of finite verbs (couched in the simplest of diction), this passage speaks a language such as we find in no other poet—abstract, changing, pleasure giving, and human.

PATRICIA PARKER

Inescapable Romance

Valéry's conception of the necessity of this evasion [poetry's evasion of the linear tendency of words] brings us finally to the figure of Wallace Stevens. We close with Stevens not simply because he is among the most recent discoverers of "inescapable romance" ("An Ordinary Evening in New Haven"), but because, unlike Mallarmé or Valéry whose work, though it revives the ancient pun on *carmina*, is less grounded in a native romance tradition, he provides a retrospect on the meaning of romance for English poetry since Spenser. In one of the *Letters on Chivalry and Romance*, Bishop Hurd remarks that modern men are "doubly disgusted" to find, in the romances, "a representation of things *unlike* to what they have observed in real life and *beyond* what it was ever possible should have existed." Stevens' project two centuries later is still the domestication of the imagination, an activity which, as he remarks in one essay, involves cleansing it of the "romantic." His own poem entitled "Re-Statement of Romance" is part of a continuing reductive quest, the search for a "neutral centre" ("Landscape with Boat") freed of all the "rotted names" ("The Man with the Blue Guitar," XXXII), the accretions of the errant imagination and its exploded fancies, and for the "poem of pure reality, untouched / By trope or deviation" ("An Ordinary Evening in New Haven," IX). The mode in which this reduction is practiced in poem after poem seems to make him part of the anti-romance of the plain style of *écriture neutre*, the poetic counterpart of the quester of "Landscape with Boat":

> he rejected, he denied, to arrive
> At the neutral centre, the ominous element,
> The single-colored, colorless, primitive.

This technique of rejection is partly Wordsworthian or Keatsian in intent: "the great poems of heaven and hell have been written and the great poem of the earth remains to be written." Stevens knows with Keats that "The greatest poverty is not to live / In a physical world, to feel that one's desire / Is too difficult to tell from despair" ("Esthétique du Mal," XV). And the "necessary angel" of his essays is the one whose task it is to enable men to "see the earth again, / Cleared of its stiff and stubborn, man-locked set" ("Angel Surrounded by Paysans"), to clear away the veil of successive mediations and to provide an "Evening without Angels."

Reduction to this center, however, is not always in Stevens a source of pleasure or a matter of choice. The "he" of "The Latest Freed Man," having divested himself of all the rotted names, describes the exhilaration of being "At the centre of reality," seeing everything as "more real." But what in this poem is experienced as exhilaration is in others a form of poverty. "Esthétique du Mal" becomes another in the long line of post-Spenserian poems which lament the progress of enlightenment and its destruction of many "blue phenomena" even as it celebrates the emergence of a "physical world":

Phantoms, what have you left? What underground?
What place in which to be is not enough
To be? You go, poor phantoms, without place
Like silver in the sheathing of the sight,
As the eye closes . . . How cold the vacancy
When the phantoms are gone and the shaken realist
First sees reality.

(VIII)

The destitution of a man for whom the moon can no longer be a "round effendi" (IX) is a poverty like that of the moment of "pain and ugliness" in Keats' *Lamia*, when nothing "is left but comic ugliness / Or a lustred nothingness" ("Esthétique," IX). And the reduction of the "paradise of meaning" to the Mammon world of "one meaning alone"—"the sky divested of its fountains"—raises the call for "Another chant, an incantation," music that "buffets the shapes of its possible halcyon / Against the haggardie."

This ambivalence, the search for the neutral center of "veritable ding an sich" beneath the "last distortion of romance" ("The Comedian as the Letter C," I) and the realization that this reduction will, finally, not suffice, is what makes Stevens' "Notes Toward a Supreme Fiction" the supreme poem it is. It begins in the search for the "first idea," the "muddy centre" which existed "before we breathed." But if it is to this reduction that the poem is driven by "the celestial ennui of apartments," there is equally "an ennui of the first idea," an awareness that it is not possible for men to remain within the "final no." If, as in the title of another poem, "Reality is an Activity of the Most August Imagination," the autumnal vision is not the "veritable season" ("Examination of the Hero in a Time of War," XVI), and "disillusion" is finally only "the last illusion" ("An Ordinary Evening in New Haven," V). Reduction in poetry to the "single-colored, colorless" center is not finally possible because figuration itself is part of the "inescapable romance." The poet of "Someone Puts a Pineapple Together" seeks a way through the "pale arrondissements," a reduction to "The angel at the centre of this rind," "the irreducible X / At the bottom of imagined artifice." But the "angel" itself remains the irreducible figure. Even the reduction to the "first idea" in "Notes" ends in an "imagined thing." The ephebe is to learn that "Phoebus is dead," to "clean the sun" of all its images. But the sun which must "bear no name" is simultaneously, and beautifully, called "gold flourisher," a kenning which reimports figuration in one of its most elemental forms.

Stevens is by no means unaware of the sorrows of being exiled from a single center or abiding presence:

> It would be enough
> If we were ever, just once, at the middle, fixed
> In This Beautiful World of Ours and not as now,
>
> Helplessly at the edge, enough to be
> Complete, because at the middle, if only in sense,
> And in that enormous sense, merely enjoy.
> ("The Ultimate Poem is Abstract")

Stevens' poems of this exile recapitulate the romance tradition of its melancholy, the perpetual sense of being on the periphery, debarred. And yet he also shares this tradition's wariness of the center: the frozen solipsist of "This Solitude of Cataracts" is a fixity, a "bronze man" breathing "his bronzen breath at the azury centre of time." In "Prologues to What Is Possible," the journey to the "point of central arrival" is described in images of fire and weightlessness like those which accompany Dante's ascent of his Mountain of Vision. But when we reach the goal of the quest, at the end of the first section, and hear the lines

> As at a point of central arrival, an instant moment,
>   much or little,
> Removed from any shore, from any man or woman,
>   and needing none . . .

it is difficult not to hear echoes of the "expunge all people" of "Sailing after Lunch" or the solipsistic "third world without knowledge, / In which no one peers" of "Esthétique du Mal" (XII). What saves this poem from this more dangerous center, however, is the corresponding outward, or less directed, movement of its second section, the fact that the journey to the center, here, is not a final end but only a "prologue" to the "possible," a pure projection.

Stevens' wariness of apocalypse or center is partly a peculiarly American preoccupation—the wariness which causes Emily Dickinson to pause before the moment of Revelation in "Our journey had advanced" or to seek in another poem to keep "Eternity / From presenting—Here—" ("Crisis is a Hair"). But the constant *andirivieni* of a poetry which incessantly qualifies even as it approaches a satisfying center or place of rest allies Stevens finally with Spenser, the other English poet who knew that "Death is the mother of beauty" ("Sunday Morning"). If T. S. Eliot inherits the purgatorial typology of romance, Stevens inherits its preference for the *clair-obscur,* however much he may proclaim that all distance from the center is a "tragic chiaroscuro" ("Notes"). The poet is, by definition, an eccentric whose vision is always slightly off center, making the visible a little hard to see ("The Creations of Sound"). Spenser begins the second Book of *The Faerie Queene* with a defense of "Faerie," the latent world of the not-yet-discovered on the threshold of the actual. Stevens' "Faerie" is the shadowy "spirit's universe" of the poem "Description without Place," an "affair / Of the possible; seemings that are to be, / Seemings that it is possible may be."

It is this preference for, or interposition of, the "possible" which imports a contradiction into the quest for the "neutral centre" or for a poetry exactly coincident with "Things as they are" ("The Man with the Blue Guitar"). In "The Noble Rider and the Sound of Words," one of the essays in *The Necessary Angel,* Stevens writes:

> There is, in fact, a world of poetry indistinguishable from the world in which we live, or, I ought to say, no doubt, from the world in which we shall come to live, since what makes the poet the potent figure that he is, or was, or ought to be, is that he creates the world to which we turn incessantly and without knowing it and that he gives to life the supreme fictions without which we are unable to conceive of it.

The shift from "the world in which we live" to "the world in which we shall come to live" is unobtrusive and as characteristically Stevensian a feint as the equivocation ("Invisible or visible or both") in "Notes" ("It Must Be Abstract," VI). But the temporal disjunction is crucial. The imagination's locus is finally not the "veritable ding an sich" which Crispin confronts when freed from the "last distortion of romance," but something closer to that pregnant virtuality Keats called a "shadow of reality to come," the promise of "the possibilities of things."

This necessary disjunction or gap applies, finally, even to the Supreme Fiction of the "Major Man." If he is the figure whose "solitaria / Are the meditations of a central mind" ("Certain Phenomena of Sound," XI), it is a centrality "eccentric" in relation to the present circumference of vision, "not too closely the double of our lives, / Intenser than any actual life could be" ("Description without Place," VI). The hermitage at this center is not the fixed and frozen point of solipsistic withdrawal because it is a sphere which is, in the words of "The Sail of Ulysses," the "centre of the self" but of "the self / Of the future" (IV). The "major men" of "Paisant Chronicle" are finally

> characters beyond
> Reality, composed thereof. They are
> The fictive man created out of men.
> They are men but artificial men. They are
> Nothing in which it is not possible
> To believe . . .

In a tradition in which, as Yeats complained, romance and the Mammon of relevance were very early at odds, this eccentricity necessarily involves Stevens in one of the romance tradition's characteristic anxieties, from the potential limbo of Spenser's "Faerie" to the darker aspect of Keats' "shadow of reality to come." The poet who cannot sing of "things as they are" is potentially the creator of nothing but a barren "abstraction," however much he might deny that "abstraction is a vice" ("A Thought Revolved"). For the poet of "Notes Toward a Supreme Fiction," the two qualifications of the Fiction—"It Must Change" and "It Must be Abstract"— are flanked by the perversions of each pole. The perversion of "It Must be Abstract" is "abstraction" in the sense of mere "evasion" ("The poet evades us / As in a senseless element"). The other side of "It Must Change" is the endless round of the cycle of nature, the reason, finally, why the "muddy centre" of the "first idea" will not suffice. Each of these extremes leads to the same dead end, a fact which may explain why the song of mere being in "It Must Change" ends on the same note as the description of the human abstract, the statue of General Du Puy. Both share the essential stoniness of a "granite monotony," the one part "Of an earth in which the first leaf is the tale of leaves" and the sparrow a "bird / Of stone, that never changes," the other "Of a suspension, a permanence so rigid / That it made the General a bit absurd," where "Nothing had happened because nothing had changed."

For Stevens, the alternative to the radical sameness of these extremes is the "pendant," or "dependent," relation of that section of "Notes" which comes between the two:

> Two things of opposite natures seem to depend
> On one another, as a man depends
> On a woman, day on night, the imagined
>
> On the real. This is the origin of change.
> Winter and spring, cold copulars, embrace
> And forth the particulars of rapture come.
>
> Music falls on the silence like a sense,
> A passion that we feel, not understand.
> Morning and afternoon are clasped together
>
> And North and South are an intrinsic couple
> And sun and rain a plural, like two lovers
> That walk away as one in the greenest body.

This fruitful dependency is Stevens' *Concordia,* a Creation or "mundo" made possible by a tempering of both kinds of possession, the violence from without and the violence from within. It is neither a collapse of subject and object into oneness, nor their estrangement: the "Supreme Fiction" remains both "a part" and "apart." It is, rather, part of the ongoing process Stevens calls "taming the monster of the incredible," an activity which does not divest itself of romance and its ghostlier demarcations, but moves instead towards a concord of opposites, "the imagined and the real, thought / And the truth, / Dichtung und Wahrheit" ("The Man with the Blue Guitar," XXIII), a dependency which makes these "Notes," dedicated to Henry Church, into Stevens' Legend of Friendship. And it is finally what makes this strain in Stevens, so different from either Mallarmé or Valéry, still part of the metamorphoses of a romance still open-ended.

ISABEL G. MacCAFFREY

"Le Monocle de Mon Oncle"

H*armonium* is one of the monuments of the modernist movement in America, however much it has come to seem, in our hindsight, relatively nonradical in its experimentalism. Some of Stevens' experiments sprang from his short-lived interest in imagism. Others, more prophetic of the innovations that were to characterize his late poetry, reveal an early interest in discontinuous, even disjunctive forms as shattered mirrors of certain preoccupations in the modern consciousness. Helen Vendler's judgment that "the poetry of disconnection is Stevens' most adequate form" is an insight that could be illustrated many times over from the poetry of *Harmonium* to *The Rock*. Of the two most famous poems in *Harmonium*, "Sunday Morning" and "Le Monocle de Mon Oncle," the former is much less radical in its abandonment of the civilities of discourse. It is in fact discursive, a dialogue in which certain propositions are argued by shadowy participants, proceeding at a steady pace that admits few interstitial gaps. The spaces between stanzas have not yet become eloquent with inexplicit meanings.

If "Sunday Morning" is "the only truly great 'traditional' poem that Stevens wrote," [A. Walton Litz] "Le Monocle" has impressed most readers as a genuinely original work. Its dispossession by "influence" authenticates its claim to modernism:

> This great poem abrupts into Stevens' poetic world with such energy and polished perfection that its origins must remain partly in mystery. Like "Sunday Morning," it towers over the poems which precede and follow it; but unlike "Sunday Morning" it does not fit easily into the tradition of English poetry. [Litz]

From *Wallace Stevens: A Celebration*, edited by Frank Doggett and Robert Bittel. Copyright © 1980 by Princeton University Press.

One of Stevens' famous adages can take us close to the heart of [what Frank Kermode calls] "this great and obscure" work: "Every poem is a poem within a poem: the poem of the idea within the poem of the words." This formula is unsatisfactory insofar as it suggests that "the poem of the idea" can somehow be arrived at without the help of "the words." But it indicates that Stevens himself was aware of a peculiar relationship in his most characteristic poetry between medium and message, language and referent. We can say that the rhetoric and the subject in "Le Monocle" and a large number of later poems, including "Notes Toward a Supreme Fiction," approach each other by meanders rather than forthrights, or that sometimes they seem not to approach at all, but rather to shout at each other across an abyss of noise, raising echoes and alarming hoo-has from the icy elysées en route.

It is not strange, therefore, that attempts to identify the subject of "Le Monocle de Mon Oncle" have been more than usually tentative. The title is only the beginning of the poem's elusive inarticulateness. It is "a poem about language and love," says Litz. Yes, indeed. But the key terms contain multiple possibilities of meaning and are problematically related to one another. We may well be tempted to resort, with Frank Kermode, to the Cerberus principle: "with such verses it is true that one needs to quiet the housedog of the mind with any meat so that the poem may do its work." Yet Stevens does provide us with a few clues as to how his poem should be read, notably in the opening stanza, which he divides into two parts, the second commenting upon the first—perhaps to encourage the reader to take over a commentator's role in later stanzas.

After the mock-heroic invocation, spoken "aloud" in quotation marks, the speaker turns to contemplate his own motives, that is, the sources of "magnificent measure":

> And so I mocked her in magnificent measure.
> Or was it that I mocked myself alone?
> I wish that I might be a thinking stone.
> The sea of spuming thought foists up again
> The radiant bubble that she was. And then
> A deep up-pouring from some saltier well
> Within me, bursts its watery syllable.

"The sea of spuming thought" characterizes the action, namely, the incessant alterations of the organism that eventuate in what we call "thought"—a kind of spume that is the vocalized evidence of depths below. "I wish that I might be a thinking stone" is a cry for stillness, for an end to the eternal restless change that is the measure of living. But to think and to be a stone are incompatibles, as Aquinas knew. So we sink deeper into the well of the unconscious, into an extraordinarily visceral sequence of appeals to voiceless sensation. Imagination "foists up" the memory of what "she was," an image out of the drowned past that floats for an instant to the mind's surface to be contemplated. "Foist" is the perfect verb for the intrusiveness and fraudulence of memory, palming off its irresistible bygones upon the unwilling consciousness, which can no more inhibit their formation than the ocean can prevent a bubble rising to *its* surface. But the bubble is only a "watery syllable" in the interior world; and indeed, all syllables have watery origins, as the stanza makes clear. The "deep up-pouring" is a rush of sensation and emotion, of flooding awareness, as the springs of feeling open unexpectedly. They are salty with the taste of sex, of blood, of the sea that is within us as well as all around us. The movement is regressive, for the salty well is, above all, a source, and by the end of the stanza Stevens has gotten to the bottom of the splendid mockery of the initial sentence.

He later said that "the Mother of Heaven was merely somebody to swear by," the point being that all this gorgeous rhetoric, while not exactly meaningless, is misleadingly expressive; its true referents lie in the interior world, at the feeling source. The pompous phrases move associatively, from the Queen of Heaven to "regina of the clouds," and then to her heavenly paraphernalia—sun and moon, scepter and crown. It is easy to piece together an explication of these epithets in terms of Stevens' sun/ moon imagery elsewhere, to say that the heroine of "Le Monocle" unites male reality with female imagination, or to invoke literary analogues, such as Britomart's dream at the Temple of Isis in *The Faerie Queene*—another concordant image, where the dreamer sees the statue's transfiguration of costume from a "Moone-like Mitre to a Crowne of gold" (V.VII.13). Such an exercise would be otiose, for Stevens' lines merely let us hear the imagination babbling out loud in the way it always has, turning over the watery syllables on its tongue to articulate its salty sensations.

A more exact Spenserian parallel, and one that does shed some light on the subject of "Le Monocle," is the vision evoked by Colin Clout's music on Mount Acidale in Book VI. The maiden at the center of the concentric garlands of dancers is as anonymous as Stevens' lady— simply "she that in the midst of them did stand," and by so standing, caused the pattern to form:

> But that faire one,
> That in the midst was placed paravaunt,
> Was she to whom that shepheard pypt alone;
> That made him pipe so merrily, as never none.
> (VI.X.15)

While Frank Kermode quite properly identifies the object of Stevens' address as the Interior Paramour, there is nothing to prevent her also being an actual paramour, for the Muse has many avatars. Hence the arguments about whether these lines refer to a "real" or an "ideal" woman usually miss the point, and Spenser's stanzas show why this is so: the laws of psychic necessity require that feeling always be immediate and concrete in its attachment to objects, and only feeling is potent enough to generate the construction of cloud-capped towers or reginas who preside there. Imagination draws its strength from the viscera, feeds upon who-knows-what nameless orts of emotion. It is almost impossible not to stumble over alimentary and sexual metaphors in trying to verbalize imaginative process. The embrace of poet and Muse rationalizes events that transpire at a subverbal level, and Stevens' poem is an attempt to intimate, if not completely to articulate, the nature of these events. "A deep up-pouring from some saltier well" gives rise to the high talk of the apostrophe; the woman addressed is "somebody" to whom emotion is attached and therefore the cause, in all senses of the term, that the poem comes into being. "That made him pipe so merrily."

The opening pomposities of "Le Monocle" are thus deflated by a visit to their oceanic origins in "The Creations of Sound":

> We do not say ourselves like that in poems.
> We say ourselves in syllables that rise
> From the floor, rising in speech we do not speak.

It is always the speech we do not speak that Stevens is striving to articulate; hence the snares spread in the nets of discontinuous form that the poet weaves:

> Tell X that speech is not dirty silence
> Clarified. It is silence made still dirtier.

To make the silence dirty, thick with the syllables we do not speak, Stevens contrives a rhetoric of intermittences, of false starts and misleading clues, of centerless labyrinths, hollow resonances, eloquent silence, visionary blankness. Many of these tricks are evident in "Le Monocle," and so is one of the consequences of employing them: a willingness on the part of the poet to appear foolish, precious, dandified, superficial. Stevens creates surfaces behind which essential meanings can emerge and gambol, meanings too shy to be observed directly and lying, as Wordsworth said, "far hidden from the reach of words." The large assurances, positive gestures, confident assertions are attention-getting devices by the sleight-of-hand man, so that we shall be distracted from the urge to paraphrase long enough for significances to form unobserved. The result is not only a perverse use of language in the interests of silence, but also a persistent duplicity of voice. Parallels can be found in Wordsworth, some of whose assumptions about language were shared by Stevens. The swervings and changes of tack in *The Prelude* have been often remarked, and "Resolution and Independence" is another poem in which a dithering, or flat, or loftily inconsequential surface makes a protective shell for the delicacies of self-accusation, self-doubt, condolence, and consolation that are Wordsworth's real subjects.

Style in such poems moves away from the mimetic to a kind of anti- or counterexpressionism. An ostensible speaker is permitted to maunder, "expressing" his perceptions or feelings or thoughts in a manner that is visibly inadequate, bombastic, bland, or self-deceiving. Meanwhile, by devious means (such as the impervious though taciturn integrity of Wordsworth's Leech-gatherer) these verbal gestures are shown up for what they are and replaced by a "meaning" that, while never completely articulate, can be apprehended behind the words. The first stanza of "Le Monocle de Mon Oncle" exposes this strategy with special clearness while at the same time introducing us to the most important of the poem's unspoken premises. Its most general form has been stated by Hugh Kenner: "language . . . can mime the wordless world only by a kind of coincidence." Magical theories of language, to which most poets subscribe at one time or another, assert that coincidence is a version of fate, that the poet uses language in a way that will bring out the hidden logic of its affinities with "the wordless world." Stevens resisted magic on principle, and almost consistently; in "Le Monocle" he created a poem that accepts Kenner's principle and its consequences for poetry, but without resorting to occult explanations. It is possible, then, to reconstruct a skeletal system of assumptions that lie behind this poem and of which the actual stanzas on the page are the symptoms; but it is hard to feel that in doing this we have found a "subject" in any traditional sense.

The reconstruction would proceed as follows. Poetry's most important subjects belong to "the wordless world," the world of Eros, who, alas (or perhaps fortunately), is dumb. This world generates language and the need to use it, but it does not speak directly to us. So Stevens' poem invites us, and the speaker, to verbalize experience, yet perpetually repudiates or mocks the result, as the "I" mocks his own magnificent measure in stanza I. "Love and language," to be sure: love is the source of language, and also its destroyer. A discontinuous form is the inevitable vehicle for this theme; its interstitial white spaces can become dirty silences, and its perpetual new beginnings can palliate, if not cure, the bad faith of poets who would claim too much for their fictive music.

The hostility between poetry and its subjects, between language and experience, manifests itself in two ways, both unacceptable to a serious poet. On one hand, it produces a self-nourishing but irrelevant rhetoric, as in Stevens' first stanza; on the other hand, awareness that words "in giving form and order to emotion also kill the true feeling" [Joseph N. Riddel] may produce the poet's ultimate despair: silence. This is not a new predicament. Philip Sidney, repudiating traditional rhetorics in the first sonnet of *Astrophil and Stella,* followed his Muse's advice and looked into his heart. But it led him, at the climax of the sequence, to poetically unwelcome conclusions:

> Come then my Muse, shew thou height of delight
> In well raised notes, my pen the best it may
> Shall paint out joy, though but in blacke and white.
> Cease eager Muse, peace pen, for my sake stay,
>   I give you here my hand for truth of this,
>   Wise silence is best musicke unto blisse.
>
> (Sonnet LXX)

"Well raised notes" or "wise silence"—does the poet's choice reduce to these forbidding alternatives? Innovating poets have always denied it. So we find Wordsworth brilliantly defending the fiction-making power of imagination in its role as mediator between unexpressed feeling and an uncommunicating world. At issue is the meaning of the Leech-gatherer, a "reality" that must somehow be shown to be linked with obscure sources of emotion in the poem's speaker. In his revision, Wordsworth added a stanza that, through two similes ("As a huge stone is sometimes seen to lie . . ."), creates this link. The maker of the fiction justifies his conceits as an instance of imagination's legitimate function: "In these images, the conferring, the abstracting, and the modifying powers of the Imagination, immediately and mediately acting, are all brought into conjunction."

In thus acting to unite the world without and the world within, imagination is taking a liberty. It is putting words between experience (the speaker's feelings) and uninvented images (the mysterious presence of the old man). These words, the similes in Wordsworth's ninth stanza, have no immediate referents in the poem but are "conferred" upon, "abstracted" from, and "modify" the given raw materials. Stevens defined imaginative liberty of this kind as "an intervention." Many stanzas in "Le Monocle de Mon Oncle" are instances of intervention, the creation of fables or parables like Wordsworth's stone and sea-beast that will exemplify the proper function of a healthy and self-chastising imagination. But Stevens' demonstrations complicate Wordsworth's. His distrust of imagination's megalomania went deeper; Wordsworth, after all, had spoken approvingly of its "indestructible dominion." Stevens was bothered by the notion that "Things as they are have been destroyed" ("The Man with the Blue Guitar") in modern art by an imagination conceiving of itself as indestructible; hence his choice of discontinuous forms, which permit him to wipe out successive attempts at articulation and begin again. He was also less confident than Wordsworth that language could *ever* render the plain sense of things. Thus in "Le Monocle" and other major poems of his middle period there is nothing to correspond to the factuality of "Resolution and Independence," which surround stanza IX and allow us to see how "mediation" occurs.

Instead, there are dirty silences and enigmatic self-mockery, as in stanza II of "Le Monocle":

> A red bird flies across the golden floor.
> It is a red bird that seeks out his choir
> Among the choirs of wind and wet and wing.
> A torrent will fall from him when he finds.
> Shall I uncrumple this much-crumpled thing?
> I am a man of fortune greeting heirs;
> For it has come that thus I greet the spring.
> These choirs of welcome choir for me farewell.
> No spring can follow past meridian.
> Yet you persist with anecdotal bliss
> To make believe a starry *connaissance.*

The first four lines represent imagination's effort to introduce the third major term of the poem's "subject": it is "about" not only love and language, but also death, about the fact that Eros and Thanatos must embrace, and imagination must find words for their love affair. The words that speak of a red bird and a golden floor are nonreferential within the poem's world, like Wordsworth's stone and sea-beast, but more like the latter. Stones, after all, are "sometimes seen to lie" on eminences; imagination, in noting the fact, is behaving mimetically, at least to begin with. "A sea-beast crawled forth" onto a shelf of rock is much more rarely seen—is seen, perhaps, by imagination's eye alone when it requires a link between inorganic and organic being to complete the mediational circuit. But Wordsworth, in his later explanation, uncrumples his invention much more fully than Stevens allows the speaker of "Le Monocle" to do. The later poet refuses at this stage to make the fiction-devising power seem natural and inevitable; rather, he presents us with an extreme case, enigmatic and tantalizing, of imagination at its hermetic games.

The uncrumpled "meanings" that follow line four do not satisfy as explications. They have some reference to the dark brilliance of the initial images, but in trying to work out the relationship, we are frustrated. The effect is to make the parable of the red bird more opaque, mysteriously significant, and mute when parable gives way to ineffectual paraphrase: "I am a man of fortune greeting heirs"; "No spring can follow past meridian." Stevens employs "statements" like these to undermine the adequacy of statements and so, at last, to convince us of the need for parabolic utterance, the dark conceits that mediate between the "wordless world" and that articulateness that is the mark of consciousness.

Having rebuked high talk in stanza I and commonsense explication in stanza II, Stevens proceeds in eight of the remaining stanzas to propose additional parables that will close in upon and gradually circumscribe the poem within the poem, which concerns in part, of course, the problem of meaning itself. It is a fact, however deplorable, that meanings entail some sort of articulation. In his essay "The Effects of Analogy," Stevens defends, even celebrates, the use of words to articulate "the objects of . . . passions,"

> the objects before which [poets] come and speak, with intense choosing, words that we remember and make our own. Their words have made a world that transcends the world and a life livable in that transcendence. It is a transcendence achieved by means of the minor effects of figurations and the major effects of the poet's sense of the world and of the motive music of his poems and it is the imaginative dynamism of all these analogies together.

The "sense of the world" given body in "Le Monocle" is Stevens' awareness of the transient fragility of every human moment and every human contrivance, including the contrivances of poetry. They are "trivial" and evanescent, but necessary: "This parable, in sense, amounts to this"; "This trivial trope reveals a way of truth." Dissolving his parables at the end of every stanza, Stevens resumes after the white space the incessant effort to speak "The speech of truth in its true solitude" ("Things of August").

"The imaginative dynamism" of multiple analogies, as it emerges from this poem, requires attentiveness to Stevens' "figurations" as they attract and repel one another. The final quatrain of stanza III is one of the poem's most obscure patches; Kermode admits that the "last two lines are among the most beautiful in Stevens, and I do not know what they mean." The poet himself explained them "as meaning simply that the speaker was speaking to a woman whose hair was still down." But the questions posed by this speaker are not answered:

> Alas! Have all the barbers lived in vain
> That not one curl in nature has survived?
> Why, without pity on these studious ghosts,
> Do you come dripping in your hair from sleep?

The study of "inscrutable hair in an inscrutable world" ("The Comedian as the Letter C") is questioned: "Is it for nothing, then . . . ?" Yes and no. Hair, in China, Japan, and eighteenth-century England, has been twined into a metaphor for various deep significances: the philosophy of old men, "the end of love" in both senses of the word "end." "The mountainous coiffures" that expressed their makers' sense of meaning have perished. But the urge to educe meanings, and to devise forms for them—"all-speaking braids" or poems—does not perish. The dying of things, Stevens wrote three years before, goes on like "A wave, interminably flowing" ("Peter Quince at the Clavier"); and yet Venus arises again from the sea every time a woman enters a lover's consciousness, "dripping" in her hair, to motivate his poems.

The watery imagery of this line harks back to the salty well of stanza I and anticipates the lily pool of stanza XI and its "odious" frog music. Deep in the belly's dark, love has its source; but what human beings do with it once it is born is the main focus of interest:

> I pursued,
> And still pursue, the origin and course
> Of love. . . .

The course of love brings decay and loss; it also brings high talk. And it brings "Doleful heroics, pinching gestures forth / From madness or delight. . . ." These rhetorical gestures are efforts to express the nature of love (or, indeed, any human emotion), which alters from minute to minute:

> But in our amours amorists discern
> Such fluctuations that their scrivening
> Is breathless to attend each quirky turn.
> When amorists grow bald, then amours shrink
> Into the compass and curriculum
> Of introspective exiles, lecturing.
> It is a theme for Hyacinth alone.

But Hyacinth is aphasic. Experience can only be captured—in contemplation or in art—after the fact, by men of forty, introspective exiles, dull scholars, and dark rabbis. The predicament is not altogether remote from Wordsworth's struggles in the "Immortality Ode" to find in the lucid contemplation of mortality compensation for the loss of childhood's intensity.

> O joy! that in our embers
> Is something that doth live,
> That nature yet remembers
> What was so fugitive!

Stevens' subjects in "Le Monocle"—love, death and change, poetry—often come close to Wordsworth's in the "Ode," and an offhand description he gave of his own poem could refer to either. Protesting against his correspondent's "much too close" reading, he insists that "I had in mind simply a man fairly well along in life, looking back and talking in a more or less personal way about life." The retrospective point of view establishes each poem as an instance of what both poets are talking about: the fact that an unbridgeable gap yawns between experience and the articulation of experience. The intensities of childhood or first love—"fiery boys" and "sweet-smelling virgins"—contrasted with the sobrieties of middle age, manifest this troublesome disjunction: the distance between words and things, reality and its reflection in art, the deep sources of poems and poems themselves, all surface and bravura.

These paradoxes are pursued by both Wordsworth and Stevens through two principal techniques: disjunctive stanzaic forms and the self-conscious use of taciturn myths or mythical images. Wordsworth's preference for the continuous form of blank verse gives way in the "Ode" to the irregular stanzas of the revived Pindaric, whose disjunctiveness is underlined when we recall the poem's slow gestation. Stevens' unrhymed stanzas are less irregular but even more ostentatiously unrelated to one another; and as in Wordsworth's poem, their separateness is insisted upon by Roman numerals. Wordsworth invokes the May mornings of conventional pastoral in stanzas III, IV, and X; in stanza V he has recourse to the less predictable Platonic myth of recollection, and in VII and VIII, to his own version of childhood's primitive and potent imaginative life, which offended Coleridge and many later readers. The poet's language, especially in section VIII, is indeed extravagant; one might surmise (remembering the Leech-gatherer and the mythic status conferred upon other unlikely personages) that Wordsworth half intended the claims made here to sound outrageous, to produce a reaction disproportionate to their literal sense. Certainly Stevens intends *his* outrageousness, for instance in stanzas VII, X, and XI of "Le Monocle." Both poems also display alterations of tone that suggest the limits of the writer's control over his material.

The point of such deliberate violations of decorum would be to deal with the inadequacy of fiction by flaunting and exaggerating it, to affirm the necessity of myths, images, all poetic inventions, at the moment of declaring and illustrating their foolish insufficiency. Both the "Ode" and "Le Monocle" are modern poems in Stevens' sense, poems in the act of finding what will suffice. Since total sufficiency is impossible, it can be most closely approximated by insisting that no invention really suffices.

> Most venerable heart, the lustiest conceit
> Is not too lusty for your broadening.

It is, in fact, never lusty enough. But, after all, he must try again:

> The fops of fancy in their poems leave
> Memorabilia of the mystic spouts,
> Spontaneously watering their gritty soils.
> I am a yeoman, as such fellows go.
> I know no magic trees, no balmy boughs,
> No silver-ruddy, gold-vermilion fruits.
> But, after all, I know a tree that bears
> A semblance to the thing I have in mind.
> It stands gigantic, with a certain tip
> To which all birds come sometime in their time.
> But when they go that tip still tips the tree.

The tree of this stanza anticipates Yeats' great-rooted blossomer as an emblem for the life principle that is eterne in mutability. It gathers the implications of three other stanzas: "this luscious and impeccable fruit of life" (IV); the golden gourds that are also warty squashes (VIII); the eternal bloom of the imagined damsel and the evanescent honey of earth (VII). Stevens' exploration of the origin, course, and curious fate of love in these conceits comes to a focus in the non-magic tree, which bears none of the silver and golden apples yearned for by Yeats' Wandering Aengus. This tree bears instead a semblance. The fops of fancy give way to the yeoman-poet, Peter Quince the carpenter, nailing together his flimsy frames of meaning. Stevens' description of the tree contains an imaginative precision within the images. The delicate tip, a perch for a successive stream of birds that never ends, is a careful analogy for "a substance that prevails," which Stevens attempted to capture again in "Martial Cadenza":

> The present close, the present realized,
> Not the symbol but that for which the symbol stands,
> The vivid thing in the air that never changes,
> Though the air change. Only this evening I saw it again,

> At the beginning of winter, and I walked and talked
> Again, and lived and was again, and breathed again
> And moved again and flashed again, time flashed again.

This stanza describes an antiepiphany: the recognition that the meaning of our lives lies in their ongoingness. The moment "out of time," the instant of mystical insight treasured by writers of all ages, and especially vivid in Yeats and Eliot, is here reintegrated with temporality, located in a season "at the beginning of winter." This experience "was like sudden time in a world without time." "The present" is realized as part of a continuum; the changeless thing never manifests itself to us except in change. In stanza X of "Le Monocle" Stevens balances the notion of enduring stillness ("that tip still tips the tree") with temporality ("all birds come some*time* in their *time*"). The birds that repeatedly serve this poet as indicators of life in time are here the means of knowing that the tree and its tip exist.

Stanza X is central to Stevens' defense of fictions in "Le Monocle"; it brings together explicitly the idea of change and the imagination's need to confront and come to terms with it. Behind the poem's title is a modern version of Blake's prayer: "May God us keep / From single vision and Newton's sleep!" In the self mockery of his one-eyed persona, Stevens calls into question the single vision of the self-deceiving fancy, but the successive fables offered in these brilliant stanzas are also a rebuke to the Newtonian sleep of those who will not dream of baboons and periwinkles. Stanza X opens on an ambiguous note but soon deepens into the serious and beautiful "semblance" of the yeoman-poet. And even the "fops of fancy" are not unequivocally dismissed. "Memorabilia of the mystic spouts" fails to conjure up any visual image that is not absurd, but it is consistent with the notion of a hidden watery source of imagination, which Stevens relates throughout the poem to spontaneity and change. "The verve of earth" has been linked with "the intensity of love" (V), and these spontaneous intensities are in turn linked with intimations of mortality: "inklings of your bond to all that dust." The "poem of the idea" in "Le Monocle" concerns the deep affinities between love and death (and, therefore, the earth that is the source and end of love) and the reluctant submission of a healthy imagination to death, if it is to devise the great poem of earth.

> This luscious and impeccable fruit of life
> Falls, it appears, of its own weight to earth.
> When you were Eve, its acrid juice was sweet,
> Untasted, in its heavenly, orchard air.

These lines condense the meaning of stanza VI of "Sunday Morning" and present us with a twentieth-century version of the Fortunate Fall. The apple falls inevitably from "heavenly orchard air" to earth because it has weight and substance; its fall and Eve's tasting are associated, as in the original myth. But in a post-Newtonian context both events take on the inexorability of natural law, and in the next quatrain Stevens diagrams this law for us in the most basic of all geometries:

> An apple serves as well as any skull
> To be the book in which to read a round,
> And is as excellent, in that it is composed
> Of what, like skulls, comes rotting back to ground.

The delicate sound patterns of "Le Monocle" rarely assert themselves as noticeably as this; the rhyme imitates the finality of the cyclical process. Hamlet, reading a round in Yorick's skull, proves that "imagination [may] trace the noble dust of Alexander" through an ecological cycle:

> as thus: Alexander died, Alexander was buried, Alexander returneth into dust; the dust is earth; of earth we make loam; and why of that loam, whereto he was converted, might they not stop a beer barrel?
>
> (V.1)

Stevens, with like severity and facetiousness, reads in apples and skulls an unsentimental "way of truth": "An ancient aspect touching a new mind." The idyll of stanza IV becomes the surreal grotesquerie of stanza VIII, the lovers

> Two golden gourds distended on our vines,
> Into the autumn weather, splashed with frost,
> Distorted by hale fatness, turned grotesque.

"This trivial trope reveals a way of truth." The truth-revealing tropes of this poem all concern the natural cycle, life bearing and death dealing, and our dependence upon it as the world in which we have our happiness, or not at all: "Yet you persist with anecdotal bliss / To make believe a starry *connaissance*." Make-believe is the product of an imagination that has failed to root itself in the deep rhythms of nature and acknowledge our "bond to all that dust." Its "anecdotal bliss" fixes on isolated moments and draws from them intimations of a heavenly wisdom that might make sense of our lives. That the hand of providence writes its hieroglyphs in the sky is a belief that many have found comforting, but Stevens throughout his life was to deny it. Although acknowledging the seductiveness of such make-believe in some enchanting lines of stanza VII, he insists that transcendental imaginings remain in the region of *if* and *may*: "Suppose these couriers brought amid their train / A damsel heightened by eternal bloom." Eternal bloom is repeatedly denied. *Suppose* has no consequence.

This is the difficult confession hammered home in the dull scholar's Hamlet-like meditation upon Eros and Thanatos in the following stanza. "A damsel heightened by eternal bloom" is an invention of fancy, imagination in its wish-fulfilling mood. "Suppose. . . ." But meanwhile there is the "ancient aspect" of actual love: "It comes, it blooms, it bears its fruit and dies." The "way of truth" that cures the ground and chastens fables insists that "our bloom is gone." So much for "eternal bloom." In these adjacent stanzas, therefore, Stevens offers his dominant, interlaced subjects in dynamic but inexplicit relationship. Imagination, the mediating and expressive power, can deal with its major theme, love, in two ways. It can perpetuate radiant bubbles, the remembered glory of time past, in fictions that make-believe the heavenly origin of beloved damsels: "The mules that angels ride . . ." and so forth. Yet, there is a darker awareness that counters the starry *connaissance*, bursts the bubble. This "deep uppouring from some saltier well" knows that love's origin lies deep, not high, in those depths from which the beloved arises "dripping in your hair from sleep." The responsible imagination of the yeoman-poet recognizes that starry fables are for fiery boys and sweet-smelling virgins unaware of their mortality and addresses itself to the difficult task of charting "the origin and course / Of love" over an entire life span. The point is that this task too requires trivial tropes, requires the oblique and self-annihilating activity of fiction making.

The last of Stevens' anecdotal meditations, before he winds up "Le Monocle" in stanza XII, speaks, tropically, of mature love. It begins with a commentary in the conditional mood. "If sex were all, then every trembling hand / Could make us squeak, like dolls, the wished-for words." It is a stanza that has given much trouble to readers, but may give less if we recognize that in it the poet knots together the strands of his imagining on the subjects of language, love, and organic mortality, and that the image of the last four lines is another version of the basic spatial model that undergirds the poem.

To say "If sex were all" is to say that it is not all. "That first, foremost law" does not dictate the words of poems like "Le Monocle de Mon Oncle." Rather, love does that—"madness or delight"—causing us to "shout / Doleful heroics" like the opening phrases of the poem. Stevens knows, of course, that sex and love are both rooted in the watery unconscious world "down there," where the frogs boom:

> Last night, we sat beside a pool of pink,
> Clippered with lilies scudding the bright chromes,
> Keen to the point of starlight, while a frog
> Boomed from his very belly odious chords.

This trivial trope reiterates the principle of relationship between opaque, visceral depths and dazzling verbal surfaces that is both the subject and the methodology of the poem. The "odious chords" arise from the same region as the "deep up-pouring" of stanza I, and the newborn Venus ascending from the world of sleep in stanza III. "Odious chords" affront imagination, which desires always to convert animal noises to articulate language and sense-making fables that will suffice for our mixed being. Lilies and starlight belong to conventional love language, and Stevens' style in these three lines is as mannered as it is in any passage in the poem. And yet, every depth has a surface, every spasm of madness or delight aspires to articulateness. "Fate" has decreed a double allegiance in us, to the dark emotions in the belly and to "the wished-for words." Stevens' image of surface and depth, like the Freudian model that lies behind it, makes us see these two motives as basically continuous, however often they may conflict in practice. Stanza XI, unexpectedly, offers a biological explanation for imagining, which allows for mutuality of effect between the emotions yearning for words and their visceral origins. "If sex were all," odious chords would be enough. But we are not stirred by "every trembling hand," only by a particular hand at a particular moment of a temporal "curriculum." The hand belongs to the "she" who brings words into being and is endowed with her love-attracting power by the feeling and imagining being in the grip of the "foremost law" of his being.

The philosophic roots of Stevens' poem lie close to those expressed in Spenser's Garden of Adonis.

> That substance is eterne, and bideth so;
> Newhen the life decayes and forme does fade,
> Doth it consume and into nothing goe,
> But chaunged is, and often altred to and froe.
>
> (III.vi. 37)

"There is a substance in us that prevails." The speaker's awareness of himself as implicated in dying generations, his effort to come to terms with the indifferent substrate of his biological and temporal being, is the situation for which Stevens provides successive parabolic comments. He must discover how to speak accurately about an ever-changing world in which love, and every loved object, "both comes and goes at once." A saying of the truth about a fluent mundo can never be definitive; any lapidary claims it may make will betray the superficiality of its source, and it will end up on the dump. "The dump is full / Of images" that have lost their verve:

> Is it a philosopher's honeymoon, one finds
> On the dump? Is it to sit among mattresses of the dead,
> Bottles, pots, shoes and grass and murmur *aptest eve:*
> Is it to hear the blatter of grackles and say
> *Invisible priest;* is it to eject, to pull
> The day to pieces and cry *stanza my stone?*

The aptest Eve is the one who becomes a warty squash in "Le Monocle." The stanzas of the poem do not profess to be stones; thinking stones, in particular, are dismissed at the beginning. The tropes are effective precisely *because* they are trivial, ephemeral, because they trace intensities and verves through their fluctuations with a breathless scrivening. Stevens' twelve stanzas show him to be a master of repetitions in the terms of his own later definition. The poem shows why repetition is necessary for faithful speech, and it awards its instances precisely the degrees of credence and skepticism that they deserve. They will grow more shrunken and distant from their origin as the years go by:

> When amorists grow bald, then amours shrink
> Into the compass and curriculum
> Of introspective exiles, lecturing.

As the "man fairly well along in life" is exiled from the fiery boy he once was, so the poet is exiled from the experiences that supply him with his materials:

> the hiding-places of man's power
> Open; I would approach them, but they close.
> (*The Prelude,* XII, 279–80)

The introspective exile continues, however, to lecture, to read, and to write. He wields a compass that can trace, though now on a flat surface, the circles of skulls and apples. *Curriculum* is a dry word for the lecturer's paradigm, but it is also *curriculum vitae,* the necessary course of a life. In a late poem, Stevens associates it with the flowing "river of rivers":

> It is the third commonness with light and air,
> A curriculum, a vigor, a local abstraction . . .
> Call it, once more, a river, an unnamed flowing,
>
> Space-filled, reflecting the seasons. . . .
> ("The River of Rivers in Connecticut")

Scrivenings are shrunken, flattened, and attentuated versions of "reality," but they can reflect the seasons of a human life if the scrivener will take chances, discard dead decorums, and resist the temptation to lapidary utterance and premature closure. Both Wordsworth and Stevens shocked their early readers, and both were accused of triviality and deliberate obfuscation. From the 1970s they look like heroes precisely because they admit the foolhardiness of what they do and are capable of allowing themselves to assume a fool's role in some of their poems.

Stevens' last persona in "Le Monocle" is the rose rabbi who in the final stanza reads yet another round, the eloquent figures traced by the birds, who in stanza X visited the gigantic tree of reality. Now they make a final sense of "a moving chaos that never ends" in a close that manages to evade finality. The poem's ultimate conceit perfectly adumbrates the poise of vision that rewards imaginative *ascesis*:

> A blue pigeon it is, that circles the blue sky,
> On sidelong wing, around and round and round.
> A white pigeon it is, that flutters to the ground,
> Grown tired of flight.

One hesitates to mangle the delicacy of implication in these lines. The "it is" of lines one and three is an early example of a stylistic device that later pervaded Stevens' poetry; and like the late examples, these *its* have indefinite reference. The blue and white pigeons are figures for whatever comes to life and makes its mark on the isolation of the sky—birds, human beings, loves, poems. The circles are related to the apples and skulls of stanza IV; all are books "in which to read a round." Stevens in his next volume celebrates "The Pleasures of Merely Circulating" and queries the "secret in skulls," concluding, "Yet that things go round and again go round / Has rather a classical sound." He is after something more subtle than the classical notion of cycles. The classical sound is avoided in "Le Monocle" by breaking the "round and round" of the first two lines with the ravishing cadences of the next two. Nevertheless, this stanza has more end rhymes than any other in the poem: *round* rhymes with *ground* and *found*; *pursued* and *knew* is a near miss. So the classical sound is not altogether denied. Stevens is working for a conclusive cadence that will imitate the inconclusiveness of the "inner poem."

The blue pigeon circles; the white pigeon settles to a dying fall. Stevens is speaking of the ends of things, but so gently that repose seems as desirable as it is inevitable. The poet and the bird both grow tired of flight and return to rest in the ground of their being. But flight is natural to them, and they, or others like them, will fly again. The stanza's middle lines turn the speaker's irony upon himself again; his mincing machine mutilates what it devours. But in modulating from the presumptions of the dark rabbi to the hesitations of the rose one, Stevens achieves an eloquent seriousness.

> Like a rose rabbi, later, I pursued,
> And still pursue, the origin and course
> Of love, but until now I never knew
> That fluttering things have so distinct a shade.

The poem ends in the evanescent present moment of insight. As Wordsworth regards the meanest flower that blows, Stevens observes the fluttering thing that casts its intensely significant shadow. "Shade" carries many meanings; it touches lightly the territory of the "studious ghosts" in stanza III and the place where shades and ghosts live. Shadows and substance change places in the last line: "real" things flutter and distinctness belongs to shades. This is a commentary upon distinctness. We cannot know, or embody, or grasp anything more distinct than a shadow, and so the shadows that imagination conjures up are as enduring, and as fleeting, as the solemn temples, the great globe itself.

By concluding the great "Ode" with a reference to "thoughts that do often lie too deep for tears," Wordsworth confesses a final inarticulateness. Thoughts too deep for tears are also too deep for linguistic expression, and indeed, they remain unspecified. The poem ends, having approximated, as best it may, the poem within. Both the "Ode" and "Le Monocle de Mon Oncle" illustrate Stevens' proposition in "Man Carrying Thing," that "The poem must resist the intelligence / Almost successfully"; they also, to some extent, explain why.

Poetry and its sources are connected only through "intimations," Wordsworth's stubbornly precise word for "what remains behind" in the poet's cabinet. Yet all men desire to know themselves and to speak of their knowing; the instinct to understand, to contemplate, to express, is almost as deeply rooted in *nature* as the primary experience itself. From these features of "our climate," Wordsworth deduced his theory of poetry and Stevens the propositions concealed behind "Le Monocle." The effort to understand, which for the language animal means the effort to speak, will continue as long as the human race continues; expression will invariably be inadequate to intuition, and therefore unsatisfying; "what will suffice" will forever elude us, but forever retain its power to re-enchant the imagination to yet another adventure.

JOHN HOLLANDER

The Sound of the Music
of Music and Sound

The whole of "The Whole of Harmon-
ium" is a musical trope, but it is a kind of master trope of such complexity
that merely to catalogue its elements can be bewildering. Pianos, oboes,
orchestras, mandolins, guitars, claviers, tambourines, and songs; the mu-
sics of Mozart and Brahms, and all the bird songs and other noises of
nature; the sounds of language deconstructed into vocables; the visionary
phonetics of transcendent tongues; music claimed for language as well as
language claimed for music; music abstract and concrete; music simply or
complexly figurative—from the clattering of bucks to a scrawny cry from
outside, Stevens' poetry is suffused with systematic sound. To say that all
this music—high, low, noisy, verbal—is metaphorical is surely not enough.
And even to map those metaphors—the movement between "music" and
"a music" in "Peter Quince at the Clavier," say, and the kinds of
transition from section to section within the poem that are those of
program music ("clavier" or no, the *poem* is playing Schumann)—is to
deal with dense terrain. Figures of persons, things, or activities in Stevens
are always full of shadows and echoes of other figures, and most impor-
tantly, figurations of previous tropes. It is almost as if the analogue of the
process by which verbal wit can reanimate a cliché or dead metaphor (for
example, by momentarily literalizing it) were the imagination's making
figures of figures. When "the theatre was changed / To something else"
("Of Modern Poetry"), then the truly poetic had to twang "a wiry string
that gives / Sounds passing through sudden rightnesses," not an old and

From *Wallace Stevens: A Celebration*, edited by Frank Doggett and Robert Bittel.
Copyright © 1980 by Princeton University Press.

prettified, but soundless, lyre. Nowhere is this more locally evident in Stevens' verse than in his imagery and mythology of music and of the traditionally figurative "music" of natural sound.

There is no manifesto about musical figures more powerful or more direct than the beginning of "The Idea of Order at Key West," where the voice of the singing spirit and the "constant cry" of the sea are emphatically denied a relation that their forerunners have had throughout the history of our poetry. After an initial correction of what might be an inevitable mistake in interpretation ("The sea was not a mask. No more was she"; that is, neither is a mere per-sona through which some hidden or higher voice is sounding) there is another corrective adjustment:

> The song and water were not medleyed sound
> Even if what she sang was what she heard,
> Since what she sang was uttered word by word.
> It may be that in all her phrases stirred
> The grinding water and the gasping wind;
> But it was she and not the sea we heard.

The "medleyed sound" is no less than one of the oldest and most powerful tropes of eloquence: that blending of human music, whether vocal or instrumental, and natural sound that I have elsewhere referred to as "the mingled measure." Drawing upon two conventions of literary pastoral— the echoing of poetic song by nature and the catalogue of pleasant sounds in the *locus amoenus* (the wind in the trees, the eloquence of moving water, bird song, etc.)—the figure undergoes a romantic transformation, becoming the basis in all but few English poets for a new authentication of human music as an instance of something transcendent (a status it had lost when neoclassic rhetoric and rationalist cosmology had disabled *harmonia mundi* for poetic purposes, and *musica humana* had become the busy institutional churning of opera house, salon and concert hall). The blending of contrived, human music with the spontaneous noises of nature, the blending of mere literal music with sounds that are only figuratively so, becomes a dominant romantic musical image. In English and American poetry, at least, the layered blendings of natural symphony and human singing and playing is the only poetic sound.

In the lines quoted above, Stevens is rejecting the possibility of using the old figure in any unfigured way. To have heard and reported on nothing but grinding of water and gasping of wind would have constituted modernist poetic journalism of a sort still, alas, too much with us. To have heard and celebrated a "medleyed sound" would have been humming slightly new, but not inappropriate, words to a very corny old tune. The wind and water music stirred "in all her phrases " (although of her text or melody we are, significantly, not told—such is the magic of verse) because it is her song that can "make" by being able to imbibe, digest, and transform literalness.

Perhaps we can see this more clearly by turning to some American romantic instances of the medley and its versions. William Cullen Bryant's "Summer Wind" comes heroically upon a scene of attentive silence (save for the "interrupted murmur of the bee" at his sweet and sexual work on "the sick flowers"): hills, "With all their growth of woods, silent and stern, / As if the scorching heat and dazzling light / Were but an element they loved." The poet awaits the coming of this heroic bridegroom, lying "where the thick turf, / Yet virgin from the kisses of the sun, / Retains some freshness." He woos the wind, and, after a preceding vision of natural declarations of fealty (the pine "bending his proud top," etc.),

> He comes;
> Lo, where the grassy meadow runs in waves!
> The deep distressful silence of the scene
> Breaks up with minglings of unnumbered sounds
> And universal motion. He is come,
> Shaking a shower of blossoms from the shrubs,
> And bearing on their fragrance; and he brings
> Music of birds, and rustling of young boughs,
> And sound of swaying branches, and the voice
> Of distant waterfalls. . . .

Save for the remarkably deployed context of marriage and its poetic consequences (the wind is causing landscape to sing her own epithalamium, but of his composition), the catalogue of polyphonic voices is quite traditional. It is of the sort dangerously travestied in Spenser's Bower of Bliss and taken up by Wordsworth's eighteenth-century predecessors.

Or we might adduce the contrasted inner and outer soundscapes in Whittier's "Snowbound," where "within our beds" the remembered sleepers heard

> The wind that round the gables roared
> With now and then a ruder shock,
> Which made our very bedsteads rock.
> We heard the loosened clapboards test,
> The board-nails snapping in the frost. . . .

But those sounds underwent transformation in visionary sleep:

> Faint and more faint the murmurs grew,
> Till in the summer-land of dreams
> They softened to the sound of streams,
> Low stir of leaves, and dip of oars,
> And lapsing waves on quiet shores.

Imaginatively transformed or no, these are not the syllables sought by a later poetic "Vocalissimus, / In the distances of sleep" ("To the

Roaring Wind"). Emerson teaches a similar lesson, but it has to be learned from him at several removes. In "Forerunners," the writer catches the scent of poetic flowers strewn by "happy guides," as "tone of silver instrument / Leaves on the wind melodious trace." The syntax of the last three words is Miltonic, the transition from a scent to an outdoor music is one of the commonplaces of the music of earthly paradises, and the complex image of "tracing" the sound of an already figurative (neoclassical and emblematic) instrument on the more imaginatively authentic wind is confirmed in the unusual reversal of the received metaphor. The musician wind usually plays upon the figurative strings of the trees, all of nature being, in this set of instances, an Aeolian harp. Emerson has taken care, in a parable about poetic predecessors, to adapt the precursory commonplace. (I think that Robert Frost followed Emerson along the "shining trails" of the landscape in this poem, and although the same voices may not have echoed in a "harp-like laughter" of unabashed bardic power as they did for Emerson, he did keep hearing a chuckle.)

Emerson is as insistent about transforming old images for poetry as he is about quickening poetry itself, which is why in "Bacchus" music must be mingled with wine, and why in "Merlin" all the socially contrived salon music must be transfigured:

> Thy trivial harp will never please
> Or fill my craving ear;
> Its chords should ring as blows the breeze,
> Free, peremptory, clear.
> No jingling serenader's art
> Nor tinkle of piano strings. . . .

This is taken by subsequent American poetry to be a parable of form and a plea for the arrival of Whitman's free verse. But it should be read more deeply, less as a fable of scheme or formal surface than of trope, and the first line must refer, for any poet following Emerson, to "thy trivial 'harp' " as well; use and mention, as it were, become procreatively confused. Merlin's powerful banging must mingle with more than the natural voices domesticated by centuries of earlier poetry. They must chime

> with the forest tone
> When boughs buffet boughs in the wood;
> Chiming with the gasp and moan
> Of the ice-imprisoned flood;
> With the pulse of many hearts;
> With the voice of orators;
> With the din of city arts;

> With the cannonade of wars;
> With the marches of the brave;
> And prayers of might from martyrs' cave.

This chorus is represented with the batterings of anaphora; it is the sound of the strings of the major harp of the cosmos, the figurative, figuring one of major poetry, rather than the trivial synecdoche, whether "lute" or "harp" or "lyre." It heralds the coming of Whitman, but by precept.

Emerson had realized, with Wordsworth and Coleridge, that "The oratorio has already lost its relation to the morning, to the sun + the earth," but he also knew that the received rhetoric that had echoed in his own earlier poetry, the artificial music attempting to regain such relations by mixing with natural sound, had lost its own imaginative force. "The Bell" of 1823, ringing across water in a key tuned originally by *Il Penseroso*, concludes:

> And soon thy music, sad death-bell,
> Shall shift its notes once more,
> And mix my requiem with the wind
> That sweeps my native shore.

But this is itself the music of the trivial harp, and in such descriptions of natural and human music as in "May Day" Emerson transcends such easy and mechanical mixtures.

The solemnizing of older sound imagery by taking it one step further into figuration seems to be a peculiarly American poetic activity. Thoreau shares in this in his elaborate prose odes to sound and its power (in the "Sounds" chapter in *Walden*) and in the amazing, extended series of transfigurations of the romantic mythology of the Aeolian harp in what he called "the undecayed oracle" of his "telegraph harp"—the inadvertent external music of the wind in the wires, whose internal state is agitated by the transformed sounds of electrical impulses—which extend through his journal entries of the early 1850s. He frequently imposes layer upon layer of musical figure, often letting his represented sounds yield tropes of light:

> All sounds, and more than all, silence, do fife and drum for us. The least creaking doth whet all our senses and emit a tremulous light, like the aurora borealis, over things. As polishing expresses the vein in marble and the grain in wood, so music brings out what of heroic lurks everywhere.

Emily Dickinson, with her wish that "the ear had not a heart / So dangerously near," constantly performs quirky revisions and reinterpretations, whether of the musicians who "wrestle everywhere" and the various unsatisfactory readings of that noise of living consciousness itself, or of the

profuse strains of unpremeditated art in a singing bird that "was different—
'Twas Translation—Of all tunes I knew—and more—." And Walt Whitman's very mode of rewriting the audition of transcendent music has itself
become almost canonical. For Whitman, as for few poets writing in
English in the nineteenth century, the oratorio and, particularly, the
opera maintained a multitude of glowing relations to the morning, the
sun, and the earth:

> Through the soft evening air enwinding all
> Rocks, woods, fort, cannon, pacing sentries, endless wilds,
> In dulcet streams, in flutes' and cornets' notes,
> Electric, pensive, turbulent, artificial. . . .

This image from "Italian Music in Dakota" (ca. 1880) is the sound
of a regimental band playing operatic arrangements and paraphrases of
Bellini and Donizetti, artificial at several removes,

> (Yet strangely fitting here, meanings unknown before,
> Subtler than ever, more harmony, as if born here, related here,
> Not to the city's fresco'd rooms, not to the audience of the opera house,
> Sounds, echoes, wandering strains, as really here at home,
> Sonnambula's innocent love, tries with Norma's anguish,
> And thy ecstatic chorus, Poliuto;)
> Ray'd in the limpid yellow slanting sundown,
> Music, Italian music in Dakota.

This is not just opera in itself, of course, but opera echoed, invoked,
recalled, turned into a sublimely oom-pahed version of all that it could
ever mean.

> While Nature, sovereign of this gnarl'd realm
> Lurking in hidden barbaric grim recesses,
> Acknowledging rapport however far remov'd,
> (As some old root or soil of earth its last-born flower
>   or fruit,)
> Listens well pleas'd.

Whitman's natural choirs, then, can enlist all voices. "Strange that
a harp of thousand strings / Can keep in tune so long," goes the text of
one of William Billings' fuguing tunes, and the "varied carols" of American sound maintain in Whitman a discordia concors. A poem of 1861
consists entirely of the figuratively revised natural concert:

> I heard you solemn-sweet pipes of the organ as last
>   Sunday morning I pass'd the church,
> Winds of autumn, as I walk'd up the woods at dusk I
>   heard your long-stretch'd sighs up above so mournful,

> I heard the perfect Italian tenor singing at the opera,
> I heard the soprano in the midst of the quartet singing;
> Heart of my love! you too I heard murmuring low
> through one of the wrists around my head,
> Heard the pulse of you when all was still ringing little
> bells that night under my ear.

This is Whitman's "At a Solemn Music," and it adduces the only available form of the music of the spheres in an otherwise untuned world. It is carefully orchestrated; lines about "war-suggesting trumpets" and a lady playing "delicious music on the harp" were cut from an earlier version. The layerings of upper and lower "parts," the movement toward total musical authentification in the movement from the sounds of church music to art to the ultimate metaphorical bells calling him to an internalized worship of, and in, the body are themselves a figure for musical scoring.

Whitman's more elaborated symphonies of music, of the noise of human occupation and sounds of discourse include, on the one hand, minor, ad hoc occasional pieces like the late "Interpolation Sounds" and, on the other, a major musical ode, "Proud Music of the Storm," his adaptation of the tradition that extends from Dryden through its fugurative form in Collins to Wordsworth. The ode encompasses passing figures like those in "Song of Myself 18" ("With music strong I come") and the full-fledged chorus of 26 ("Now I will do nothing but listen"); but with that music always round him, Whitman hears polyphonically, comprehends the dramaturgy of independent part and vertical harmony striving always for phenomenological priority:

> I hear not the volumes of sound merely, I am moved by
> the exquisite meanings,
> I listen to the different voices winding in and out,
> striving, contending with fiery vehemence to excell
> each other in emotion;
> I do not think the performers know themselves—but
> now I think I begin to know them.

"The performers" are almost the voices themselves, and the act of knowing them is one of recognizing the uniqueness and universality at once of the reinvigorated trope of musical harmony for both inner and outer energies.

But Whitman's imagery of music and sound can easily harden into something brittle and empty: chant, in America, reduces in a generation to cant. A further transfiguration of the "exquisite meanings" of sound and noise that live in and outside of discourse is necessary if poetry is to renew itself by continually sloughing off its husk of rhetoric. "The music brought us what it seemed / We had long desired," begins one of the most Stevensian poems not written by Stevens, talking of the incapacitated older fictions, "but in a form / So rarified there was no emptiness / Of sensation. . . ." Even Whitmanic chorales of everything in life entering, *fugato*, the scene of awareness can become what John Ashbery goes on to characterize as "the toothless murmuring / Of ancient willows, who kept their trouble / In a stage of music." The willows almost have trivial harps hanging from them. So that

> The truth is that there comes a time
> When we can mourn no more over music
> That is so much motionless sound.
> There comes a time when the waltz
> Is no longer a mode of desire. . . .
>   ("Sad Strains of a Gay Waltz")

This is Stevens' version of the oratorio having lost its relation to the morning, and he could have gone on revising almost indefinitely—fugues unleashed from memory become tediously scampering beasts, and so forth. But his general poetic project, to be the "harmonious skeptic . . . in a skeptical music" that will be "motion and full of shadows," could not merely catalogue the nostalgias of old flowers, nor rest content in hearing a not newly new replaying of the music of the spheres:

> The heaving speech of air, a summer sound
> Repeated in a summer without end
> And sound alone.
>   ("The Idea of Order at Key West")

His project always carries him beyond these alternatives. One of the asides one mutters on the oboe concerns the obsolete fiction of the lyre somewhat loudly swept, and the implication is that the oboe itself must be abandoned, not broken like a pastoral pipe or hung on a tree, but loudly junked: one must move on to the next thing. The ultimate instrument upon which Hoon hums his hymns ("And my ears made the blowing hymns they heard") may be a subtle transformation of the most complex form of the romantic seashell, which is shaped like both ear and mouth and which adds to our own ear and speaks into it when we hold it up for news of the sea's depth and vastness. But Hoon being Hoon, every trace of this has been swallowed up. Throughout *Harmonium* Stevens reveals a restlessness with available figurations of sound, and any revision of them can become anecdotal. The reading of the winter music in "The Snow Man," the triumph of "Heavenly labials in a world of gutturals" in "The Plot Against the Giant," the epitome of all serenade when in "Le

Monocle de Mon Oncle" the frog "Boomed from his very belly odious chords" (best quitted with disdain)—these are all familiar modes of transformation of older tropes. The "spontaneous cries" of the quail at the end of "Sunday Morning" echo the "unpremeditated art" of a Shelleyan bird, even as the "casual flocks of pigeons" shadow the Keatsian swallows. And in the penultimate stanza of that poem, the moment of unqualified sublimity allows for a pre-Whitmanian natural chorus:

> And in their chant shall enter, voice by voice,
> The windy lake where in their lord delights,
> The trees, like serafin, and echoing hills,
> That choir among themselves long afterward.

The hills, more than merely affirming (in metaphor) the truth of a poetic outcry by echoing it, continue to resound with echoes of their own echoing: we are gently and implicitly reminded that the echoes outlast the primary voice, and that those lasting echoes must themselves enter the polyphony of the great imagined chanting.

We usually think of Stevens' musical metaphors as reworking and reinventing the outworn and broken instruments of the Sublime: the lyre, harp, and lute of neoclassic diction; the Aeolian harp and singing seashell of earlier romanticism, the virtuoso pianism or homely parlor upright of its later phase; personal instruments, such as the guitar ("This slave of Music" given by Shelley-Ariel to Jane-Miranda); and the bird song, to which I shall return. There is, in fact, hardly a scrap of traditional auditory mythology upon which Stevens has not improvised. At the beginning of "Evening without Angels," the familiar Christianized version of the heavenly choir of *harmonia mundi* is queried as to its right to represent the eloquent significance of our surrounding element:

> Why seraphim like lutanists arranged
> Above the trees? And why the poet as
> Eternal *chef d'orchestre?*
>
> Air is air,
> Its vacancy glitters round us everywhere.
> It sounds are not angelic syllables
> But our unfashioned spirits realized
> More sharply in more furious selves.

The answer is that there *is* such a right, but that it must be exercised in a way so as not to abrogate itself. We are, after all, "Men that repeat antiquest sounds of air / In an accord of repetitions. . . ." (As so often in Stevens, the genitive phrase is ambiguous: the sounds are made *of* air and *about* it.) But the repetitions are not elements in a unison of redundancy and monotony: "If we repeat, it is because the wind / Encircling us, speaks always with our speech."

The voices of air are like other natural sounds in that we are in them, but there is no sentimentality here. It is noteworthy that Stevens seems largely uninterested in any diachronic myth of the origin of the language of air. It clearly transcends the empty prattle of moving water: the antiquest tropes of the stream's eloquence and the pool's reflectiveness. But the figure of noise as music is almost a *donnée*. The closest Stevens seems to come to accounting for its emergence is at a tender and privileged moment, when the actual imprinting of human meaning upon nature is treated visually:

> Now, of the music summoned by the birth
> That separates us from the wind and sea,
> Yet leaves us in them, until earth becomes,
> By being so much of the things we are,
> Gross effigy and simulacrum, none
> Gives motion to perfection more serene
> Than yours. . . .
>   ("To the One of Fictive Music")

That masquelike music called up by a transformed Lucina is itself almost the music of wind and sea, yet something from beyond them both. The voices of earth and air and water alike become auditory simulacra at the same time. But this is vastly different from the witty, precise myth of origination in Frost's "Never Again Would Birds' Song Be the Same," wherein the birds, after hearing Eve's "daylong voice," added to their own voices an "undersound"—her "tone of meaning" but lacking "the words." It is always the speech, and never the music, that the Frostean protagonist is striving to hear and to decipher. "To hear is almost to understand," says Santayana, but Frost and Stevens would make very different things of this observation. Frost will wonder whether a natural noise is whispering a text, for sounds are almost like visual hieroglyphic signs. He will produce keener demarcations, ghostlier sounds; Stevens will be overwhelmed with the music of our own listening.

This distinction is particularly noticeable with respect to the two poets' respective kinds of attention to bird song. Frost's sonnet about the ovenbird is exemplary: the poem addresses itself to the philosophical bird whose song celebrates midpoints, whose inflections do not hymn but question ("what to make of a diminished thing"). The cry of the ovenbird is traditionally called "Teacher! teacher!" Stevens hears birds singing "Preacher! preacher!" and turns away in weary distaste; *or*, they say "Creature! creature!" calling him to a mode of the erotic to which he will not dance. At best, he will hear their songs as asserting their own exemplariness ("Feature! feature!"?). The "warblings early in the hilarious trees / Of summer, the drunken mother" ("Meditations Celestial & Terrestrial") do in fact undo him a bit. "A passionately niggling nightingale," however, is the hymn and flight of the vulgar ("The Comedian as the Letter C"), and it heads a catalogue of problematic songbirds throughout Stevens' poetry.

"Autumn Refrain" is a sad and beautiful poem, and its attempt to take up again the rejected nightingale of moonlight from "The Comedian as the Letter C" is fraught with the presence of silence. The silence, when it comes, is both acoustical—the silence of not being able to hear anything—and rhetorical—the silence of having nothing to utter.

> The skreak and skritter of evening gone
> And grackles gone and sorrow of the sun,
> The sorrows of sun, too, gone . . . the moon and moon,
> The yellow moon of words about the nightingale
> In measureless measures, not a bird for me
> But the name of a bird and the name of a nameless air
> I have never—shall never hear. And yet beneath
> The stillness of everything gone, and being still,
> Being and sitting still, something resides,
> Some skreaking and skrittering residuum,
> And grates these evasions of the nightingale
> Though I have never—shall never hear that bird.
> And the stillness is in the key, all of it is,
> The stillness is all in the key of that desolate sound.

Harold Bloom has pointedly called this poem "a debate between the grackles and Keats," associating the "skreak and skritter" here with the "blatter" of those same grackles in "The Man on the Dump" and their other unpleasant appearances. The Keatsian nightingale may sum up a whole tradition for Stevens. There are in America neither larks nor nightingales of the kind that have astonished English poets for their invisible voices; there are only copies of the poems about them. There are no sweetly singing English blackbirds here, only grackles, named with a skreakingly assonantal diminution of "blackbirds," worldly gutturals below the singing of more heavenly labials. But I wonder whether the nightingale is not Milton's as much as it is Keats'; the former's first sonnet broods on the voice of the nightingale and wonders what it could mean. Is it an emblem of love or of poetry? Virginal to the first, already significantly affianced to the second, the young poet complains to the bird that "thou from year to year hast sung too late / For my relief." For Stevens, it is not that the bird sings too late but that it is all too late in the year and in the day, and always will be. There will be no easily audited poetic bird for Stevens. The "skreaking and skrittering residuum" that lies below stillness is hardly a cosmic music, itself a residuum of the demythologized music of the spheres that for George Eliot lay "on the other side of silence." Even that residuum has been internalized. It "grates these evasions of the nightingale," but this statement, too, is rhetorically problematic: the typical Stevensian ambiguity lies in the "of—" phrase (archetypally, in "the malady of the quotidian," where the meanings "the malady that the quotidian condition entails," "the malady *called* the quotidian" and "the malady that *marks* it" are, significantly, not sorted out). Two evasions are grated, and their very identification is part of the poem's concern: the "measureless measures" of the old nightingales are themselves evasions, and, if used at too late a time, doubly so. But the world of grackles and the stillness that is *their* residuum are evasions in another sense. They are necessary ones, performed lest the first evasions that *are* the bird's song be unwittingly espoused in the belief that they are direct confrontations.

This is certainly, as Bloom suggests, the poem of a silent time, and it is forced back on its own meager musical resources. The refrain here is not provided by any bird song or cricket chirp from without, nor is there any of the hum and bustle of harvesting or the slow, "hours by hours" drip of some sweet *Spätlese*. The refrains in the poem are generated by its own words, repeated elegiacally as refrainlike phrases, or, almost parodistically, as conjoined word—"the moon and moon." The anapestic cadence first heard in "but the name of a bird" itself becomes a prosodic refrain, closing the whole poem with its last occurrence, which underscores the second of two corollaries about "stillness is all." The nightingale in this poem is not only like the later, blattering grackles (in "The Man on the Dump"), like Milton's later, prophetic nightingale, an "invisible priest"; he is silent, he is absent. The key of the residual sound totally contains, but is not to be identified with, silence; "that desolate sound" may only be breathing, and to that degree it is not to be associated with utter poetic death.

A word about the word "refrain." As designating a repeated line or phrase or burden, it comes from a romance term for "breaking off" (as to return again); but the verb "to refrain" (from a late Latin sense of "bridling, holding back") haunts this instance of its homonym, for the skrittering repetitions in the poem are necessitated by something (a bird, a muse, a poet) that has refrained from singing. This double refraining is all that there is, a kind of low point at the bottom of a parabola. The problem is what to make of an emptied thing—a capacity for singing, a trope for that capacity—and the poem provides no answer.

It is indeed only the continuing body of Stevens' work that will provide it, although when he can return to natural choirs and choruses of birds it will be to at least a mildly ironic accompaniment. The various instruments of metaphor that will be able to sing sufficiently of their own turnings will yield "The luminous melody of proper sound." The antiphonal choirs of "ké-ké" and "bethou me" in the sixth canto of "It Must Change" both undo the traditional work of polyphonic harmony: the first moves toward a monotony, a dead unison, the second through a quickening mockery, through a touch of reintegrated skyey harmony (but only in default: "There was such idiot minstrelsy in rain, / So many clappers going without bells, / That these bethous compose a heavenly gong"). But the chorded *bethous,* too, will fall toward that ultimate entropy of image, when trope hardens into statue and even into idol.

"A tune is a kind of tautology, it is complete in itself; it satisfies itself," observed Wittgenstein in another context. Well and good; but what if it satisfies itself only? The danger of changing and changing only to achieve this ungenerous and ungenerating situation is inherent in the unending process of variation in Stevens' "music." Whether this concerns figurations of sound, or what they are synecdochic for (the figurative life that has become more than *merely* figurative), or the rhetorical music that seems to embody the figurations—Stevens' restless ear is always able to agitate what it is hearing, and his tunes, of whatever sort, never rise to tautological purity. There is a hint of this problem in the questioning of the pianism of B. in "Esthétique du Mal":

> A transparence in which we heard music, made music,
> In which we heard transparent sounds, did he play
> All sorts of notes? Or did he play only one
> In an ecstasy of its associates,
> Variations in the tones of a single sound,
> The last, or sounds so single they seemed one?

There are monotonies of variation as well, and Stevens is constantly revising his own mode of variation, backtracking when necessary, denying significance of the wrong or easy sort, emptying a sound of sense in order to refill it.

> Item: The wind is never rounding O
> And, imageless, it is itself the most,
> Mouthing its constant smatter throughout space.
>   ("Montrachet-le-Jardin")

Stevens adduces the very problematic character of half-articulation in the course of unfolding a more complex catalogue, but the assertive value of, at least, the semiotically dirty, mumbled smattering over the possibility of the O (itself half-glossed by the preceding line's "an inaccessible, pure sound") is still clear. (Frost, a schoolmasterly decipherer, would devote himself to comprehending the smatter.)

One of the problems of Stevens' musical program is to create that smatter throughout the depths of his poetic language. It is not only in the realm of trope that the demarcations become more ghostly, but also at the surface of scheme, where the sounds are more keenly heard. His poetry contains an encyclopedia of one kind of echo: that play of sound sounding like sense in verse, that game of rhyme and assonance and alliteration used as implicit copulas of predication, that has occupied English verse since Shakespeare. Frequently, these games will play upon logical confusions of use and mention, a marriage of meta-object and meta-languages. The protagonist of "Anglais Mort à Florence," for whom the music of Brahms began to fail, remembers when it did not and when he could feel and see the moon "In the pale coherences of moon and mood." These coherences are themselves those of the assonance, and when Stevens employs his famous arrays of purely onomatopoetic syllables, he is doing something very like extracting the "ooo" from the sentimental correspondences. The level of figurative rhetorical music, the so-called music of poetry in the dimension that Pope explored in the famous passage about sound and sense in the *Essay on Criticism*, misled many early critics of Stevens into thinking of it as dandified nonsense, as high-flown joking about elevation of voice. But he was as serious about the music of his own verse as about anything external, and this provides an additional layer of complexity for the analysis of his images of music.

Stevens is always conceiving words

> As the night conceives the sea-sounds in silence,
> And out of their droning sibilants makes
> A serenade.
> ("Two Figures in Dense Violet Night")

And he does so even as evening turns the sibilance of the stressed syllables in the first of these lines into the proper initial phoneme of "serenade." The very operation of semantic punning on the word and its designatum is the operation of poetic music. The phonetic and thematic kinds of music come together elegantly and somewhat sadly in "Mozart, 1935":

> Poet, be seated at the piano,
> Play the present, its hoo-hoo-hoo,
> Its shoo-shoo-shoo, its ric-a-nic,
> Its envious cachinnation.

But the present throws stones on the roof of the poet practicing arpeggios, and as for

> That lucid souvenir of the past,
> The divertimento;
> That airy dream of the future,
> The unclouded concerto . . .
> The snow is falling.

The mingling of another voice from that of the pianist proper is required, although this is no romantic blending of piano and wind sighing in willows. The wind is the wintry follower of Shelley's autumnal voice, and the injunction to fuse wind and words moves in the opposite direction to Shelley's. The poet-pianist is urged

> Be thou the voice,
> Not you. Be thou, be thou
> The voice of angry fear,
> The voice of this besieging pain.
>
> Be thou that wintry sound
> As of the great wind howling. . . .

As if it were not enough to be oneself (be the *voice*, not *you*), it is only after that other voice has been absorbed that "We may return to Mozart," amid the snow and the streets "full of cries." The properly prepared poet can now be urged to take his place at the properly prepared piano: "Be seated, thou." (The "be thou" here is, syntactically, still Shelley's; a next stage of rewriting this injunction will be to convert the phrase to a punning verb, as in the sixth canto of "It Must Change.") The poem itself has properly prepared music to serve as a metaphor for poetry in an aftertime (Mozart "was young, and we, we are old") by combining three kinds of poetic music: *musica instrumentalis* (or, literally, music, piano and orchestral, by, say, Mozart); *musica mundana*, realized in its romantic form as natural noise of wind; and *musica loquacitatis*, the verbal music of Stevens' own poetic language. And even the older romantic fiction of blending or mingling the sounds is reworked, schematically, in the poem.

But this metaleptic process is at work in Stevens all the time, in so many areas of imagery. Music used naively is like all manifestly available public mythologies; for the imagination, they are all like statues, immobile. Metaphors reached down from a shelf cannot descend, as do resonant tenors in their shining vehicles, to ransom us from deadly literalness. Stevens represents such tropes "whom none believe" as "A pagan in a varnished car" ("The Man with the Blue Guitar"); in a figure as wittily self-descriptive as anything in Stevens, the "polished car" of the new star at the end of Milton's "Ode on the Morning of Christ's Nativity" has become tarnished for the imagination as it gets varnished for reuse. As with the metaphor of music for poetry, so with the "music" of nature. In Frost as well as in Stevens, we have seen a general transfiguration of the music of nature, but in Stevens there is an additional complexity. The very music, as it were, of that transfiguring, the sounds of the act of the mind—itself part of that natural music—must undergo renewal.

So that when we find in the late poems a return to what would have seemed withered figures of music as the vehicles for poetry, as the tenor of natural noise, it is not the result of any exhaustion. The lightly troped, almost Tennysonian choruses of bells in "To an Old Philosopher in Rome," the imitative soundscape of the defunctive music in "Madame La Fleurie" ("The black fugatos are strumming the blacknesses of black . . . / The thick strings stutter the finial gutturals"), the dampened dove of "Song of Fixed Accord," are all surely instances of this renewal. "Things of August" is almost explicit about it:

> These locusts by day, these crickets by night
> Are the instruments on which to play
> Of an old and disused ambit of the soul
> Or of a new aspect, bright in discovery. . . .

And Stevens can conclude:

> Nothing is lost, loud locusts. No note fails.
> These sounds are long in the living of the ear.
> The honky-tonk out of the somnolent grasses
> Is a memorizing, a trying out, to keep.

And, most certainly, the unidentified bird's cry in "Not Ideas about the Thing but the Thing Itself" is part of that very ancient claiming of musical status for natural sound by the language of poetry. The "scrawny cry from outside" is no self-generated echo but comes truly from outside; no mere cockcrow heralding light, no ké-ké or bethouing from the coppice, but rather a voice more like the "frail, gaunt and small" appearance of a darkling thrush at Hardy's coppice gate. In thin lines of verse and by means of a scrawny pun (on the letter c and the musical pitch it names) its unqualified heralding is made clear:

That scrawny cry—it was
A chorister whose c preceded the choir.
It was part of the colossal sun,

Surrounded by its choral rings,
Still far away. It was like
A new knowledge of reality.

The initial consonant of cry, chorister, choir, colossal, choral (and coral and coronal as well) is the note to which all the choired words are tuned, a synecdoche of the ever-primal sun—no mere alarm-clock bird, the text of whose song is the light to which it awakens one. The music of that cry, extracted by the meanest and scruffiest of poetic arts, is nonetheless an affirmation of the continuing possibilities of a world of music and sound in which more is heard than meets the ear.

ELEANOR COOK

Riddles, Charms, and Fictions

*No man though never so willing or so well enabl'd to instruct, but
if he discerne his willingnesse and candor made use of to intrapp
him, will suddainly draw in himselfe, and laying aside the facile
vein of perspicuity, will know his time to utter clouds and riddles.*

—MILTON, Tetrachordon

*But not yet have we solved the incantation of this whiteness, and learned
why it appeals with such power to the soul.*

—MELVILLE, Moby-Dick, XLII

Among the many riddling poems
Wallace Stevens has given us are some that are riddles structurally. That is,
they cannot be read with much beyond pleasurable puzzlement until we have
found the questions for which the poem provides answers. One example,
published in the last year of Stevens' life, is *Solitaire under the Oaks* (1955):

> In the oblivion of cards
> One exists among pure principles.
>
> Neither the cards nor the trees nor the air
> Persist as facts. This is an escape
>
> To principium, to meditation.
> One knows at last what to think about

From *Centre and Labyrinth: Essays in Honour of Northrop Frye*, edited by Eleanor Cook.
Copyright © 1983 by University of Toronto Press.

And thinks about it, without consciousness,
Under the oak trees, completely released.

The key to this compact little poem is Descartes: René Descartes and *des cartes*, the cards with which we play card games. The wit lies in the questions and answers implicit in the poem. What card game would a Cartesian, would M. Cards himself play? Why, solitaire, of course. We all know that our problems as *solitaires*—isolating self-consciousness, separation of nature into thinking self and outer object—stem from Descartes' principle, *cogito ergo sum*. Solitaire is the quintessential Cartesian card game. But what has M. Descartes forgotten? (He has forgotten something: 'In the oblivion of cards . . .') Answer: trees and air and indeed the cards themselves (which is to say, himself) as facts rather than as principles. Yet the card game of solitaire does offer compensating escape to principium, to meditation, as in Descartes' *Principia philosophiae* and *Les Méditations*. One escapes the burden of consciousness as long as one exists within this card-game, thinking according to its rules.

I am not interested here in Stevens' view of Descartes. (It has more to do with the Descartes of Coleridge and of Valéry, I think, than with the seventeenth-century Descartes.) I am interested in the function of the riddle-poem. Itself a game, this little riddle simultaneously enacts a game and comments on other games, both small and large—solitaire and Cartesian philosophy and poetry too. In its play with paradoxes of outside and inside, it suggests that there are multiple ways to think of a player and a game, or of a reader and a text. Poetry comes closest to game in riddle-poems, those 'generic seeds and kernels, possibilities of expression sprouting and exfoliating into new literary phenomena,' as Northrop Frye says of both riddles and charm poems. And 'those who want to study the relation between form and function in a contemporary setting' may well 'turn . . . to the rigid context of games' [E. H. Gombrich]. The topography of riddles and charms has been finely mapped by Frye in his 1976 essay, 'Charms and Riddles'; my exploration here proposes to extend that map only a little farther.

Games in riddle-poems may be multiple in less logical ways, as my second example is meant to demonstrate. What question do we ask to bridge the gap between title and couplets in the opaque poem of 1950, *The Desire To Make Love in a Pagoda*?

Among the second selves, sailor, observe
The rioter that appears when things are changed,

Asserting itself in an element that is free,
In the alien freedom that such selves degustate:

> In the first inch of night, the stellar summering
> At three-quarters gone, the morning's prescience,
>
> As if, alone on a mountain, it saw far-off
> An innocence approaching toward its peak.

We begin by noting the double sense of the title: the desire (felt by a human) to make love in a pagoda, and the desire felt by a pagoda to make love. We note also the different senses of 'peak,' and reflect that the act of making love has a peak physiologically and emotionally, and that pagodas are 'strange buildings which come to a point at the end,' as Ruskin says. We recall the old trope of the body as the temple of the Lord, and remember that a pagoda is for most of Stevens' readers a foreign or 'alien' temple. Finally, we read the second line as if the noun clause were written by Lewis Carroll. 'Rioter,' 'when things are changed,' is anagrammatically a near-complete 'erotic,' which we might expect in a poem about a desire to make love. These preparations are sufficient for a reading of the poem as the gently witty, erotic, multi-layered verse that it is: on desires of the body and of feelings; on primal desires for morning, which a temple might desire, as in love; on the desire to make riots or anagrams of letters, and to trope. The riddle takes the following form. Query: Is the body a temple? A temple of the Lord? Answer: Sometimes it is a pagoda. We begin with a sailor and a rioter and an anagram, but by the time the word-play culminates in 'peak,' only six lines later, Stevens has left behind the mode of Lewis Carroll. This is a riddle-poem whose games can touch as well as amuse the reader.

These two examples are built as riddle-poems. More often, Stevens will include a riddle as part of the larger argument of a poem. For example, why does Jerome beget the tubas in *Notes Toward a Supreme Fiction* (III.I)?

> To sing jubilas at exact, accustomed times,
> To be crested and wear the mane of a multitude
> And so, as part, to exult with its great throat,
>
> To speak of joy and to sing of it, borne on
> The shoulders of joyous men, to feel the heart
> That is the common, the bravest fundament,
>
> This is a facile exercise. Jerome
> Begat the tubas and the fire-wind strings,
> The golden fingers picking dark-blue air . . .

In his letters, Stevens' answer to my question is carefully and courteously straightforward and also carefully limited: 'Jerome is St. Jerome who "begat the tubas" by translating the Bible. I suppose this would have been clearer if I had spoken of harps.' But why tubas and not simply harps? It is true that through his translation of the Bible into Latin Jerome begat sundry *tubae*; that he begat the 'jubilas' of line I as in the best-known plural 'jubilas,' *Jubilate Deo*; that he begat the association of 'exult' and 'jubilas' through his several pairings of forms of *exultare* and *jubilare*. It is also true that he gave us the sound-association of *tuba-jubilate* in the Vulgate, to say nothing of Jubal and Tubalcain, which we also know from the English Bible. (Joyce exploited the sound-association three years before Stevens: 'jubalent tubalence,' 'tubular jurbulence.') But there is another reason. Stevens owned a Lewis and Short Latin dictionary, whose use gave him 'delight,' as he testified to Robert Frost when making Frost a present of one. There he would have found two meanings for the word *juba*: 'the flowing hair on the neck of an animal, the mane,' and 'crest.' These are precisely the tropes of Stevens' second line, in a happy mingling of nonsense-echo and metaphor, the metaphor being, 'A multitude is a lion.' Stevens' huge Christian lion—not so much the Church triumphant as the Church rampant—is related to an earlier lion in *Notes* (I.v) and also to the lion that iconography commonly places beside Saint Jerome. After all this, how could Jerome beget only harps? He begat the tubas not only through orthodox biblical association, but also for the good poetic reason that they rhyme with *jubas* (in a proper Latin feminine accusative plural ending too), and together the two words offer heterodox associations for the word 'jubilas,' whose power we might otherwise reverence unduly.

I offer these examples partly as cautionary tales, for I think that sometimes Stevens' seeming obscurity and nonsense are in fact examples of wit we have not yet come to appreciate, riddles whose sibylline ideas of order we have not yet pieced together. To christen a questing, mountain-climbing lady Mrs Uruguay has a good deal more point when we recall that the capital of Uruguay is Montevideo, as Frye once noted. To marry her to a Mr Alfred Uruguay also has a certain point when we recall that the most famed Alfred in modern poetry has as a surname Prufrock, and begins his poem thus:

> Let us go then, you and I,
> When the evening is spread out against the sky
> Like a patient etherised upon a table;

To which famous simile, Stevens' opening line to *Mrs. Alfred Uruguay* mischievously replies in an Eliot ragtime rhythm:

> So what said the others and the sun went down . . .

It does not do to underestimate the capacities for riddling and general word-play of a poet who can pun on the words 'artichoke' and 'inarticulate': . . . 'a dream they never had, / Like a word in the mind that sticks at artichoke / And remains inarticulate'—'rather an heroic pun,' as its inventor endearingly remarked.

If all Stevens' riddles worked as these and many others do, we would be dealing with a fine, formidable wit,

> Logos and logic, crystal hypothesis,
> Incipit and a form to speak the word
> And every latent double in the word,
>
> Beau linguist.
>
> (*Notes* I.viii)

Our problems as readers come when Stevens' hypotheses are clouded, when the latent doubles in the word refuse to become patent and remain half-shadowed, figurae without fulfilment. I have offered readings of some of Stevens' riddles using as means of interpretation puns, logic, well-known tropes, Latin equivalents, nonsense-rhymes, iconography, literary antecedents. Though these riddles stand in varying relations to the arguments of their poems, and though their effects differ, they may all be read coherently. The interpretive devices I have mentioned satisfy our desire as readers that consistent if multiple answers be possible for riddles in texts.

But Stevens sometimes moves toward more problematic kinds of riddle. I am not thinking so much of impenetrable lines, which await a wise reader, as of lines where the riddles appear only partly soluble, and the problem becomes not only how to answer the riddle but also how to read the answer. Such lines include sinister-metamorphosis or horrid-meta morphosis poems like *Oak Leaves Are Hands*; 'metamorphorid' is Stevens' fine portmanteau word for the process. They also include lines in which Stevens engages in intertextual word-play. For example, in *Esthétique du Mal*, part V, what are the 'obscurer selvages'? 'For this . . . we forego / Lament, willing forfeit the ai-ai / Of parades in the obscurer selvages.' We can answer this question only so far. Selvages are edges, of course, and so belong in this canto of limits and bars. They may be more precisely placed, however, by reading them against the first five lines of the opening canto of Dante's *Inferno*. There Dante finds himself in a dark wood, *una selva oscura*, and the noun *selva* is repeated in line 5, where its sounds at once expand into *selvaggia—esta selva selvaggia: selva oscura . . . selva selvaggia, oscura . . . selvaggia*, obscure selvage. *Selvaggia*, however, is cognate with our word savage and not with the word selvage. Eliot makes use of correct etymology in *The Dry Salvages*, third of the *Four Quartets*, published three years before Stevens' poem. The Dry Salvages are a small group of rocks off Cape Ann, Massachusetts, as Eliot tells us; the name, he says, was originally *les trois sauvages*. By anglicizing this name, New Englanders have brought it somewhat closer to its Latin root (*silvaticus*, from *silva*) and much closer to its Italian cognate, *selvaggia*. In Eliot's poem, there is an implicit play on salvages (the rocks), savage, salvage (flotsam and jetsam), and I think salvation (which has the same Latin root as salvage)—play that includes the metaphor of the rock of salvation and allegories of travelling. I read Eliot's title as interwoven in this word-play, and as echoing the *selva . . . selva selvaggia* of the beginning of Dante's journey.

Stevens echoes sound but dislocates denotative meaning, as he summons the ghost of a Dantean *topos* only to de-centre it. For Dante's *selva oscura* is not in the middle of life's way for Stevens—neither as doctrinal allegory nor as personal allegory nor as a place for poetry. As allegory, it is on the edge of things, peripheral to Stevens' earthly vision. Even more on the edge—and thus the 'obscurer selvages'—is Eliot's poem, *The Dry Salvages*. Yet, having answered this riddle, we find problems in reading the answer. Is this simply ironic distancing? If so, what is the angle of difference between Stevens' troping and Dante's, Stevens' troping and Eliot's? Or is this perhaps what John Hollander calls metaleptic echoing?

Another example of a problematic riddle is the passage about the Arabian in *Notes toward a Supreme Fiction* I.III. Here the relation of the reader to the text, even of the interior 'we' to his own text, shifts as we read and reread the canto. I should like to pause over these lines and to look at the different relations of reader and text, for I think they may tell us something about the functions of riddles, and of charms as well. Here is the entire canto:

> The poem refreshes life so that we share,
> For a moment, the first idea . . . It satisfies
> Belief in an immaculate beginning
>
> And sends us, winged by an unconscious will,
> To an immaculate end. We move between these points:
> From that ever-early candor to its late plural
>
> And the candor of them is the strong exhilaration
> Of what we feel from what we think, of thought
> Beating in the heart, as if blood newly came,

> An elixir, an excitation, a pure power.
> The poem, through candor, brings back a power again
> That gives a candid kind to everything
>
> We say: At night an Arabian in my room,
> With his damned hoobla-hoobla-hoobla-how,
> Inscribes a primitive astronomy,
>
> Across the unscrawled fores the future casts
> And throws his stars around the floor. By day
> The wood-dove used to chant his hoobla-hoo
>
> And still the grossest iridescence of ocean
> Howls hoo and rises and howls hoo and falls.
> Life's nonsense pierces us with strange relation.

We are not surprised to find [what Harold Bloom calls] a 'Coleridgean idealization of poetry' (lines 1–12) in a meditation upon a supreme fiction, but the presence of what appears to be nonsense-verse in such a meditation is startling, and its relation to lines 1 to 12 a problem for commentators. If lines 13 to 20 are pure nonsense with no affective function, why does Stevens say in line 21 that life's nonsense pierces us? We can hardly exclude nonsense-verse from life's nonsense when we have just been given several lines of it. And whether lines 13 to 20 are read affectively or not, what connection is there with the canto's first part? And what does the movement from the Coleridgean lines into the 'hoobla' lines have to do with a supreme fiction?

At least two different types of word-play run through this canto. The first is word-play which makes sense; the second is closer to the uses of nonsense-verse. One proliferates from the English word 'candid' and the Latin word *candidus* and dominates the first part. The other plays with Coleridgean echoes, which are submerged in the first part and surface in the second. *Candidus* in Latin, like 'candid' in English, means white, but a dazzling white as against a lustreless white (*albus*). It has been used in Latin of the moon, the stars, day; of swans and snow; of Dido's beauty; of gods and persons transformed to gods. It also means 'spotless' and is thus synonymous with 'immaculate' in Stevens' canto. Figuratively, of discourse, it means clear, open, perspicuous, and therefore the opposite to riddle or *aenigma*, which is in rhetorical tradition an 'obscure allegory' and into which Stevens moves in line 13. Until then, he weaves an entrancing web out of multiple meanings and associations of 'candid' and *candidus*.

Simultaneously, we may hear an uncanny echoing of Coleridge when we read this canto as a type of riddle poem. Thus: Stevens has transposed the dove's conventional English-language sound of 'coo' to 'hoo.' If we similarly transpose the Arabian's sounds, we hear 'coobla-coobla-coobla-cow.' Then we don't. We hear 'coobla-can,' and we begin to hear a nonsense refrain, much like something out of James Joyce: Kubla Khan but hoobla how? This refrain suggests that lines 13 to 20 function at least in part as a riddle whose answer is Coleridge's *Kubla Khan*. Once we have begun to hear this echo, other Coleridgean echoes proliferate. We ask ourselves if it is nonsense to hear subliminal assertions of power in the homonyms for 'do' and 'can' in the opening line of *Kubla Khan:* 'In Xanadu did Kubla Khan.' And to read in Stevens' canto that the poem brings back a power again that gives a can-did kind to everything. Of course it is. But in the realm of nonsense riddle, this is how we read.

Outside this realm, back in the realm of rational discourse, we recall that *Kubla Khan* came to Coleridge 'without any sensation or consciousness of effort,' to quote his phrase, and comes as close as any poem to showing the 'pure power' of the imagination. We recall also that the Khan could simply decree a stately pleasure-dome, while Stevens must work toward a supreme fiction which 'must give pleasure.' *Kubla Khan* in this reading is at least one of the poems, and I think the prototypical poem, which refreshes life in the ways suggested in lines 1 to 12 of Stevens' canto.

Lest this riddle-reading appear too arbitrary, I should observe that Stevens engaged in word-play with *Kubla Khan* elsewhere. In 1923, in *Academic Discourse at Havana*, he invented a 'mythy goober khan,' which is a peanut stand. ('Khan' as 'building' we are most likely to know from *The Arabian Nights*.) But the phrase 'goober khan' functions chiefly as a parody—'a peanut parody / For peanut people'— through its unmistakable echo of 'Kubla Khan.' (I read the entire poem as a forerunner of *Notes* I.iii, for it ends with sleepers awakening and watching moonlight on their floors, and comments of itself that it 'may . . . be / An incantation that the moon defines.') In 1942, the year of *Notes*, Stevens opened his weird and haunting *Oak Leaves Are Hands* with a parody of the opening lines of *Kubla Khan*, as Helen Vendler has noted: 'In Hydaspia, by Howzen, / Lived a lady, Lady Lowzen . . .' Coleridge is present in other ways in the work of Stevens at this time. Among Stevens' essays, he appears only in a quotation in a 1942 essay, and in the 1943 essay, *The Figure of the Youth as Virile Poet*, where Stevens calls Coleridge 'one of the great figures.' In a letter of 1942, Stevens makes use of Coleridge's phrase, 'willing suspension of disbelief,' along with William James's 'will to believe,' in a discussion crucial to an understanding of *Notes*. In *Notes* itself, he echoes part of Coleridge's definition of the primary imagination (III.viii). Coleridge is pretty clearly one of the ancestral voices with whom Stevens does battle, or records past battles, in *Notes Toward a Supreme Fiction*. A *Kubla Khan* riddle, given other parodies of the great Khan's name and poem, and given Coleridge's place in *Notes*, does not seem to me an overly arbitrary reading.

How do lines 13 to 20 function in Stevens' debate with Coleridge? They work, I think, as a reversal of lines 1 to 12, and their first function is to demonstrate how disabling such a reversal may be. 'Hoobla how?' sings or plays or challenges the Arabian, and the phrase is 'damned' because one answer is: Kubla Khan but you cannot. The voice of this canto's first part talks about a power in which the reader feels invited to share as part of a communal 'we.' To give a 'kind to everything' is to bring about unity and kinship, a process quite unlike 'strange relation.' Power in the second part is exercised by the Arabian certainly, but it is a power that excludes the reader in the sense that we cannot agree on even an approximate common stance for reading lines 13 to 20. If the first part shows us the power of the human imagination, just as *Kubla Khan* does, the second part shows us the helplessness of that same imagination, just as the longer *Kubla Khan* we do not have also and most painfully does. (Coleridge's preface to *Kubla Khan* makes a useful gloss on this canto; the return to 'his room' and to a dissipated, fragmented vision is, I think, one source for Stevens' Arabian lines. Yet one hardly likes to bring a hoobla-how-Kubla-Khan riddle too close to the memory of Coleridge, even in fancy.)

We can work out the reversal: suggestions of white magic to suggestions of black; radiance to night, with eerie moonlight and broken constellations; openness to riddle; the future as immaculate end to the future as something cast—a context of fate rather than destiny. The visual becomes vague or erratic; the oral reduces itself to the same limited series of sounds as if the Arabian made the memory of the wood-dove chant to his own tune and allied himself with the ancient continuing hooing of the ocean. Language, once glowing with power and moving outward in its ex-prefixes, becomes fitful and nothing to read by or into. The Arabian splits fores and casts, and into the split he throws the future. By line 20, the salt ocean has prevailed over the freshening of line 1. Incantatory multilingual echoes cry through this line, with its monosyllabic equivalent of a Latinate ululate-undulate word-play, and an implicit French-English pun on *houle* (sea-swell) and 'howl.' 'Oh! Blessed rage for order . . . The maker's rage to order words of the sea.' But the Arabian with his damned words is master now, the moon at its most unpropitious (the connection is presumably through the figure of the crescent). Against the human 'will' and 'can' of lines 1 to 12, another voice says 'how?' The puns move away from vanished chant and down toward incantation: adnominatio to paronomasia to monotonous echo. How, hoo, who, indeed.

The movement to wood-dove and then to ocean is toward losses other than the loss of poetic power, one of love and the other (I think) in death. A sequence of 'gross, grosser, grossest' is implied in the superlative form of the adjective at the end; iridescences may also be of the moon and of doves, and if we use the word 'gross' in the sense of 'material,' we may see here a logical sequence of downward imagery (moonlight, bird, ocean) and of loss (of poetic power as the least fleshly, then of love, finally of the body itself). I think also that the memory of the erotic dove merges with some memory of the poetic dove who broods creatively over the abyss—descendant of the biblical and Miltonic bird of the Holy Ghost through Wordsworth's 'brooding mind' to Joyce's 'Coo' and Stevens' chanter of hoobla-hoo. The poetic voice has now lost the voice of the dove; the operative forces are the Arabian and the howling, hooing sea. The three realms here (moon, woods, ocean) are those of the triform goddess (Luna, Diana, Hecate) if we accept the ocean as Stevens' form of the underworld. The chanting of hooblas and how and hoos, a circle woven thrice as in the charm-poems of Theocritus and Virgil, resounds like some mage's spell to undo the white and shining enchantment of the first part.

Stevens' riddling here verges on the type of poetry Frye calls charms, poetry whose rhetoric 'is dissociative and incantatory,' uses repetitive devices ('refrain, rhyme, alliteration, assonance, pun, antithesis'), and seeks to 'break down and confuse the conscious will.' Charms and riddles are two different kinds of play with language; 'Magic would disrupt Nonsense,' Elizabeth Sewell argues. But the two may converge: 'the game or the dream, logic or irrationality, may lead us to the same point in the end.' For 'charms and riddles . . . are psychologically very close together, as the unguessed or unguessable riddle is or may be a charm' [Frye]. That is what I think we have here: a riddle-and-charm poem with two contrasting parts. 'Like primitive astronomers, we are free to note recurrences, cherish symmetries, and seek if we can means of placating the hidden power: more for our comfort than for theirs' [Hugh Kenner on Beckett]. But there is minimal comfort, if any, in the dwindling symmetries which the reader can ascertain in Stevens' nonsense-lines. The moon has come down from heaven and brought a most uncandid charm, one potentially damning and disabling.

What Stevens accomplishes here is a systematic undoing of his first world, and with it all such 'immaculate,' idealized first worlds—childhood or erotic or religious paradises—and perforce all idealized theories of poetry. The strategies of undoing dominate the first cantos of Notes, and

Kubla Khan, with its magical transformations of biblical and Miltonic paradises and with its yearning poet, serves Stevens' purposes wonderfully well. Such an undoing may be disabling, as it is, for example, in a lunar sequence in *The Man with the Blue Guitar* which moves from 'immaculate' (vii) through 'unspotted' (xiii) to 'the spot on the floor' (XV). But for Stevens such an undoing may also be a defence. I have read 'we say' as 'we find ourselves saying' and so have followed the voice of the poem into the power of the fiction of the Arabian. But Stevens' cryptic 'we say' also bears the sense of 'it is we who say.' As soon as we read not 'an Arabian . . . with his damned hoobla-hoobla-hoobla-how,' but 'it is we who say an Arabian . . . with his damned hoobla-hoobla-hoobla-how,' another response to his riddle becomes possible: not the accuser saying Kubla Khan but you cannot, but rather the self saying Kubla Khan and I cannot. This is to acknowledge poverty but not helplessness. It is a defensive strategy against the authority of words, including the words of supreme fictions, say 'candid' or *candidus.* Riddles and charms do not merely assert that we are makers of our own words, but demonstrate this by showing how words may be reversed and fictions undone. Stevens' nonsense-lines read to me like an archetypal riddle-and-charm poem, the precise opposite of the archetypal 'original spell to keep chaos away' [Frye], the Word of God or Logos.

'To indulge the power of fictions and send imagination out upon the wing is often the sport of those who delight too much in silent speculation,' Imlac says in *Rasselas* (XLIV). 'Then fictions begin to operate as realities . . .' He is speaking of an astronomer, who is persuaded he has the power to control the weather, the sun and even the planets, and so could if he wished do just what Stevens' astronomer does. The astronomer is for Imlac an admonitory example of the hazards of taking fictions for realities. Imlac's idea of what constitutes a fiction differs from Stevens', of course; his religious beliefs are not to him fictions. For Stevens, they are, and Stevens was sensitive to the hazards as well as the benefits of all belief, including poetic belief: 'Suppose the poet discovered and had the power thereafter at will and by intelligence to reconstruct us by his transformations. He would also have the power to destroy us.' This would be to make art, including sacred art, into magic, and the poet, including the writer of scripture, into an arch-magician and arch-riddler. For Stevens, it is a necessary knowledge that we say and therefore can unsay all our fictions, including our most august stories. Riddles and charms, which by definition are distanced from referential discourse, can make this point very clearly. We not only can unsay all our fictions, but must, for this is how one part of the imagination works, as Stevens says in 1947 in what I read as comment on canto I.iii of *Notes*:

> It must change from destiny to slight caprice . . .
> . . . move to find
> What must unmake it and, at last, what can,
> Say, a flippant communication under the moon.

We are by now so familiar with the ways of deconstruction that my argument thus far appears to claim simply that Stevens is a modern poet. For example, my first reading of *Notes* I.iii.13–20 would be seen by Derrida as an example of non-radical 'illegibility,' that 'non-sense' (*le non-sens*) which is still 'interior to the book, to reason or to logos.' My second reading would open the possibility of 'radical illegibility' (*l'illisibilité radicale*) or the deconstruction of the traditional doctrine of logos, reason, and the book. Yet the implications of these readings may be disquieting for the reader and lover of fictions. If we deconstruct the old, unifying Coleridgean theories of the imagination, as it seems we must, do we lose the power of illusions, the ability to suspend disbelief? Do all our fictions become Arabian fictions of nonsense, powerful within themselves but without much power over us? Or mirrors of another imagination, Coleridge's perhaps, as the sea mirrors the moon and the moon mirrors a greater light? We seem to be caught. When we are knowledgeable enough and defensive enough about the ways language works, how far can it then affect us? This is a question that John Bayley raises in another context, and it lies behind speculation about the end of narrative. For Stevens, there is the further question: how can we then create or hear a supreme fiction?

Riddles and charms can show us in a nutshell three relations of reader to text. The reader may enter and share the assumed power of the text, answering riddles and feeling exquisite enchantments (in other terms, playing the game or dreaming happily). He may enter the assumed power of the text, unable to answer riddles and feeling sinister enchantments (in other terms, becoming the played-with or experiencing nightmare). Or, he may step outside the blessing and damning power of words, observing that we make the rules of the games and (as we now say) 'privilege' the text. But in so far as we still use words, or they us, what power do they then retain?

It takes the whole of *Notes toward a Supreme Fiction* to answer that question fully. Two parts of the answer are pertinent here. The first is suggested in Stevens' final line to *Notes* I.iii: 'Life's nonsense pierces us with strange relation.' Not 'relations,' as we might expect, but 'relation,' which includes more pointedly than the plural noun a relation that is a fiction. The word 'pierce' is unexpected too. It is a powerful word in Stevens: one use makes it a function of speech ('the acutest end / Of speech: to pierce the heart's residuum'; another use makes it an effect of illusion, and here we need to remember that there is benign as well as harmful illusion for Stevens '. . .the laborious human [of *Notes* II.v] who lives in illusions and who, after all the great illusions have left him, still clings to one that pierces him'. In *Notes* I.iii, for all the possible defence in the clause 'we say,' Stevens does not end defensively. He ends with a piercing or wounding, even by nonsense-language, even by the 'hoo' we hear the ocean saying, even in the full knowledge that we say these things ourselves. If we read the poem's last line as in part Stevens' gloss on his own nonsense-lines, then he is putting before us the possibility of words as not only a power to bless and damn, a power against which we must defend ourselves, but also a power to pierce and to which we cling because (not although) it pierces us. In *Notes* III.viii, Stevens asks: 'Am I that imagine this angel less satisfied?' Are we who say the riddle and charm of the Arabian less pierced? Only if we defend ourselves completely against the power of all fictions. And a self that cannot be pierced by words cannot be healed or refreshed by them either.

How words 'wound' has been explored by Jacques Derrida and more recently by Geoffrey Hartman. This canto suggests another pattern for such speculation through its echoing of religious diction, including the language of grace in line 1 and the language of sacrifice in line 21. Stevens may be said to prefigure here the only version of the incarnate Word which he could accept: the human imagination re-entering and being wounded by a world of language that it has itself created. This is, in effect, what happens in Poe's story, *The Power of Words*, a story which Stevens admired.

A further answer to my question is suggested by *Notes* III.viii, a companion-piece to canto I.iii and part of the beautiful climactic develop-ment of the whole poem. Here the assertive statement that the poem 'satisfies / Belief' becomes interrogative: 'What am I to believe?' Satisfac-tion is implied but limited: 'Am I that imagine this angel less satisfied?' 'Is it I then that . . . am satisfied.' All the sentences are interrogative, though one modulates through its clauses into a sufficiently assertive mood to drop the question-mark. This canto does not send us 'winged by an unconscious will.' 'I' both sees as spectator and experiences as angel, and sees his experience, of a movement downward 'on his spredden wings,' a movement protracted and without landing, a suspension. The time of fulfilment is not in terms of undefined beginning and end, but is specifically limited: an hour, a day, a month, a year, a time. Ex- words here (expressible, external) are limited in comparison with the outward movement—the ex-ness, so to speak—of such words in I.iii (exhilaration, excitation). We might suppose that a movement from first-person plural to first-person singular, from assertive to interrogative mood, from winging our way from immaculate beginnings to immaculate ends to seeing and being a falling angel, from extended to modified adjectives, from excited participation in power to a multiple stance where power is questioned— that all these limitations would make for a lesser canto. But this is not what happens. Stevens' enchanting first world is presented anew here in strength. His canto both enacts and comments on 'that willing suspension of disbelief for the moment, which constitutes poetic faith.' Coleridge's definition and Stevens' canto are powerful and live for us not in spite of their careful limiting but because of it. Stevens' 'I am' claims no more than he can sustain: 'I have not but I am and as I am, I am.'

At the end of this canto, the Cinderella story reverses the angelic moment, as the Arabian's story reverses the world of 'candid' and *candidus,* the two reversals being very different. It also reverses the Miltonic and biblical world of the aspiring Canon Aspirin in the three preceding cantos (v–vii). 'Candid' is used only once elsewhere in Stevens' poetry ('candor' never again) in a way that associates it with 'canon' and 'canonical.' When we note that a candidate may also be an Aspirant (*OED,* 'candidate,' 2.a), the candid-Canon-canonical association appears firm. In 1909, age twenty-nine, Stevens noted the Cinderella story in his journal in a one-word entry: 'pumpkin-coach.' The entry follows immediately on these lines:

> What I aspired to be,
> And was not, comforts me—

The lines, unidentified, are from Browning's *Rabbi Ben Ezra,* so that Browning's rabbi must take his place as another of the aspirers who make up that compound ghost, Canon Aspirin. For all Stevens' love for the white worlds and aspiring figures of a biblical, Miltonic, Coleridgean, and Browning heritage—rather, because of his love—their power has to be undone, whether by riddle or by charm or by fairy tale. Only then can Stevens lead us toward the exquisite fiction of his fat girl in the final canto of *Notes.* Only then can he write at all, can he 'patch together' (Stevens' revisionary version of the word 'compose'). For *Notes* ends with a Stevensian poet who

> Patches the moon together in his room
> To his Virgilian cadences, up down,
> Up down. It is a war that never ends.

CHARLES BERGER

The Mythology of Modern Death

Stevens wrote so frequently in the elegiac mode and drew such strength from it, that any attempt to isolate pure elegy in his poetry would be pointless. A sophisticated anatomy of his work would produce innumerable forms of farewell: for, like his alphabetical persona Omega, Stevens seems always to have been "refreshed at every end." If we glance back to the earlier poetry, perhaps the most interesting elegiac expressions can be found in those poems which associate death with poetic failure: "The Comedian as the Letter C," "Anglais Mort à Florence," "Landscape with Boat." These poems serve Stevens as a means of exorcising dangerous tendencies within himself; by tracing the decline of a substitutive persona, Stevens manages to save himself for poetry. But the predominant form of elegy in the earlier Stevens is captured in spare, epitaphic poems such as "The Death of a Soldier," which evoke the ghostliest of figures. Accustomed as we are to think of Stevens as a poet of earth, it still ought to surprise us when we realize how thoroughly he has excised the eschatological dimension from the elegy. If traditional elegies can be said to enter "the enlarged space that the dead apparently create for the living" [Peter Sacks], however fearful that space, then Stevens can be said to avoid speculation upon such *terra incognita,* as well as the formal or traditional apparatus of the elegy which transports us there.

"The Owl in the Sarcophagus" (1947) is the obvious exception in the Stevens canon, although I will argue in my next chapter that the brief lyrics composed at the very end of Stevens' career, the cluster of poems following "The Rock," should also be read as meditations upon the shape

From *Forms of Farewell: The Late Poetry of Wallace Stevens.* Copyright © 1984 by University of Wisconsin Press.

of the poet's survival. But "The Owl" is the most overt poem of discovery in the Stevens canon, rivalled only by "The Auroras," written a few months afterward. "To an Old Philosopher in Rome," composed five years after "The Owl in the Sarcophagus," is the only other poem by Stevens which might be read as a formal elegy, although, in complex ways which I will explore, it works to revise the prophetic or visionary mode of elegy advanced in the earlier poem.

"The Owl in the Sarcophagus" has been called "the least accessible of Stevens' major poems" [Harold Bloom], and it has certainly drawn the fewest readings. The complexity of its imagery is daunting even by its author's standards, and the density of internal reference to other Stevens poems, generally an aid to interpretation, seems to be kept deliberately low. The poem might also be regarded as the least assimilable of Stevens' long poems, for its speculations on the end of imagination are not of the sort that easily generate other poems. They remain fixed in the mind, visionary prodigies rather than paradigms.

The occasion for the elegy was the death of Stevens' closest friend, Henry Church. It is axiomatic that great elegies concern the poet's own fate more than that of the deceased, whether the latter is a rival poet or hero. I would suppose that the most salient fact to keep in mind about Henry Church is that he was a patron of the arts and that he and Stevens had intended to establish what they called a Poetry Chair. This investment in the institution of poetry is worth considering in the context of what "The Owl" reveals about what might be termed the afterlife of imagination. For if the poem avoids the relentless self-allusiveness of other major poems of Stevens', it compensates by gathering up the whole of elegiac tradition in the great image of the winding-sheet, a flowing robe or tapestry of the imagination. Harold Bloom has centered the ancestry of "The Owl" in "The Sleepers" and "When Lilacs Last in the Dooryard Bloomed," especially in the latter's triadic configuration of the poet and the two figures Whitman calls "the knowledge of death" and "the thought of death." For the genesis of Stevens' three forms that move about the night, one might also point to a lesser poem, Keats' "Ode on Indolence," where we encounter a linked ensemble of "Poesy," "Love," and "Ambition." That last figure interests me the most in terms of "The Owl," for it bears most closely upon the elegiac poet's inevitable placement of himself within tradition. And, as my reading will demonstrate, Yeats once again hovers over the scene, as he tends to when Stevens is writing in the Sublime mode.

A last word, however, on the question of elegiac tradition before turning to a reading of "The Owl in the Sarcophagus." Bloom points to

Stevens' repression of Whitman as a source of the poem's power, but the extent of Stevens' deliberate forgetting or eliding of primordial elegiac metaphors might go even deeper. For Whitman, the assassination of Lincoln in the early spring was a solemn coincidence verifying the elegiac poet's seasonal trope of death and rebirth. The severity of internalization in "The Owl" can best be seen in the avoidance of any reference to spring in the poem: for not only did Henry Church die in the early spring but, as it happens, he died on Good Friday. Perhaps the depth of Stevens' feeling for Church and for his vision can best be measured by the excision of any occasional detail from the poem, even when those accidents might validate the enduring tropes of poetic mourning and consolation. It is as if "The Owl in the Sarcophagus" discovers a haunt of prophecy that endures beyond April's green.

I

> Two forms move among the dead, high sleep
> Who by his highness quiets them, high peace
> Upon whose shoulders even the heavens rest,
>
> Two brothers. And a third form, she that says
> Good-by in the darkness, speaking quietly there,
> To those that cannot say good-by themselves.
>
> These forms are visible to the eye that needs,
> Needs out of the whole necessity of sight.
> The third form speaks, because the ear repeats,
>
> Without a voice, inventions of farewell.
> These forms are not abortive figures, rocks,
> Impenetrable symbols, motionless. They move
>
> About the night. They live without our light,
> In an element not the heaviness of time,
> In which reality is prodigy.

The most intriguing of these figures is certainly the third form, the woman. She is situated between life and death, but enjambment nudges her toward death's side, for the utterance can be read: "And *death* cries quickly." She is past life, but not yet into death; this is a region Stevens will come to explore increasingly in the last poems. In "Of Mere Being," for example, it becomes the space between the last thought and the end of the mind.

The odd thing about this cry is that the woman almost seems to be the dying one: "I am gone." She beseeches the departing ones—"those that cannot say good-by themselves"—to remain true to her memory of them:

> Keep you, keep you, I am gone, oh keep you as
> My memory.

This is intensely interesting and difficult. Are we meant to supply "of you" in brackets after the last two words: "My memory [of you]"? In other words, are the dead being implored to remain true to the earth-mother's memory of them as they were? In this reading, the mother would be the source of memory. But it also seems possible to regard the phrase as meaning that the dead *are* "My memory"; the dead embody the memory of the world. The dead *remember* where they came from and that memory somehow keeps the world alive. Dead poets especially are keepers of the world's memory, are kept alive insofar as they keep memory alive. "Keep you" is an archaism and also an irrational or onomatopoetic construction, resembling a bird's cheeping. (Compare the bird's "scrawny cry" in "Not Ideas About the Thing but the Thing Itself.") The phrase can be brooded upon until its stable meaning, if it has any, is dissolved; surely Stevens intended this for the cry between life and death. On any level, however, the phrase does read like an exhortation to faithfulness. Whether the mother does the work of memory, or the dead do the keeping, this is the earth's voice crying out, not the voice of the dead. "Keep you, keep you," can easily glide into the contrary: keep me, keep me. In any case, *keeping* may be viewed as the prime labor of poetic elegy, if not of poetry itself.

The second canto might have opened the poem, since it presents an image of the poetic quester setting out on his journey:

> There came a day, there was a day—one day
> A man walked living among the forms of thought
> To see their lustre truly as it is . . .

Stevens seems to be stuttering over the phrasing of this dark day, perhaps the day of Henry Church's death, as he approximates the elegist's traditional trouble in beginning his lament. "Among the dead," from the last canto, has now become "among the forms of thought," the underworld in which the structure of things at last reveals itself. It has been suggested [by Harold Bloom] that "A man walked living" refers to Church, but surely it is the poet himself who goes to the underworld in order to "Follow after, O my companion, my fellow, my self." The four stanzas of this canto provide a lyric abstract of the motives for the descent in the great epics—those instances of "abysmal melody"—and do so in phrases which are almost all Stevensian key signatures at this point in his career:

> And in harmonious prodigy to be,
> A while, conceiving his passage as into a time
> That of itself stood still, perennial,
>
> Less time than place, less place than thought of place
> And, if of substance, a likeness of the earth,
> That by resemblance twanged him through and through,
>
> Releasing an abysmal melody,
> A meeting, an emerging in the light,
> A dazzle of remembrance and of sight.

The first four words of canto III—"There he saw well"—capture the visionary clarity attained on this journey. "There" is the peculiar marker of the visionary realm, while "saw" conveys a privileged or prophetic mode of seeing which Stevens gives uncanny emphasis to by adding "well." "There he saw well" corrects the limitations of earthly sight; Yeats' line from "The Wild Swans at Coole," "I saw before I had well finished," may be in Stevens' mind at this point, providing an example of partial vision.

But what exactly does Stevens see, what is the content of his vision? Despite the promise of revelation, the poet seems to see coverings rather than uncoverings:

> There he saw well the foldings in the height
> Of sleep, the whiteness folded into less,
> Like many robings . . .

Even at this height, things are still hidden for the "living" man who walks among the dead. The living man sees the folds which either will be unfolded upon death—and which Henry Church, the subject of the elegy, sees now—or sees that the truth will always remain folded, the book remain closed. If "foldings" are taken to mean seals, then it would require a greater apocalypse than that of mere death to open the Book. Stevens, as epic follower in the land of the dead, sees what can be seen upon death, which is to say that he sees the folds that require unfolding. Considering the nature of Stevens' temperament, such an unfolding will probably only reveal further coverings. As a living man, furthermore, Stevens situates himself on the near side of the vanishing point, the outer side of the gold. Indeed, if we see the fold as a shroud—Yeats' "Cuchulain Comforted" comes to mind—it is clear why Stevens remains on the outer side of "the whiteness folded into less." Following after, Stevens discovers that the dead are in motion, perhaps moving away from him:

As a moving mountain is, moving through day
And night, colored from distances, central
Where luminous agitations come to rest,

In an ever-changing, calmest unity,
The unique composure, harshest streakings joined
In a vanishing-vanished violet that wraps round

The giant body the meanings of its folds,
The weaving and the crinkling and the vex,
As on water of an afternoon in the wind

After the wind has passed.

The vision here seems closer to that of the mountainous body of all the death in "Esthétique du Mal," VII. The bodies of the dead become "the giant body," as Stevens substitutes the figure of the mountain for the traditional pile of fallen leaves.

Canto III closed with a true flight "beyond the fire." After describing what he sees in terms of folds, wrinklings, and vexed robings, Stevens focusses on the blazing "whiteness that is the ultimate intellect."

Sleep realized
Was the whiteness that is the ultimate intellect,
A diamond jubilance beyond the fire,

That gives its power to the wild-ringed eye.
Then he breathed deeply the deep atmosphere
Of sleep, the accomplished, the fulfilling air.

It is impossible to tell who has experienced "sleep realized," but it seems most likely that the quester in the land of the dead is casting his "wild-ringed eye" upon a surmise of what the dead themselves must know; he himself cannot pass beyond the fire, but he imagines the realm of ultimate intellect. Stevens can only approach this region, although he comes close enough to breathe in its atmosphere. "Breath" and "breathing" are strong terms in Stevens, almost always used to signify the poetic faculty and the climate in which it thrives. That climate is usually naturalistic; to breathe deeply means to inhale the essence of life on earth:

Tonight the lilacs magnify
The easy passion, the ever-ready love
Of the lover that lies within us and we breathe

An odor evoking nothing, absolute.
We encounter in the dead middle of the night
The purple odor, the abundant bloom.

> The lover sighs as for accessible bliss,
> Which he can take within him on his breath.

"The Owl in the Sarcophagus" shows Stevens breathing in the atmosphere of the beyond, and though he must return to earth, his sense of what air nourishes the deepest inhalation has been changed.

The central figure in the poem's triad is also its most puzzling. In a poem as mystery-laden as "The Owl in the Sarcophagus" it is redundant to talk of puzzles, but the fourth canto presents tonal, if not verbal complexities, surpassing those of any other canto. The lines on peace, or "peace after death," are disturbing as well as enigmatic, since more than a touch of the sinister creeps into the representation of this centaur-like guardian, "the godolphin and fellow."

> There peace, the godolphin and fellow, estranged, estranged,
> Hewn in their middle as the beam of leaves,
> The prince of shither-shade and tinsel lights,
>
> Stood flourishing the world. The brilliant height
> And hollow of him by its brilliance calmed,
> Its brightness burned the way good solace seethes.

In the epigraph to "Notes Toward a Supreme Fiction," Stevens characterized peace as a "vivid transparence." Here it is anything but transparent. As the figure of peace flickers across Stevens' sight it will assume a number of phantasmagoric shapes, but none more difficult to decipher than this opening one. A godolphin is an Arabian stallion, a "godolphin and fellow," presumably, a horse and rider, or equestrian statue. (Just as one should not overlook the presence of god in godolphin, so "dolphin" should not be ignored, with its Yeatsian resonance. I will soon show what the state of peace-after-death has in common with Yeats' "Byzantium.") Statues fill Stevens' poems where generally they are regarded as premature ideas of order, states of peace achieved at the cost of living change. Most memorably, from "Notes," there is the mounted General Du Puy, cast in "the nerveless frame / Of a suspension, a permanence, so rigid / That it made the General a bit absurd." Peace seems to be both horse *and* rider, animal and human, a condition Stevens sees as estranged—as if peace, oddly enough, were not at peace with itself. This would be in accord with the dictum that "the imperfect is our paradise," and yet such a note of division does not appear comforting. But there is little about peace that soothes—indeed, the peace that he brings *seethes*. Stevens chooses to see him in these opening tercets as something of a poseur, another of those suspicious sleight-of-hand men. Does the elegy, then, move to uncover a falsehood in our conception of peace?

Perhaps the question can best be approached by hearkening to Stevens' recognition of the figure before him as "peace after death." "The Owl in the Sarcophagus" proceeds in a region where all the tropes come true, but in the case of peace such truth borders dangerously upon falsehood. No longer is peace the aim of a summer prayer, as in "The House was Quiet and the World was Calm," or "Credences of Summer." Nor is Stevens leaving peace unimaged as Eliot does at the end of "The Waste Land," where "Shantih, Shantih, Shantih" invokes the peace that passes understanding. Peace has been attained, but at the price of a death. Such a price demands scrutiny of the reward to which the subject of the elegy has gone and where the poet will soon follow. Rewards have to do with ends, and Stevens is now beholding not only an end to an imaginative man, Henry Church, but the end of the imagination as well. For in the preceding canto, Stevens-as-quester seemed to be exerting his power of visionary sight even as he observed the bourne of "sleep realized." He remained still within the circle of the wild-ringed eye; his ability to breathe deeply indicated that the poetic spirit was suspiring, not expiring. In fact, the canto on sleep seems to have nothing to do with the notion of death. Moving into the realm of peace, however, changes everything. Peace is an end-state, the place where the imagination finally comes to rest. Another way of describing the difference between the cantos centers on the distinction between the "ultimate intellect" of canto III and "generations of the imagination" in IV. The former, a condition of sleep, posits a continuity between earthly faculties and what is left to us "beyond the fire," even if the material foundations of intellect are shed. But, as the hieratic robe swathing peace makes clear, the imagination is literally wrapped up in its material. This dialectical distinction between imaged and unimaged intellect lies at the very heart of Stevens' late poetry.

Stevens sees peace as being clothed in a ceremonial robe or shroud. Unlike the condition of the shades in Yeats' "Cuchulain Comforted," who sew their shrouds in the afterlife, this robe is composed of the "fictive weavings" (to quote the character of Ozymandias in "Notes") spun by the living; in other words, their poems.

> Generations of the imagination piled
> In the manner of its stitchings, of its thread,
> In the weaving round the wonder of its need,
>
> And the first flowers upon it, an alphabet
> By which to spell out holy doom and end,
> A bee for the remembering of happiness.

> Peace stood with our last blood adorned, last mind,
> Damasked in the originals of green,
> A thousand begettings of the broken bold.

Stevens never achieved a more totalizing vision than this extraordinary glimpsing of the whole body of imagination. Its only rival would be his sighting of the mother's face in "The Auroras." The temporal generations are laid out in spatial simultaneity upon this grand tapestry (really a tapestry-within-a-tapestry), since the figures who parade through the poem are also woven around the urn-like sarcophagus. The sight of the "generations . . . piled" is one we associate with the epic quester's vision of all the dead heaped on the shore: "I had not thought death had undone so many." And the products of imagination do seem to strike Stevens as more than a little deathly, as if all the sheets of composition, in the end, came down to winding-sheets. The alphabet ("A bee"), the flowers, are items in a Book of the Dead, with peace its mummified priest. The corner of this particular mausoleum is hardly a poet's paradise. However resplendent its flowing robe of texts, peace guards over a dead tradition, tradition regarded as the equivalent of death.

As I mentioned in regard to the word "godolphin" and the possible puns it contains, "The Owl in the Sarcophagus" engages the Yeats of "Byzantium," but Stevens draws close only to reinforce the distance between the two. "A thousand begettings of the broken bold" summons Yeats most overtly, highlighting as it does the crucial verbs "break" and "beget" in the final stanza of "Byzantium":

> Astraddle on the dolphin's mire and blood,
> Spirit after spirit:
> The golden smithies of the Emperor!
> Marbles of the dancing floor
> Break bitter furies of complexity,
> Those images that yet
> Fresh images beget,
> That dolphin-torn, that gong-tormented sea.

Most commentators agree that Yeats is standing in Byzantium and looking outward—*sub specie aeternitatis*—as the living are converted into the dead. How much he rejoices at this vision, where his sympathies lie, is at question; the stanza splits power both ways, between the force of "break" (belonging to the artisans of eternity) and "beget" (belonging to the fecundity of the living). "Peace after death" is more of a weaver than a smithie, but he also converts living material into eternal forms. Stevens, however, shows considerably less ambivalence than Yeats when it comes to the value of earthly begettings, and his sense of the "broken," though less overtly violent than Yeats', contains more elegiac pathos. Stevens' fervor is displayed in the choice of "bold" as a trope for the poet, a revelation of his heroism in the aftermath of ruin.

The conclusion to this unsettling canto hypostatizes "peace after death" in terms that are all wrong for Stevens:

> This is that figure stationed at our end,
> Always, in brilliance, fatal, final, formed
> Out of our lives to keep us in our death,
>
> To watch us in the summer of Cyclops
> Underground, a king as candle by our beds
> In a robe that is our glory as he guards.

By wrong, I mean intolerable. This Statue at the World's End appropriates all glory to himself, in a robe that is a rob, since it is our glory. As will also be true in "Of Mere Being," we are left uncertain as to who has stationed this figure, who formed it. Whoever set it, the task of this guardian is clear: he is meant to keep us in place after death—compare the aim of the mother's keeping—and to insure that the dead do not wander back to disturb the living. "Peace after death" fixes tradition, assigning place at the cost of mobility. Since the dead here are poets, they are offered the aesthetic inducement or charm of beholding their own works in the tapestry of imagination. And yet Stevens tells us that the dead must be guarded: ever-Odyssean, they will try to escape the cave of the Cyclops in order to accomplish their return.

The "she" of canto V is a wisdom figure, indeed a goddess of wisdom, reminiscent of Yeats' early symbol of the Rose. The connection to Yeats' imagery might account for the gnomic "rosed out of prestiges / Of rose." Just as the wisdom figure leaves behind self-consciousness in her perfect selfhood, so she leaves behind the symbol or prestige of the Rose—etymologically, "prestige" derives from *praestigium*, an illusion or juggler's trick—in her attainment of knowledge. A favored word for knowledge with Stevens is "discovery," and so "She held men closely with discovery." But since this figure conducts men across the threshold, her revelation has to do with the knowledge of death:

> She was a self that knew, an inner thing,
> Subtler than look's declaiming, although she moved
> With a sad splendor, beyond artifice,
> Impassioned by the knowledge that she had,
> There on the edges of oblivion.

Possessing all the attributes of a Muse, she nevertheless conducts to oblivion, not Fame. Just as Stevens seemed to be enforcing a distinction between ultimate intellect and generations of the imagination, so he now forces us to brood on the possible discrepancy between that intellect and this "knowledge that she had." Perhaps the distinction has to do with the dissociation between intellect and selfhood. In the region of ultimate intellect, there is no longer any room for the self. So we find the wisdom figure, "a self that knew, an inner thing," on the point of extinction.

In the opening canto we are told that "the third form speaks, because the ear repeats, / Without a voice, inventions of farewell." The "flash of voice" in which she speaks comes close enough to *flesh* of voice (as in word-made-flesh) to bring out her status as *logos*. But as she says good-by she also seems to be speeding into invisibility, detaching herself from the poet. The exhalation spoken of in the final tercet of canto V may indeed be the departing poetic breath, the poetic psyche, while the "reddened" form of the departing muse blends into the light of the setting sun. The principle of inwardness has been transformed into "a motion outward." The separation between Muse and poet is marked by his use of the more distant pronoun "her" in the last line, where the logic of the vocative address leads us to expect the intimacy of "your":

> O exhalation, O fling without a sleeve
> And motion outward, reddened and resolved
> From sight, in the silence that follows her last word—

Before looking at the complex act of disengagement performed by Stevens in the concluding canto, we should try to determine where he has brought us thus far. As an elegy, "The Owl in the Sarcophagus" must present a surmise as to the shape of survival, whether literary or personal. What does this poem tell us of the beyond? The poem's dense imagery makes it seem almost crude to pose such a blunt question, but "The Owl" does represent itself as a far flight of imagination. First of all, it is extremely difficult to determine the relationship between the "three forms." Stevens tells us that "peace is cousin by a hundred names," but the problem I am discussing is not a question of kinship. Are the forms linked in a temporal progression, so that we "climb" in hierarchical ascent from sleep to peace to the mother? Or is Stevens playing with the spatial concept of the urn, so that the figures simply revolve into view? Do the three figures represent competing or complementary visions of the poetic soul's fate? Are we to understand Stevens' vision as a dream-blending of all three realms? Certainly, no fully worked-out credo can be found in the poem, yet Stevens has left some rigorous clues, which I have tried to expound in my reading, to guide us in differentiating the figures and the poet's reaction to them. The state of "sleep realized," whether achieved by the quester or the dead themselves, is the state of celebration proper, since it represents the whiteness of "the ultimate intellect." All questions of individuality fade in the light of that "diamond jubilance." But when the poem goes on to ask the question Wordsworth asked in Book V of *The Prelude* concerning the "consecrated works of Bard and Sage"—"Where would they be?"—the mood darkens. The canto devoted to peace unveils the ending place of imagination. We find out that the products as well as the producers (both are "generations") are preserved, but in a mausoleum. And the mother's abrupt break-off indicates another state of dead-endedness ("her last word") for the imagination.

The three figures seem to portend three separate, if not congruent fates, depending on how one defines the essential activity of man and poet. "Sleep" foresees a future least discontinuous with the past, but constructed on the principle of visionary impersonality and immateriality. The pathos at the heart of "peace after death" comes from the realization that the material forms of art have no place in this domain, except to dress "An immaculate personage in nothingness." And yet poets cannot break the spell of their narcissistic attraction to those glittering forms. "She that says good-by" stands halfway between sleep and peace, less materially grounded than the latter, more so than the former, since her being belongs to speech. Though Stevens can foresee continuity between earthly and higher vision, speech cannot follow beyond the fire. He is not the first to make this observation, but to envision the truth of the end-point oneself means experiencing it anew. So Stevens suffers the wounding force of the muse-mother's disappearance into "silence," the slashing mark of discontinuity which ends her section. Selfhood vanishes and so does the poetry of the self. If "peace after death" spells the obsolescence of our only true begettings, then the disappearance of she who sponsors selfhood removes the begetter as well. If we are to survive, Stevens seems to be saying at the end of the vision proper in "The Owl in the Sarcophagus" (the end of canto V), we will survive in the refining and self-extinguishing fire of ultimate intellect.

But it is also necessary to live in the here and now, to keep the poetic career going until the end, and so Stevens must enact the difficult return from the site of vision. The dash which concludes the fifth canto is the most radical break in all of Stevens' poetry; unlike an enticing ellipsis, it offers little room for interpretation, serving rather to divide than to bridge. The final canto seems at first to deflate what the poet has seen "there," with its talk of mythology, mufflings, and monsters:

This is the mythology of modern death
And these, in their mufflings, monsters of elegy,
Of their own marvel made, of pity made,

Compounded and compounded, life by life,
These are death's own supremest images,
The pure perfections of parental space,

The children of a desire that is the will,
Even of death, the beings of the mind
In the light-bound space of the mind, the floreate flare . . .

It is a child that sings itself to sleep,
The mind, among the creatures that it makes,
The people, those by which it lives and dies.

Mythology is generally not a favored word in Stevens, nor is "modern" ("Of Modern Poetry" notwithstanding). The two words together can comprise something of an oxymoron. As "A Mythology Reflects Its Region" will put it: "We never lived in a time / When mythology was possible." "Mufflings" make us aware that Stevens observes no faces in this poem; "the mother's face" will be unveiled only in "The Auroras." (In the "Ode on Indolence" Keats addresses his three figures in these words: "How came ye muffled in so hush a masque?") "Monsters" takes us back, through etymology, to "reality is prodigy," in the first canto, since these are *monstra* or omens. There is the further implication that, as "monsters of elegy," they have somehow become outsized projections of the elegiac impulse, threatening to overburden the occasion as well as its author, were his identity clear. I add this last qualification because even though Stevens asserts that they were "Of their own marvel made, of pity made," the identity of the fashioner is problematic. This ambiguity prevails until the end in Stevens, where it informs the question of who has created the fire-fangled bird in "Of Mere Being." Clearly, these elegiac figures have not made themselves, yet they have attained an hypostatized self-sufficiency and self-identity—"of their own marvel made." So, on the one hand, Stevens is insisting upon their status as fabrications, even while according these concepts a quasi-natural status, in that they seem native to the human mind. If they had not been invented, they would have had to exist. "Compounded and compounded, life by life," these figures are secreted out of the genius of the race. The opening four lines of canto VI represent an effort to ground the vision Stevens has borne, to anchor it in the collective mind, though we should always remember that it took one man—*a* man—to walk living among the forms of thought.

This final canto contains only one sentence and is rivalled in elusiveness only by that other single-sentence tease, "The Snow Man." The sentence may not be unreadable, but it is virtually ungraspable, as clause after clause glides into place, deferring finality for as long as possible. The chiastic structuring of these clauses makes meaning especially difficult to decide. Each cross-coupling involves another interpretive decision, one that must be made if the entire sequence of terms in this last canto is to be understood. Lines four through eight in the sixth canto constitute its heart, setting up a stunning series of appositions, as clauses rock back and forth, preparing us for the lullaby of "a child that sings itself to sleep." Let us try to line up these clauses in their logical columns, straightening out the chiasmus:

compounded and compounded	life by life
supremest images	death's own
pure perfections	parental space
the children	a desire that is the will /
the beings of the mind	even of death

In the crossing between "life by life" and "these are death's own," Stevens glides over the divide separating these states. An effacing of distinctions is the basic strategy of this method, as begetter and begotten image are blurred in our reading (as opposed to our schematic charting of the lines). Making it this hard to sort out appositives disguises the shock-value of some of these equations. The asserted continuum between life and death has the ring of solace to it, but the realization that Stevens is equating death with parental space is more jolting. One is tempted to soften the statement by substituting "ancestral" for "parental" but since Stevens goes on to link "a desire that is the will" with "parental," this ameliorating gesture is difficult to justify. It is legitimate, though, to ask which parents Stevens intends: the biological or the cultural parents? Or have they merged at this point? In any case, the death wish, as Stevens sees it, seems to grow out of a desire to return to parental space, as inhabited by the consanguine characters of the poem. Return, perhaps, is not the precise word, since Stevens envisions a joining of parent and child in that space, a joining of origin and end. By calling the mind a child, Stevens blends begetter and begotten, since the child of the last tercet is no longer an aesthetic offspring of the mind, but the mind itself. It has been said that men die because they cannot connect their beginning and their end; Stevens might argue that death ensues exactly at the moment of such connection, with the erasure of a saving distance between producer and product.

   The poem's closing image rewards endless reading, however simple it may seem at first. What is "a child that sings itself to sleep"? On the one hand, such a child seems terribly alone, forsaken almost. And yet, a proud sense of self-sufficiency lodges in the image as well, as if the child were a solitary swan drifting off in song. Child as "childe" might be a secondary meaning at work here, giving a heroic dimension to the death song which is also a lullaby, a lyric of entrance and departure, fitting for a child who is also an old man. But the intimations of immortality aroused by this evocation of the child have already been spelled out: the prophet has been preceded by his prophecy. By proclaiming the mind's generative powers even on the verge of death, Stevens in no way evades or revises the severity of the vision he has witnessed. The emphasis upon *makes* in the penultimate line, then, becomes all the more extraordinary, since we know the ultimate fate of those begettings. The poetic will, though, simply has no choice but to continue making, for the fate of "the people" depends upon it. The creative instinct survives even the projection of its own consignment to oblivion, survives the rejection of any teleological solace for the poet and his creatures.

II

"To an Old Philosopher in Rome" was written some months before the actual death of Santayana in Rome, but it nevertheless seems fitting to call the poem an elegy, though at times it verges on eulogy. The poem remains "On the threshold of heaven," even in its final lines when the lifetime's design of the philosopher "is realized." To say that the poem is about dying rather than death would be one way of accounting for the utter difference of its tone and vision from "The Owl in the Sarcophagus"; more to the point, I think, is the fact that Santayana was a man who gave up poetry for philosophy. As Stevens put it in a letter, "He [Santayana] had definitely decided not to be a poet." Most readers will simply assume that Stevens uses Santayana as an example of what his own preparation for death should be like, but the distinction Stevens has drawn between poet and philosopher ought to be brooded upon. The central personage in "To an Old Philosopher in Rome" treats his approaching death reasonably, even in his metaphors of transformation, all of which can be clearly traced to the objects lying about him: "the blown banners change to wings"; "the newsboys' muttering / Becomes another murmuring." This discovery of the realm of "another" lacks the true *otherness* displayed in "The Owl in the Sarcophagus." But the latter is a poet's vision, not a philosopher's meditation. (I would never make such a bald assertion of difference between poetry and philosophy if I did not think that the two poems read together insist upon it.) Whatever it was about the death of Henry Church that sparked Stevens' flight of imagination, "The Owl" became the vehicle for exploring what happens to the poet's creations after his death. "To an Old Philosopher in Rome" reveals no such narcissistic anxiety over the survival of the image, an absence that might be explained by the poem's emphasis on the ideality of vision, as well as its ability to exclude or repress uncertainties about the spirit's final resting-place.

As a poem of declaration, "To an Old Philosopher in Rome" comes upon no startling discoveries, though its sense of poise upon the threshold ought to startle us in the wake of Stevens' visionary jaunt in "The Owl." What relation exists between the two poems? Can they be complementary? Are we meant to reconsider the status of vision in "The Owl," or must we regard "Santayana" (and that in Stevens which most responds to him) as holding only the noblest of illusions? "To an Old Philosopher in Rome" will probably remain the more "popular" of the two poems, and continue to be regarded as the more "orthodox" version of Stevens' beliefs, if only because its avoidance of eschatological speculation makes it the more comfortable poem to read. One effect of consigning "The Owl in the Sarcophagus" to this realm of the heretical, or peripheral, is to limit its ability to disrupt orderly notions about Stevens.

From the opening lines of "To an Old Philosopher in Rome," Stevens conveys his desire to write a less severe elegy than "The Owl in the Sarcophagus," to bridge heaven and earth rather than disrupt any continuity we might project between the realms. Choosing the unrhymed, five-line stanza over the tercet allows him to be less elliptical in his transitions. (The poem's literal ellipses are among the smoothest in all of Stevens.) Such breaks as there are come in the inevitable glide between enjambed lines—"The figures in the street / Become the figures of heaven"—where they cause no breach. The poem stops comfortably on the threshold, avoiding that searing "passage" into the beyond which gives "The Owl in the Sarcophagus" its sense of trespass and menace. Vision in "To an Old Philosopher in Rome" is governed by "parallels" and "perspective":

> The threshold, Rome, and that more merciful Rome
> Beyond, the two alike in the make of the mind.
> It is as if in a human dignity
> Two parallels become one, a perspective, of which
> Men are part both in the inch and in the mile.

These plotted ratios of surmise correct the outrageous assertions of unmediated vision in "The Owl": "A man walked living among the forms of thought / To see their lustre truly as it is"; "There he saw well. . . ." One could go on and on in this vein, pointing again to a phrase from the third stanza of "To an Old Philosopher"—"the horizons of perception"—in order to establish what might be called the decorous sense of boundary in the later elegy, its refusal to push too far into an afterlife that might prove inhospitable to the imagination's desire. So that when Stevens writes,

> The human end in the spirit's greatest reach,
> The extreme of the known in the presence of the extreme
> Of the unknown,

we measure words such as "greatest" and "extreme" against the cast of mind displayed in "The Owl in the Sarcophagus," and we realize that Stevens is using a different rule of mind and metaphor in this poem. Perhaps only in the lines on fire does he come close to evincing a desire to take flight:

> A light on the candle tearing against the wick
> To join a hovering excellence, to escape
> From fire and be part only of that of which
>
> Fire is the symbol: the celestial possible.

The corresponding moment in "The Owl in the Sarcophagus" is pitched in a higher rhetorical key, appropriate to the poetic quester nearing a state of identity with ultimate intellect; here, any possible identification is distanced by dependency upon the poetic trope, beautifully and exactly rendered, of the candle. *This* candle, though, will not be hypostatized into "a king as candle by our beds."

The stanzas following the invocation of fire comprise the eulogy proper, Stevens' most sustained rhetoric of praise. The delicacy of his apostrophe to the unnamed Santayana comes partly from Stevens' realization that he stands in the anomalous position of a student addressing his master. This indeed may account for "the pity that is the memorial of this room":

> Be orator but with an accurate tongue
> And without eloquence, O, half-asleep,
> Of the pity that is the memorial of this room,
>
> So that we feel, in this illumined large,
> The veritable small, so that each of us
> Beholds himself in you, and hears his voice
> In yours, master and commiserable man . . .

Stevens gently subverts Santayana's religiosity (however sceptical) by hearkening the reader to the "commiserable man" at the center. Indeed, throughout the poem Stevens unobtrusively translates Santayana's faith into the aesthetic realm, so that the emphasis in the final stanza on "the design of all *his* words," rather than God's Word, evokes no surprise. The nature of this aesthetic faith rests on two noble idealizations. The first would assert the possibility of completing the career to one's satisfaction, bringing about "a kind of total grandeur at the end." The achievement of totality in "To an Old Philosopher in Rome" is seen as the fulfillment of a self that exerts its power of choice until the very end:

> It is a kind of total grandeur at the end,
> With every visible thing enlarged and yet
> No more than a bed, a chair and moving nuns,
> The immensest theatre, the pillared porch,
> The book and candle in your ambered room,
>
> Total grandeur of a total edifice,
> Chosen by an inquisitor of structures
> For himself. He stops upon this threshold,
> As if the design of all his words takes form
> And frame from thinking and is realized.

In the late lyrics surrounding "To an Old Philosopher in Rome," the prospect of completion is not regarded with such serenity, nor is the question of poetic afterlife so elided. But perhaps the philosopher receives a premonition of what his fate will be in the tolling of the bells heard from his chamber. This brings us to the second of the idealizations I have mentioned, for the bells may be regarded as bodying forth a message about the company into which the dying philosopher will be absorbed, his version of tradition:

> The bells keep on repeating solemn names
>
> In choruses and choirs of choruses,
> Unwilling that mercy should be a mystery
> Of silence, that any solitude of sense
> Should give you more than their peculiar chords
> And reverberations clinging to whisper still.

Acceptance into the chorus is a figure for acceptance into tradition—described earlier as the urge "to join a hovering excellence"—here conceived as having the power to vanquish the shadows of silence and solitude. This solemn order promises to perform the elegiac function of preservation, as the bells "keep on repeating solemn names" across the divide of life and death, culminating in "choruses and choirs of choruses."

For contrast, we might set this vision of the bells against Yeats' carilloners in *Per Amica Silentia Lunae,* those "ringers in the tower who have appointed for the hymen of the soul a passing bell." The concept of tradition as a harmonic whole in which the solemn names are nevertheless preserved, marks the convergence of desire and vision in the poem, as well as the extent of its divergence from "The Owl in the Sarcophagus."

But the question of whose desire is being fulfilled, whose vision expressed, remains crucial to any interpretation of "To an Old Philosopher in Rome." Answering this question comes down to trying to decide the nature and extent of Stevens' identification with Santayana. No such problem exists in reading "The Owl" where the man who "walked living among the forms of thought" is meant to discover the poet's own fate, however difficult to decipher. Though much less oblique on the verbal level, "To an Old Philosopher in Rome" forces us to confront the status of its vision at every turn by making the question of identification paramount but elusive. Does Stevens privilege the stance of the old philosopher as a reflection of his own, or does he distance himself implicitly from the very figure he eulogizes? In other words, do the very terms of praise for the philosopher's way describe a set of impossibles for the poet?

Questions such as these force the interpreter to judge authenticity of voice and vision and thereby to reveal his or her deepest sense of Stevens' poetic temperament. The self-contained sphericity of "To an Old Philosopher in Rome," its commanding poise, its gestures toward totality ("a total grandeur"), all combine to give the poem an appearance of central authority, especially when read against the shorter, more fragmentary lyrics of the same period, or even when opposed to the deep ambivalences set out at length in "The Owl." The fact that "To an Old Philosopher in Rome" does not literally have the last word in Stevens, but is itself survived by a number of gnomic lyrics which spill over its threshold, might be used to rebut the idea that Stevens achieved an orderly end to his career, but it does not weaken the case against his desire to sum up like Santayana, with a gesture of near self-congratulatory closure. To argue that Stevens would regard such an ending as both illusory and undesirable is to make a presumptuous claim about the poet's temperament, but I would insist that "To an Old Philosopher" forces us to assess the validity of its rhetoric—its "constant sacrament of praise"—which returns us to the question of the poet's identification with his central figure.

As a version of the hero, Santayana is both more perfect and more human than any of Stevens' earlier models, for the proximity of death sanctifies the plainness of plain life. No disabling return of the merely ordinary is allowed to undo the philosopher's achieved position. Santayana belongs to that class of purer and narrower consciousnesses created by Stevens for the purpose of measuring his own nature against a hypothetical ideal. Sometimes the comparison generates a bad conscience, but more often than not it leaves the ideal looking rather hollow. "To an Old Philosopher in Rome" represents the subtlest case of such comparison, complicated as well by the elegiac mode. The interpreter who scans the poem for overt marks of disengagement or distancing will circle endlessly, for the dying philosopher has indeed brought about the enclosure of his own system, even at the price of controlling or limiting the horizon of perception by suppressing the prophetic element of elegy. Though in many of his late poems, Stevens prepares to encounter death as *the known*, some proleptic shadow of the uncanny generally intrudes to disturb that equipoise. By opening himself to casts of metaphorical speculation on the shape of survival, Stevens brings the inexplicable into the realm of language. Since this is precisely what the figure of Santayana will not or cannot do—since he has renounced poetry—I would judge Stevens' praise, finally, to be eulogistic of another, rather than prescriptive for himself. For the order Santayana prepares to join is not the company Stevens would keep; the poet's place is with the broken bold.

Chronology

1879	Born October 2 in Reading, Pennsylvania, the second of five children born to Garrett Stevens and Margaretha Zeller Stevens.
1892–97	Studies at Reading Boys' High School.
1897– 1900	Special student at Harvard.
1900–01	Works as journalist in New York City.
1901–03	Student at New York Law School.
1904	Admitted to New York Bar.
1909	Marries Elsie Kachel in Reading on September 21, after a five-year courtship.
1911	Death of Garrett Stevens.
1912	Death of Margaretha Zeller Stevens.
1914	Publishes first poems since undergraduate years.
1916	Joins Hartford Accident and Indemnity Company; moves to Connecticut.
1919	Death of poet's youngest sister, Mary, in France.
1923	Publication of *Harmonium*.
1924	Birth of daughter, Holly Bright Stevens.
1931	Second, enlarged version of *Harmonium*.
1932	Moves into permanent home.
1934	Promoted to a vice-presidency of his company.
1935	First edition of *Ideas of Order*.
1936	Public edition of *Ideas of Order*; private edition of *Owl's Clover*.
1937	*The Man with the Blue Guitar* published.
1942	*Parts of a World; Notes Toward a Supreme Fiction*.
1945	*Esthétique du Mal*.
1947	*Transport to Summer*.
1949	Delivers short version of "An Ordinary Evening in New Haven" at the Connecticut Academy of Arts and Sciences in early November.
1950	*The Auroras of Autumn*.
1951	*The Necessary Angel*.

1954   *The Collected Poems of Wallace Stevens.*
1955   Dies August 2.

Contributors

HAROLD BLOOM, Sterling Professor of the Humanitites at Yale University, is the author of *The Anxiety of Influence, Poetry and Repression* and many other volumes of literary criticism. His forthcoming study, *Freud: Transference and Authority,* attempts a full-scale reading of all of Freud's major writings. He is the general editor of *The Chelsea House Library of Literary Criticism.*

HELEN VENDLER is Professor of English at Boston University and at Harvard University. Her books include studies of Stevens, Yeats, George Herbert and Keats, as well as *Part of Nature, Part of Us,* a survey of contemporary poetry.

J. HILLIS MILLER is Gray Professor of Rhetoric at Yale University. His many critical works include *Poets of Reality* and *The Disappearance of God.*

HELEN REGUEIRO, a native of Uruguay, is Professor of English at the State University of New York, Albany. Besides her study of Wordsworth, Yeats, and Stevens, her publications include essays on A. R. Ammons, John Ashbery, and on contemporary critical theory.

MARIE BORROFF, Professor of English at Yale, has published widely on medieval literature and modern poetry, with a focus on problems of language.

PATRICIA PARKER, Professor of English at the University of Toronto, has written on Shakespeare, Renaissance comparative literature, and modern poetry.

The late ISABEL G. MACCAFFREY was Kenan Professor of History and Literature at Harvard University. Her principal works are *Paradise Lost as "Myth"* and *Spenser's Allegory: An Anatomy of Imagination.*

JOHN HOLLANDER, poet-in-residence and Director of Graduate Studies in English at Yale, is equally distinguished as poet and critic. *Spectral Emanations: New and Selected Poems* and his study *The Figure of Echo* are among his major achievements.

ELEANOR COOK, Professor of English at the University of Toronto, is the author of *Browning's Lyrics* and of a forthcoming book on Stevens.

CHARLES BERGER teaches English at Yale. Besides his book on Stevens, *Forms of Farewell,* he has published essays on the poetry of John Ashbery and James Merrill.

Bibliography

Baird, James. *The Dome and the Rock: Studies in the Poetry of Wallace Stevens.* Baltimore: Johns Hopkins University Press, 1968.

Benamon, Michel. *Wallace Stevens and the Symbolist Imagination.* Princeton: Princeton University Press, 1972.

Bloom, Harold. *Wallace Stevens: The Poems of Our Climate* Ithaca: Cornell University Press, 1977.

Borroff, Marie. *Language and the Poet: Verbal Artistry in Frost, Stevens and Moore.* Chicago: University of Chicago Press, 1979.

————, ed. *Wallace Stevens: A Collection of Critical Essays.* Englewood Cliffs, N.J.: Prentice-Hall, 1963.

Brazeau, Peter. *Parts of a World: Wallace Stevens Remembered* New York: Random House, 1983.

Brown, Ashley, and Haller, Robert S., eds. *The Achievement of Wallace Stevens.* Philadelphia: J. B. Lippincott Co., 1962.

Buttel, Robert. *Wallace Stevens: The Making of Harmonium.* Princeton: Princeton University Press, 1967.

Buttel, Robert and Doggett, Frank, eds. *Wallace Stevens: A Celebration.* Princeton: Princeton University Press, 1980.

Doggett, Frank. *Stevens' Poetry of Thought.* Baltimore: Johns Hopkins University Press, 1966.

Frye, Northop. "The Realistic Oriole: A Study of Wallace Stevens." *The Hudson Review* 10, no. 3 (Autumn 1957).

————. "Wallace Stevens and the Variation Form." In *Spiritus Mundi.* Bloomington: Indiana University Press, 1976.

Fuchs, Daniel. *The Comic Spirit of Wallace Stevens.* Durham: Duke University Press, 1963.

Kermode, Frank. *Wallace Stevens.* New York: Grove Press, 1960.

Litz, A. Walton. *Introspective Voyager: The Poetic Development of Wallace Stevens.* New York: Oxford University Press, 1972.

MacCaffrey, Isabel G. "The Other Side of Silence: 'Credences of Summer' as an Example." *Modern Language Quarterly* (September 1969).

Martz, Louis L. *The Poem of the Mind.* New York: Oxford University Press, 1966.

Middlebrook, Diane Wood. *Walt Whitman and Wallace Stevens.* Ithaca: Cornell University Press, 1974.

Miller, J. Hillis. *Poets of Reality.* Cambridge: Harvard University Press, 1965.

Morse, Samuel French. *Wallace Stevens: Poetry as Life.* New York: Pegasus, 1970.

Pack, Robert. *Wallace Stevens: An Approach to His Poetry and Thought.* New Brunswick, N.J.: Rutgers University Press, 1958.

Pearce, Roy Harvey, and Miller, J. Hillis, eds. *The Act of the Mind: Essays on the Poetry of Wallace Stevens.* Baltimore: John Hopkins University Press, 1965.

Riddel, Joseph. *The Clairvoyant Eye: The Poetry and Poetics of Wallace Stevens.* Baton Rouge: Louisiana State University Press, 1965.

Stevens, Wallace. *The Collected Poems of Wallace Stevens.* New York: Alfred A. Knopf, 1954.

———. *Letters of Wallace Stevens.* Selected and edited by Holly Stevens. New York: Alfred A. Knopf, 1966.

———. *The Necessary Angel: Essays on Reality and the Imagination.* New York: Alfred A. Knopf, 1951.

———. *Opus Posthumous: Poems, Plays, Prose by Wallace Stevens.* Edited by Samuel French Morse. New York: Alfred A. Knopf, 1957.

———. *The Palm at the End of the Mind: Selected Poems and a Play.* Edited by Holly Stevens. New York: Alfred A. Knopf, 1967.

———. *Souvenirs and Prophecies: The Young Wallace Stevens.* Edited by Holly Stevens. New York: Alfred A. Knopf, 1977.

Sukenick, Ronald. *Musing the Obscure.* New York: New York University Press, 1967.

Vendler, Helen H. *On Extended Wings: Wallace Stevens' Longer Poems.* Cambridge: Harvard University Press, 1969.

Walsh, Thomas, F., ed. *Concordance to the Poetry of Wallace Stevens.* University Park: Pennsylvania State University Press, 1963.

Acknowledgments

"Introduction" by Harold Bloom from *Figures of Capable Imagination* by Harold Bloom, copyright © 1976 by Harold Bloom. Reprinted by permission.

"The Sausage Maker" by Helen Vendler from *On Extended Wings: Wallace Stevens' Longer Poems* by Helen Vendler, copyright © 1969 by Harvard University Press. Reprinted by permission.

"Stevens' Rock and Criticism as Cure" by J. Hillis Miller from *The Georgia Review* 30 (Spring 1976), copyright © 1976 by J. Hillis Miller. Reprinted by permission.

'The Rejection of Metaphor" by Helen Regueiro from *The Limits of Imagination* by Helen Regueiro, copyright © 1976 by Cornell University Press. Reprinted by permission.

" 'An Ordinary Evening in New Haven' " by Harold Bloom from *Wallace Stevens: The Poems of Our Climate* by Harold Bloom, copyright © 1977 by Cornell University Press. Reprinted by permission.

"An Always Incipient Cosmos" by Marie Borroff from *Language and the Poet* by Marie Borroff, copyright © by The University of Chicago Press. Reprinted by permission.

"Inescapable Romance" by Patricia Parker from *Inescapable Romance* by Patricia Parker, copyright © 1979 by Princeton University Press. Reprinted by permission.

" 'Le Monocle de Mon Oncle' " by Isabel G. MacCaffrey from *Wallace Stevens: A Celebration*, edited by F. Doggett and R. Bittel, copyright © 1980 by Princeton University Press. Reprinted by permission.

"The Sound of the Music of Music and Sound" by John Hollander from *Wallace Stevens: A Celebration*, edited by F. Doggett and R. Bittel, copyright © 1980 by Princeton Univeristy Press. Reprinted by permission.

"Riddles, Charms, and Fictions" by Eleanor Cook from *Center and Labyrinth; Essays in Honour of Northrop Frye*, edited by Eleanor Cook, copyright © 1983 by University of Toronto Press. Reprinted by permission.

"The Mythology of Modern Death" by Charles Berger from *Forms of Farewell: The Late Poetry of Wallace Stevens* by Charles Berger, copyright © 1984 by University of Wisconsin Press. Reprinted by permission.

Index